WARRIORS FOR THE WORKING DAY
CODFORD DURING TWO WORLD WARS

Codford High Street, World War One (detail from postcard reproduced on page 22)

Warriors for the Working Day

Codford
during Two World Wars

ROMY WYETH

Dedication

This book is dedicated to my grandfather Sidney Ernest Butt, to the men who fought and died in two World Wars, and to warriors everywhere.

Romy Wyeth

First published in the United Kingdom in 2002 by
The Hobnob Press, PO Box 1838, East Knoyle, Salisbury SP3 6FA

British Library Cataloguing in Publication Data
A catalogue record for this book is available from the British Library.

ISBN 0-946418-12-8

Typeset in 10.5/12.5 pt Souvenir Light
Typesetting and origination by John Chandler
Printed in Great Britain by Salisbury Printing Company Ltd, Salisbury

Contents

Acknowledgements

This book owes a great deal to many people whose generosity with copyright permissions, military information, personal stories, old postcards and family photographs have made it possible. Special thanks are owing to the Commonwealth War Graves Commission.

For personal information to Will Collins, Ron Sutton, Walt Conduit, Joan Cole, John Selby, Joyce Dodd, Derek Morris, Clem Hill, Jeremy Unsworth-Joss, Doreen Rafdal, Arthur Meyrick, David Westley, Lord Bath, Patricia Windsor, Derek Williams, Pete Stacey and Ian Roney-Dougal.

To the authors of regimental histories, many unnamed, who recorded life on the Plain and the battlefield for future generations. To the regimental historians who made regimental histories, diaries and records available: Simon Jones M.A. – Kings Regiment; Ken Treanor [Capt]– Royal New Zealand Army Medical Corps Museum; Brigadier K A Timbers – Royal Artillery Historical Trust; R L Barrett-Cross – Royal Army Medical Corps; Colonel D A Whatmore – Regiments of Gloucester Museum; Professor Peter Dennis – Dept of History, University College, the Australian Defence Force Academy, Canberra; Brigadier A I H Fyfe – Somerset Light Infantry; David Chilton and Major P J Ball – Royal Gloucestershire, Berkshire and Wiltshire Regimental Museum; Fran McGowan – New Zealand Military Defence Library; Colonel T J Isles – Duke of Wellington's Regiment; Lieut-Colonel C D Darroch – Royal Hampshire Regt; Colonel W R H Charley, Major M B Murphy – Royal Ulster Rifles; and Andrzej Suchcitz – Polish Institute and Sikorski Museum.

For copyright permission to Terry Crawford, Dr Roger Freeman, Jim Stingl, Sydney Jary, and Tony Martin [publisher of *Plain Soldiering* by the late N.D.G. James].

For additional information to General Sir Roger Wheeler, Brigadier David Shaw, Roy Purcell, John Chandler, Christopher Green, Rod Priddle, Gary Poole, Owen Pearce, Roger Hedley, Dr Jack Barrow and Peter Ranger.

To those who told their stories: Gordon Norris, Bert Doughty, Sue Poolman, Cathy Lock, Edith Le Cocq, Ralph Ansay, John Waite, Lieut-Colonel Thomas Hyslop.

Finally, to the keepers of the flame of Codford history, the members of the Cole family. To Gwen Twist, Doreen Szeliga , Maurice, Godfrey and the late Paul Cole, all of whom have readily shared their memories, and made family papers and photos available for research over many years.

Photograph / postcard credits
Ralph Ansay, Joan Cole, Walt Conduit, Joyce Dodd, Bert Doughty, David Falcke, Lieut-Col. Thomas Hyslop, David Lee, Cathy Lock, Brian Marshall, Arthur Meyrick, Gordon Norris, Sue Poolman, Ian Roney-Dougal, Jim Stingl, Ron Sutton, Doreen Szeliga, Gwen Twist, Jeremy Unsworth-Joss, Derek Williams, Patricia Windsor.

Illustrations/maps
Martyn Lock, Brian Marshall, Gordon Norris, Ken Treanor, Owen Pearce and the AIF Project, University College, Australian Defence Force, Canberra.

About the Author

During the First World War my grandfather, Sydney Ernest Butt, lied about his age and ran off to join the Isle of Wight Rifles. He fought the Turks on the Middle East Front, across Turkey, Egypt and Palestine and I grew up listening to his stories of the Holy Land, of Gaza and Gallipoli. After his service in the Army he worked as a civilian operator and later as the Supervisor at Bulford Military Exchange, retiring after more than forty years in the mid 1960s.

During the Second World War my uncle Cecil was in the Merchant Navy. His first ship, the *Manchester*, was sunk on one of the Malta convoys and he was in the water for many hours before being rescued. My mother worked for some time in a Spitfire factory and also folding parachutes in Salisbury. As a child I was growing up in the aftermath of a war that had ended before I was born, but the echoes of the conflict were everywhere.

My grandfather was the most dominant figure in my life – he encouraged the tom-boyish tendencies that no amount of effort made by my mother or grandmother could suppress. I hated the frilly dresses and bows in my hair – yearning for jeans and wellingtons, playing with farmyards, cowboys and Indians in preference to dolls. Every Saturday afternoon from the age of three, Grandad would take me to the cinema, so I grew up on a diet of war films and cowboy movies. On Sunday mornings, rain or shine, I would get up at the crack of dawn and walk into Salisbury to go to work with him. We would catch the bus across the Plain to Bulford and I would spend the morning at the Military Exchange, riding on the 'bumper' used to polish the floor, eating my cheese and Daddies sauce sandwiches while reading my new cowboy comic, being spoilt by successive pairs of operators, and sometimes being allowed to use the switchboard. At lunchtime we would return home, but not before stopping off at the British Legion Club, to be greeted with the cry of 'Crisps Grandad' from the regulars who knew I was always seated away from the bar with my glass of Lemonade and a packet of crisps with the salt wrapped in blue paper.

When I moved to the Plain village of Codford in 1973, I had no inkling that I was being transplanted into an environment where the military past was so diverse and accessible. I was always in love with history and in the circumstances it isn't surprising that I have always had a passion for warriors. Given the place where I was born and the influences surrounding my formative years, my thirst for the past and battles seems inevitable.

Introduction

Codford is a place where the military are ever present. There are regular exercises with soldiers from many nations training on Salisbury Plain, their tank convoys and army vehicles are a familiar sight on local roads. The droning sound of helicopter rotor blades beyond the horizon, fighter planes screaming overhead, and giant Hercules aircraft circling in the skies above the village are part of the fabric of our lives. For one hundred and thirty years the Army has trained on Salisbury Plain. Safeguarding our freedom and the unique archaeological and natural landscape, they are a part of the Wiltshire heritage. The muffled sound of the great guns echo in the night, a lullaby for the children of the Plain. Through two World Wars the military have co-existed with the villagers of Codford, at the beginning of the third millennium many retired Army officers are living in the community.

Warriors for the Working Day captures brief moments during momentous times when the world was aflame. It tells the stories of ordinary people of extraordinary courage, of two settlements transformed and invaded as a result of global conflict and of the men who marched to war to fight and to die on far-off battlefields. Marcus Aurelius once said that every instant of time is a pinprick of eternity – I have only scratched the surface of the fragile and fragmented world of one Plain village during two World Wars.

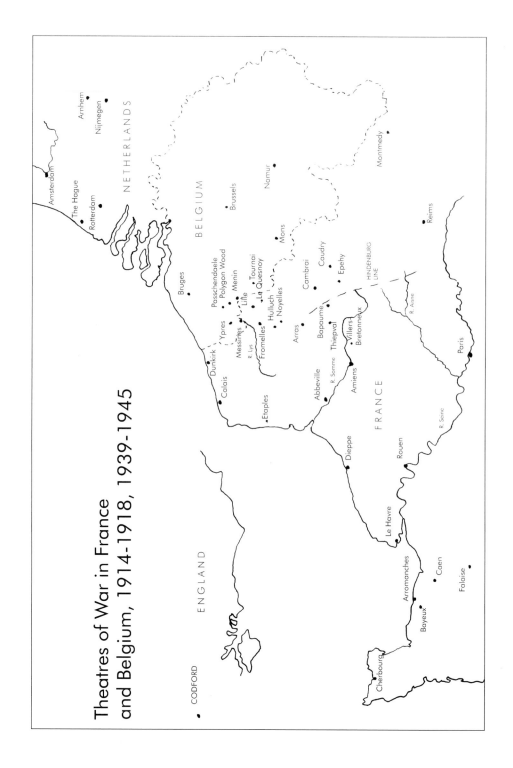

Theatres of War in France
and Belgium, 1914-1918, 1939-1945

WORLD WAR ONE

The Great War

It began with high spirits, national pride and a belief, 'it would all be over by Christmas.' This was the first global conflict, the War to end all Wars. Young men from across the Empire joined up in a patriotic fervour, often groups of pals enlisted together in 1914 to fight for King and Country. Four years later the battlefields had claimed a generation of young men, death in France, in Flanders fields and in the deserts of the Holy Land, in Palestine, Egypt and Turkey. Death on the high seas, beneath the wind whipped waves and troughs of turbulent oceans. Death in the sky, as fledgling pilots, many trained on Salisbury Plain, plummeted from the clouds to oblivion.

Both Codford St Mary and Codford St Peter as well as the surrounding settlements of Boyton, Corton, Sherrington, Stockton and Upton Lovell were almost immediately engulfed in the preparations for war. The small villages of Codford St Mary and Codford St Peter turned overnight into military encampments, with thousands of troops and a miscellany of hastily erected buildings, shops along the streets and barracks across the fields. This is the story of those chaotic and exciting years, individual tales from the 'tin city' on the edge of Salisbury Plain.

The Corporation Dust Cart
[*circa* World War One]

Sure a Corporation mud-cart
Overturned itself one day,
And all its fragrant contents
In a Wiltshire ditch did lay.
        And when Headquarters saw it,
It looked so wondrous damp,
They said, 'Oh what a lovely place
Suppose we build a camp.'
        They thought they'd call it Codford,
 With the accent on the Cod,
And they put the 3rd line in it
And commended us to God.
        And then they built some rat-traps
Which down here they call huts,
And we only wish they'd shove them
Where the monkeys shove their nuts.

One form of this poem is courtesy of Will Collins of Manor Farm. Will believes he first heard it from John Stratton, and remembers the first three verses in a slightly different format. This version was on a postcard in David Falcke's collection.

Extracts from *Plain Soldiering – A History of the Armed Forces on Salisbury Plain*
by N. D. G. James

In September 1914 the *Warminster Journal* recorded: 'A portion of the new Kitchener's Army is coming to this district for training, and during today and tomorrow, no less than 24,000 will arrive in the neighbourhood of Codford where they will be encamped for this purpose.'

A week later it was reported that, 'Codford had been transferred from a village of little more than five hundred people to a military town of many thousands' and that 'camping grounds' for the tents were located at 'the Fisherton Delamere end of

Codford.' These were mainly on Manor Farm, although the 2nd Wessex Royal Engineers were in camp near Codford Station.

On 25th September the *Journal* reported that, 'the camps are divided into two divisions, the 25th and the 26th. The former is situated in the Codford and Fisherton Delamere area . . . while the latter is around Sherrington.'

The author lists the fifteen Codford Camps occupied by the 25th Division:

Camps 1 and 2 were on the north side of the Warminster road between The Manor at Fisherton and Malmpit Hill. Camps 3 and 4 were on the south side of the

Camp No. 1, Codford St Mary

road opposite Foxhole Bottom. Camp 5 lay between Little Wood and Codford St Mary Church, Camp 6 was to the north of the church and Camp 7 to the west. On the east side of, and close to the Chitterne road were five more camps, 8 to 12. Camps 13 and 14 stood beside the road to Manor Farm. Camp 15 was opposite Ashton Gifford to the north of the Warminster road.

There were a further twelve camps spread along the Wylye Valley close to the villages of Sherrington, Boyton, Upton Lovell and Corton which were allocated to the 26th Division.

A Red Cross Hospital was established near St Mary's Church but in the middle of October, 'erection of huts to replace tents had begun, starting at the Fisherton side.' Codford Military Hospital was situated in Punch Bowl Bottom and extended down to Chitterne Road.

In October 1914 it was announced that an area of fifty acres at Knook, some two and a half miles north-east of Codford St Peter, had been selected for a camp, and according to the late Reverend E. D. Ginever, Knook was laid out as an artillery camp in 1914 while at the same time Heytesbury House was taken over for officers' quarters.

The expansion of Codford as a military centre was, to a large extent, dependent on a railway connection. In August 1914 it was clear that improved railway facilities

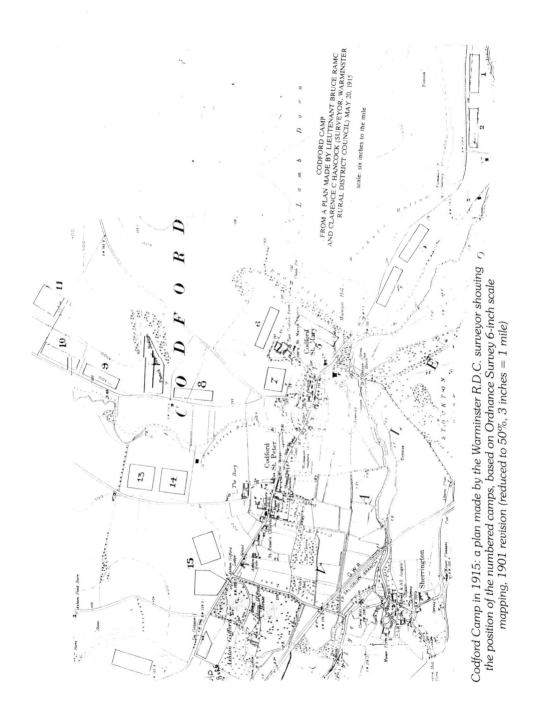

CODFORD CAMP
FROM A PLAN MADE BY LIEUTENANT BRUCE RAMC
AND CLARENCE C HANCOCK (SURVEYOR, WARMINSTER
RURAL DISTRICT COUNCIL) MAY 20, 1915

scale: six inches to the mile

Codford Camp in 1915: a plan made by the Warminster R.D.C. surveyor showing the position of the numbered camps, based on Ordnance Survey 6-inch scale mapping, 1901 revision (reduced to 50%, 3 inches = 1 mile) were needed at Codford station and by October, the constructions of new sidings was 'well in hand.' However the sidings were only a beginning and the following issue of the *Warminster Journal* reported that 'the extension of the railway is being pushed ahead rapidly'.

On leaving Codford station, the Codford Camp Railway swung eastwards to complete a half circle, passing to the north of Ashton Gifford before crossing the main road about 700 yards north west of Codford St Peter Church. From here it continued westwards through Camp 15, to cross the road from Codford St Peter to Manor Farm. The line turned north for some 200 yards before bearing due east between camps 13 and 14 and over the Chitterne Brook. At this point it swung north again over the Codford–Chitterne Road to the north-west of Codford Hill where this section of the line terminated. The railway divided and a branch ran southwards over the Chitterne Road opposite the punchbowl, and then besides the road. Here it bore to the east along the present road on the north of Codford St Mary, running between camps 6 and 7, where it swung south before it ended besides Camp 5. The total route length was a little over two and a half miles.

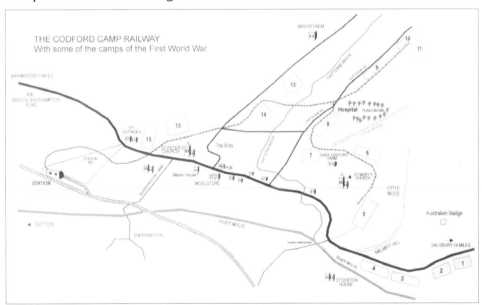

The Codford Camp Railway, illustrated by Brian Marshall, based on an original map by Martyn Lock

The sudden arrival of a large number of soldiers in a rural area was bound to have a considerable impact on village life. At Boyton 'the church has been given up entirely to the use of troops', while at Codford temporary shops, cafes, barbers saloons and so on, sprang up on any vacant site and even in front gardens beside the main street.

At first the welfare of so many soldiers was a problem but by early October the situation had improved. The Bristol YMCA erected a commodious marquee in the centre of Codford which could accommodate about a thousand men. Some six months later a YMCA hut had been built thanks to the generosity of an anonymous donor.

By the middle of October 1914 the fine autumn had come to an abrupt end and a long period of rain followed. Codford had its share of wet and cold. Extensive flooding occurred in the village especially in the area around the railway station and the camp became known as 'Codford on the Mud.'

The 26th Division left Codford in September 1915 for Salonica, and later the 25th Division went to France where it remained for the rest of the War. Although these Divisions were replaced with other British troops, in July 1916 Codford Camp was chosen as the New Zealand Command Depot for men who, having been wounded or sick, had completed their convalescent period but were not yet fit for active service. Since the Depot held some 2,500 men it was essential to provide a hospital in the immediate vicinity, and Codford Camp Hospital was taken over by No 3 New Zealand General Hospital. It contained beds for 10 officers and 980 soldiers.

Codford Camp was not popular for its surroundings or its exterior attractions. Less than a mile from the camp headquarters lay the old-fashioned Wiltshire village from which the camp derived its name – the only oasis of interest in the midst of a drab environment. Men usually went to Codford after a period of fourteen days convalescent leave which did not enhance its popularity.

Under such circumstances it was particularly important to provide adequate facilities for relaxation during off duty hours. 'Probably the most popular of Codford's institutes was the New Zealand War Contingent's Club, Aotea Roa . . . claimed inside and outside the Depot as the best equipped club on the Plain. Its management was in the hands of ten capable ladies of the War Contingent Association whose arduous work . . . was very faithfully done.' Aotea Roa is the Maori name for New Zealand.

On 31st October 1918 the strength of the Depot was 33 officers and 2,382 soldiers, while the hospital had 40 officers and 979 soldiers making a total of 3,361 for all ranks.

Little is recorded about Australian troops at Codford but since there are graves of 31 Australian soldiers as well as those of 66 New Zealanders in Codford St Mary New Churchyard it would appear that some Australians were admitted to the New Zealand Hospital.

During the First War a reproduction of the badge of the Australian Forces was cut on the side of the hill above Foxhole Bottom. Although No 1 Australian Command Depot was at Sutton Veny, this site may have been chosen because of its prominent position.

[Extracts from *Plain Soldiering: a history of the armed forces on Salisbury Plain*, by N D G James (Salisbury: Hobnob Press) 1987, chapters 11 and 13. James's text has been adapted and paraphrased in places (with the publisher's permission), with additional information from the *Warminster Journal* and elsewhere.]

The Wirral Camp at Codford
13th Cheshire Regiment – Autumn 1914

At the Gladstone Hall meeting on December 23rd [1914], for the promotion locally of the Volunteer Training Corps movement, Sir William H. Lever, who presided, gave an account of his meeting with the Wirral Battalion Men at Codford. He said:

> I went to the camp at Codford on Monday, and perhaps you would like to hear a word or two of what I saw there. First of all, I bring a hearty message of greeting to all, and an assurance of the very great pleasure it gives them to know that we are holding this meeting tonight. They are all very fit and well – I did not see a man there who did not look very much younger than when I saw him last before he went into camp. And yet they have not had ideal conditions. I don't think I ever saw so much mud in my life as I saw in Codford. It is a very sticky sort of mud. It is a chalky soil, and even in a field where there is grass, after a shower like that which fell about noon before we arrived, you would slip two steps back for every one you took forward.
>
> Then the drilling is done on the side of a hill about as steep as Heswall Hill. It is certainly steeper than any other I think in the neighbourhood, and therefore they have good practice over hard country. They have got out of their tents and into their huts, which is a great comfort. They had only taken the tents down a week or ten days before my visit. I saw the places where they had been. A trench had been dug around each tent so that the centre of the tent was fairly dry, and fairly above the level of the mud, which was a lake all around the tents in every direction. They are very comfortable now, and happy.
>
> Their food is good; they speak very highly of their officers; they are perfectly happy and are getting hard and fit, ready to give a good account of themselves and to be an honour and a credit to you and to Port Sunlight, and to all their comrades everywhere.

Before the close of the meeting, the Chairman received and read, amid applause, the following message from Codford, to which, it was agreed, he should send a reply:

> Wirral Battalion send to you and to Port Sunlight and to Wirral Heartiest Christmas Greetings and thanks for practical kindness shown by gifts and by your personal visit. We hope to send you best year's greetings from Berlin or sooner. – Lieut-Col. Field, Commanding 13th Cheshire's, Codford.

The camp was muddy and partly flooded at the time of the Chairman's visit, but the wooden huts indicated a marked improvement on the conditions of camp life. The Chairman addressed the men whilst in the midst of their drill, and afterwards by the kind arrangement of General Allan, who happened to be present, and the Colonel, in the YMCA Home which had recently been provided, the officers having fallen out and the men left standing easy, they were free to demonstrate, which they did by cheering to Chairman vigorously and laughing at his jokes and anecdotes. Two specimens of the Roll of Honour were shown, and left in the camp with information that a copy was being sent to the homes of each of the employees of Port Sunlight who were on active duty.

The Wirral Battalion, it is pleasant to hear, have now left the camp they called Codford-on-the-Mud, and are doing duty in Bournemouth.

[Extract from 'Our chairman and the Wirral Camp at Codford', *Progress*, 1914]

Sudden Death at Codford Camp
Lance Corporal dies at Church Parade

Mr. F.A.P. Sylvester [coroner] on Monday afternoon held an inquest at Manor Farm Dairy, Codford concerning the death of William Cooper, a lance corporal in the 10th Cheshire Regiment, who is training at the army camp. The deceased, who was aged twenty years, was taken ill suddenly while on church parade on Sunday morning, and he died within a few minutes.

George Hope, a lance corporal in the 10th Cheshire Regiment, identified the body, and said the deceased was a personal friend of his. Witness had known him when they were at home, and they slept in the same tent in the camp. Deceased told him on Sunday that he rose at five o'clock in the morning and had been down to 'the town' and had got a breakfast of bacon and eggs. He did not say where he got the food. Witness left the tent after that and did not see deceased again until about ten minutes before the parade at 9.30. Deceased called to him on parade, and the next thing witness saw of him was when he was on the ground.

> *The Coroner* You were not near him when he was picked up?
> *Witness* I was about seventeen paces away.
> *The Coroner* When he called to you at 9.30 he was perfectly all right?
> *Witness* He seemed to be quite all right then.
> *The Coroner* Have you ever known him to have a fit?
> *Witness* No, sir.
> *The Coroner* Did he ever tell you he suffered from fits?
> *Witness* No, sir.
> *The Coroner* How long has he been training?

Witness A fortnight on Wednesday.

The Coroner Do you know his family?

Witness Yes, sir.

The Coroner You would have heard if he had had any fits before?

Witness Not necessarily so.

The Coroner Probably?

Witness Yes. He had complained to several of our friends in the tent of a dizziness in the head when he was on watch that morning. He did not say it was a headache, but that it was a dizziness in the head.

The Coroner Had he been a man of pretty robust health do you know?

Witness From all I know of him he was.

The Coroner And I suppose he was passed by a doctor – undoubtedly.

Witness Yes.

Edward Johnson, a private in the 10th Cheshire's said he slept in the same tent with the deceased and the last witness. Deceased slept well the night before his death, and there was no disturbance in the tent.

The Coroner You have not heard of his having any quarrel with anyone?

Witness No, sir.

The Coroner What did you see of him in the morning?

Witness He told me his head did not ache but that it felt dizzy. That would be about 7.30. Before that he had had breakfast in the village.

The Coroner Has he had any attacks of dizziness before?

Witness No.

The Coroner Or had any fit while he has been here?

Witness No.

The Coroner You were on parade at 9.30?

Witness Yes.

The Coroner What happened then?

Witness He fell backwards.

The Coroner Suddenly?

Witness Yes.

The Coroner Had you started your drill or just got into line?

Witness We had just got into line.

The Coroner What happened?

Witness They took him and carried him out of the ranks under a tree.

The Coroner Did he go for breakfast by himself?

Witness When he went into the village he did.

The Coroner You don't know where he went?

Witness No.

John Lamb, a private in the 10th Cheshire's, said he saw them carrying the deceased and asked them to put him on to the ground. His face was flushed, his teeth were clenched, and he was moving in an agitated way. Witness thought it was apoplexy and loosened his clothing. Witness was with him when he died about seven minutes later.

William Thomas Wevill, a corporal in the R.A.M.C., said his attention was called to the deceased and he found him cold. Witness tested his pulse and found it was not beating. He tested his breathing with a piece of looking glass, but that was also unsatisfactory. Witness then summoned a medical man and applied artificial respiration. Witness could find no signs of life.

The Coroner Deceased had not been in the hospital before?
Witness No.

Lieut. Henry William Spaight, R.A.M.C., said he saw the deceased after death. There were no marks on the body.

The Coroner Had the deceased done anything in the way of work before that parade?
Witness No. It was a church parade.
Witness added that he was of the opinion that the deceased suffered an epileptic fit and the immediate cause of death would be asphyxia.

An officer of the 10th Cheshire Regiment who was present replied, in answer to the Coroner, that the deceased's conduct had been quite satisfactory as far as he knew.

The Coroner said that there was no doubt that the cause of death was asphyxia suffocation, as often happened in such cases. There were no marks on the body, and they had evidence to the effect the deceased was quiet during the night and that there was no quarrel or anything of that sort in which deceased might have received a blow. He recommended the jury to return a verdict of death due to asphyxia suffocation due to an epileptic fit. The jury accordingly returned a verdict to this effect.

[From *Warminster Journal* 2nd October 1914]

Warning to Photographers
Snapshotting at Codford camp

At Warminster on Thursday, before Colonel Alexander and Dr. Charles Alcock, Herbert William Nutley, of 46, Alexander Road, Frome, described as a printer, was charged with taking photographs in the lines at Codford Military Camps, against the Defences of the Realm Act, 1914.

Lieutenant Abell, of the Cheshire Regiment, stated that a sentry reported to him that the prisoner was taking photographs of the camp without their permission.

He reported the matter to the Colonel, who gave orders that the prisoner should be handed over to the custody of the civil authorities, and PC Pearce said he took the prisoner into custody.

Prisoner stated that he was unaware that he was doing anything wrong, and was sorry for what he had done.

Supt. Scott said he had made enquiries at Frome, where the prisoner resided, and found that he was a respectable young man.

Lieutenant Abell said the colonel of the regiment wished the case brought forward as a warning to people entering the camp and photographing it without permission. He was satisfied that in this case the young man acted innocently.

The Chairman (Colonel Alexander) said prisoner had done an improper thing, and placed himself in a serious position. If he did such a thing again and was brought before the Bench, he would be seriously dealt with. Under the circumstances he would be dismissed. Prisoner was allowed his camera, but the negatives of the photographs he had taken were confiscated by the police.

[From *Devizes and Wilts Gazette* 22nd October 1914]

World War One
Codford Camp

There's an isolated, desolate spot I'd like to mention,
Where all you hear is 'Stand At Ease,' 'Slope Arms,' 'Quick March,' 'Attention.'
It's miles from anywhere, by Gad, it's a rum 'un,
A chap once lived there for fifty years and never saw a woman.
    There are lots of little huts, all dotted here and there,
For those who have to live inside, I've offered many a prayer,
Inside the huts there's RATS as big as any nanny goat,
Last night a soldier saw one trying on his overcoat.
    It's slutch up to the eyeballs, you get it in your ears,
But into it you've got to go without a sign of fear,
And when you've had a bath of slutch, you just set to and groom,
And get cleaned up for next Parade, or else it's 'Orderly Room.'
    Week in, week out, from morn til night, with full Pack and a Rifle,
Like Jack and Jill, you climb the hills, of course that's just a trifle.
'Slope Arms,' 'Fix Bayonets,' then 'Present' they fairly put you through it,
And as you stagger to your Hut, the sergeant shouts 'Jump To It.'
    With tunics, boots and puttees off, you quickly get the habit,
You gallop up and down the hills just like a blooming rabbit.

'Heads backward bend,' 'Arms upward stretch,' 'Heels raise,' then 'Ranks change places,'
And later on they make you put your kneecaps where your face is.
       Now when this War is over and we've captured Kaiser Billy,
To shoot him would be merciful and absolutely silly,
Just send him down to Codford, there amongst the Rats and clay,
And I bet it won't be long before he droops and fades away.
       WE'RE NOT DOWNHEARTED YET.

[This poem exists in various forms, on postcards and elsewhere]

Communicating with the Enemy
Charge under the Defence of the Realm Act at Warminster

At Warminster Town Hall, on Tuesday – before Colonel the Hon. W.P. Alexander and Dr Charles Alcock – Private George Bader, of 13th Cheshire Regiment, No. 3 Camp, Codford, was charged with communicating with the enemy, to wit, a prisoner of war confined in camp at Lancashire, under the Defence of the Realm Act, 1914.

Supt. Scott said that on the previous day Colonel Blair, a chief officer of the 26th Division at Codford, communicated with him about prisoner, whom he described as a German alien enemy, and asked witness to deal with him. Witness took charge of him, and found in the meantime that he was an English subject but was the son of a German prisoner of war and his mother was a German woman.

The Chairman What is your age now, boy?
Prisoner Nineteen.
The Clerk Where were you born?
Prisoner Liverpool.

Supt. Scott said that he found that prisoner had been communicating with his father, who was an alien enemy. He had written to his father, who was in a Lancashire detention camp, saying he was anxiously waiting a reply, and under the Act no communication was allowed. Under the circumstances as they could not deal with him as being an unregistered alien, he asked that the prisoner be handed back to be dealt with by the military authorities.

The Clerk The only charge is that he communicated with his father, who is an alien prisoner at the Lancashire detention camp?

Supt. Scott Yes. I may say the officers commanding consider him to be dangerous, especially as he had a letter from his mother telling him not to go on foreign service.

The Clerk said it was a case for Court martial, and the Bench had no jurisdiction. The Chairman said he would be handed back to the military authorities to be dealt with.

[From: *Warminster Journal* 23rd October 1914]

The King's Man

The third son of the Reverend Edward Denny of Codford St Peter was one of the first local casualties of the Great War. Second-Lieutenant Barry Maynard Rynd Denny was a member of the 1st Battalion The King's [Liverpool Regiment]. He had been gazetted to the Special Reserve of the King's in April 1914, so had volunteered before there was any hint of the coming conflict. Two months later, on 28th June, the assassination of the heir to the Austrian throne, Archduke Francis Ferdinand and his wife at Sarajevo set in motion a train of events that led to four years of unprecedented global warfare and the death of a generation.

On 12th August 1914 he proceeded overseas to the Western Front. Barry Denny was to die of wounds received at Polygon Wood in the first of the Ypres Battles, fought in Flanders fields in October 1914. In the *History of the King's Regiment [Liverpool] 1914-1919* Everard Wyrall sets the scene in which the twenty-nine year old officer played a hero's role, mortally wounded in the first Act.

Sir John French had primarily considered his I Corps to reinforce the II, III, Cavalry and IV Corps, [IV Corps was composed of the 3rd Cavalry and 7th Divisions under Sir H. Rawlings; they had been used in the Antwerp operations], who, on 19th October, occupied a front of some 25 miles – much wider than their strength warranted. But the enemy was threatening the Belgians with a strong turning movement, the British Commander-in-Chief, therefore, directed the 1st Corps [Sir Douglas Haig] to move to the north of Ypres, and the right of the Corps – the 2nd Division – to pass through Ypres itself. These orders were received by the Corps Commanders on the evening of the 19th October, and are of considerable interest, since they give briefly some idea of the intentions of the higher command, and the reason the 1st King's Regiment became involved in the Battle of Langemarck. The text of the orders were as follows:

The enemies' strength on the front Menin–Ostend is estimated at about a corps and no more. [The enemies' real strength between Menin and Ostend on 20th October was approximately five corps, i.e., the whole of the newly formed Fourth German Army. The

Army had been formed secretly.] The 1st Corps will advance via Thorout with the idea of capturing Bruges. The enemy will be attacked and driven on Ghent [25 miles south-east of Bruges]. The right of the 1st Corps will pass through Ypres. After passing through Ypres the G.O.C., 1st Corps is to decide according to the situation whether to attack the enemy lying to the north or that portion of the hostile forces reported in the direction of Courtrai [six miles north-east of Menin]. During the advance the 1st Corps will have the French cavalry on its left and the 3rd Cavalry Division [General Byng] on its right.

Second Division Operational Orders, however, issued at 1.30am on 20th [verbal orders having been given some hours earlier] are prefaced by the following sentence: 'Hostile columns are reported to be moving west and south-west from Menin, Roulers and Thorout'. In point of fact that the enemy was advancing with the intention of turning the left flank of the Allies. Thus the opposing forces were each engaged in similar operations, which ended in the desperate struggle for Ypres, and the formation of the now notorious Ypres Salient.

The 1st King's Regiment did not actively become involved in the Battle until the 24th; that is to say, the Battalion did not exchange shots with the enemy. At 10pm on 20th, 1st Corps Operational Orders ordered an advance in two stages on the morning of the 21st; the first to the line Passchendaele–Poelcappelle, the second to a line about one and a half miles northwards through Westroosebecke. French Territorials and refugees blocked the road along which the 1st Division was to advance, and it was somewhat after 9am [instead of 7am] before the general advance of the 1st Corps took place. The 6th Brigade, in Divisional Reserve, moved from billets at 5am, having been ordered to assemble on each side of the road just south-west of Wieltje, ready to move forward if required. The King's marched off at 4.55am until they reached the village, where the Battalion halted in a turnip field for several hours. In front the continuous rattle of machine-gun and rifle-fire, and the roar of the guns, intimated that heavy fighting was in progress. On the right the 7th Division, already worn out, were being heavily attacked by two practically fresh German divisions. In the centre and left of the line, three more hostile divisions were attacking the 1st and 2nd Divisions; the comparative strength of the opposing British and German troops, being on the 21st, about 2 to 5. Nevertheless, in the face of this superiority, the 1st Corps made a slight advance, though not as much as was hoped for, General Headquarters being then ignorant of the strength of the enemy.

After two hours or more in the turnip field, the King's men moved on about three-quarters of a mile and again halted. But apart from watching the shrapnel bursting in the distance above a wood on the right, and other signs of the struggle going on in the front, the day passed without incident for the battalion. At nightfall the King's men marched back to St Jean and billeted in the village.

The morning and early afternoon of the 22nd were spent in billets, but at 4pm sudden orders were received by the King's to 'fall in' preparatory to marching off. The 2nd Cavalry Division, between Zandvoorde and Ypres–Comines Canal, had captured a German orderly who was carrying a message ordering an attack at night on the line held by the 2nd Cavalry Division. The latter had asked Corps Headquarters for reinforcements, and troops in reserve to 1st and 2nd Divisions had been ordered to proceed immediately to Klein Zillebeke. The 1st King's marched via Potijze and Zillebeke, reaching the latter place about 6.15pm. Only one company of the King's ['B'] was sent up to the trenches, which were on the ridge between Zandvoorde and Hollebeke. But, although rifle-fire was going on on both flanks, not even a stray bullet came the way of the King's men.

At dawn on the 23rd, the enemy not having made their expected attack, the 1st King's marched back to St Jean to their old billets. Throughout the day the Battalion was again in reserve, though the 6th brigade was much split up, the 1st K. R. R. and the 2nd South Stafford's having been sent up to Pilckem to assist the 1st Division, and the 1st Royal Berkshires to billets and bivouacs just south of the main road at Frezenberg. Only the 6th Brigade Headquarters and the 1st King's, therefore, remained at St Jean on the night of the 23rd October.

During the 22nd and 23rd fighting along the whole front had been heavy, and although the line changed very little, the 7th Division was fast becoming exhausted. Gradually the German forces were increasing, and, whereas on the 21st only five hostile divisions attacked the 7th, 2nd and 1st British Divisions, the German divisions increased on 22nd to six, and on the 23rd to seven; and they were all practically fresh troops. With dogged pluck, however, the 4th and 1st Corps troops fought the enemy to a standstill and killed enormous numbers of his infantry as they advanced in massed formation, the British artillery also frequently having splendid targets, of which they took the fullest advantage.

On the 24th October, however, the King's men entered into the battle. It is an unforgettable day in the history of the 1st Battalion, for at dusk, when the day's fighting was practically over and when British and Germans were seeking what rest was possible before renewing the desperate struggle on the morrow, their gallant Commanding Officer – Lieut.-Colonel William Stirling Bannatyne – was shot down and died a little while after receiving his wound.

At 7.10pm on 23rd orders were received at 2nd Division Headquarters that the division was to be relieved by the 17th French Division, the relief to be completed by 11pm. The 6th Brigade [as already stated], on relief was billeted in the Potijze–Frezenberg–St Jean area; the 5th Brigade was in billets and bivouacs about the 'Halte 2nd kilometre' [later known as 'Hell Fire Corner'] on the Ypres–Menin road; the 4th [Guards] Brigade was to march to Zillebeke.

On 24th, the King's men, after crossing the railway south of the Ypres–Zonnebeke road, struck across country, and, with the Berkshires, were formed up under cover about half a mile east by north of Westhoek. On arrival in this position the information was received that the 5th Brigade, with troops of the 7th Division had already cleared the Polygon Wood. Extra ammunition was now served out to the King's men, and the battalion prepared for action. The village of Westhoek stood on the summit of a slight rise, and after extra ammunition had been issued, the 1st Kings moved to the forward slope on the eastern side of the village and awaited further orders. The battalion was now behind the Polygon Wood, which was under shell-fire, shrapnel and high explosive shells bursting over the wood continuously. Zonnebeke, away on the left of the battalion was also under fire, heavy fighting for the possession of the village being in progress.

Orders were then received by Colonel Bannatyne to take over the trenches held by the 1st South Stafford's belonging to the 22nd Brigade. These trenches were duly taken over, but a few minutes later the King's were ordered to attack the village of Molenaarelsthoek, with the Berkshires on the left and a French division on the left of the Berkshires. The two British battalions were to take the time of the advance from the French, who were to attack Zonnebeke. The 5th Brigade had been ordered to come upon the right of the King's men and fill the gap between the battalion and the Guards, who were opposite Reutel Ridge [Spur?].

The formation of the 1st King's in this attack was- 'B' Company [Lieut. P.J. Furneaux] on the right, 'A' Company [Capt. J.H.S. Batten] on the left. As the 5th Brigade had not come up as expected, 'C' Company [Capt. D.G.H. Scott] was put in to fill the gap on the right of the battalion to keep in touch with the Guards, who were to advance simultaneously but did not do so. This necessitated the right of 'C' Company being sent back, with the result that a gap was caused between the left of 'C' and the right of 'B' Companies; two platoons of 'D' Company were, therefore, sent up to fill the space between 'C' and 'B'.

The village of Molenaarrelsthoek was on the Broodseinde–Becelaere road, and about half a mile from the north-east corner of Polygon Wood. The latter, at this period, practically unspoilt by hostile shell fire, occupied the centre of the eastern face of a rough triangle formed by Ypres and the villages of Gheluvelt and Zonnebeke. Within this triangle the King's were to spend thirty days, fighting many a bitter battle with the enemy, and before they left the area, about the middle of November, the Polygon Wood had already acquired an evil reputation. The places of interest in this area, known chiefly to the King's men were [besides the already mentioned] Black Watch Corner [at the south-west corner of Polygon Wood], Polderhoek, Veldhoek, the Nonne Bosschen Wood [Nun's Wood], Hooge, Bellewaarde Farm, and numerous other farms which lay north, south and west of the Polygon Wood.

In the long years of the War, under the merciless shelling to which they were subjected, all these places practically disappeared, the Polygon Wood being reduced to a shapeless mass of tree stumps, blasted and torn by the incessant storm of shrapnel and high explosive shells which swept the area.

In good order the three companies of the King's men advanced on Molenaarelsthoeke and all went well until they reached the western outskirts of the village. The houses had, however, been well prepared for defence by the Germans, who had loop-holed all buildings, in some of which they had mounted machine-guns. 'A' Company was the first to be brought to a standstill by a perfect hurricane of bullets from the loop-holed houses. Casualties now became numerous, but, not to be denied, the King's men charged the houses and cleared the Germans from them. With the exception of about half a dozen outlying houses on the eastern side of the village, Molenaarelsthoeke was in the hands of the 1st Kings, but it was from these buildings that the heaviest machine gun fire came. Twice they were charged by the two platoons of 'D' Company under Second-Lieut. B.M.R. Denny, without success, the gallant young subaltern falling mortally wounded, and eventually the platoons fell back about fifty yards to a hastily-dug trench in which, for the time being, they took shelter.

In all the total King's losses on 24th October, besides Barry Denny, were their Commanding Officer Lieut.-Colonel Ballyntyne, shot through the heart and killed outright by sniper fire, Captain Hudson shot through the wrist, with twenty-four N.C.O.'s and men killed and wounded. The following day two more officers died, Capt. J.H.S. Batten was shot by a sniper in the houses and Lieut. H.B. Wallace killed in the advance. The battalion had eighteen further casualties. On 26th October all of 'B' Company's officers had become casualties, Company Sergeant Major Connolly took command only to be killed almost immediately.

The day had gone well for the King's; they had cleared the houses in the village, gained the ridge, and had established themselves in the positions won. 'The advance of the King's,' records the 6th Brigade Diary, 'was most gallantly carried out.' The cost had, however been heavy. Two officers – Lieuts. P.T. Furneaux and E.B. Baker – were killed, and Capt. H.S. Oppenheimer and Lieuts. A.M.Savage, R.G. Tudor, R.W. Coode-Adams, and D.L. Lumsden, were wounded; thirty-four N.C.O.s and men were also killed and wounded.

As the King's advanced, Barry Denny died of the wounds he had suffered two days earlier at the start of the battle for Polygon Wood. He is buried in Ypres Town Cemetery, Ieper, West Vlaanderen in Belgium. Everard Wyrall wrote:

> Coming generations may pardonably assume from the official nomenclature of areas and dates of the Battles of Ypres, 1914 that between the Battle of Langemarck, 1914, [21st-24th October] and the Battle of Gheluvelt [29th-31st October] the opposing forces were not engaged. But even a cursory glance at the war diaries of units in the field, and those kept privately, will reveal that although the 25th,26th, 27th and 28th October were days of comparative quietude, the grim struggle went on unceasingly as the story of the 1st King's Regiment will show.

[Sources: adapted from Simon Jones M.A., Curator – Kings Regiment; *The History of the King's Regiment [Liverpool] 1914-1919* by Everard Wyrall; Commonwealth War Graves Commission]

Daily Life at Codford Camp

When Terry Crawford wrote his excellent book *Wiltshire and the Great War*, now sadly out of print, he unearthed a treasure trove of intimate details about life in the camps. He discovered that soldiers quartered in surrounding camps such as Boyton and Corton were sometimes regarded as being based at Codford, a fact that is reflected in the casualty lists when men living in Stockton and Chitterne are listed as residing in Codford. His research has satisfied him that the Boyton/ Corton and Heytesbury Camps were the base for the British and Australian artillery units, with the infantry being quartered at Codford.

By December 11th 1914 the Great Western Railway had carried out work required by the War Office on five local stations, the improvements at Codford were the second most expensive at £7,812, Westbury station cost £9,642, with Wylye, Heytesbury and Warminster £1,404, £1,715 and £2,801 respectively. The GWR War Reports of the General Manager to the Board of Directors 1914-1919 gives the length of Codford track as 4 miles 212 yards, including 2¾ miles of running line. As early as October 1914 the GWR's General Manager was writing to the Board of Trade to point out that 'the War Office have formed a camp at Codford, and we are experiencing considerable difficulty in connection with daily supplies.' He proposed an extra siding, whose points would be closer to a level crossing than was allowed by the Board's regulations. The Board agreed that this would be permitted under the circumstances.

Codford Station

Many of the men arriving in Codford at the beginning of World War One had to live in tents until huts could be built to house them. Mr Crawford records that, 'Some of the arrivals were wearing clogs, most were in civilian clothing: when after some weeks uniforms arrived, these were a hotchpotch that included obsolete blue and red jackets. Some NCOs [the senior ones being 'old sweats', the junior ones

Postal delivery in the flood, Codford St Mary, January 1915

often arbitrarily selected from the recruits] wore bowler hats as a sign of authority.'
By September 25th instructors from the Duke of Cornwall's Light Infantry, the
Grenadiers and Royal Marines had arrived – no doubt these professionals were
horrified at the task facing them!

At Codford platoon commanders were issued with 1909 [unamended] editions
of *Small Arms Training* and other manuals often had to be shared.

Eight hundred men of the 10th Cheshires had no change of clothing and
were given a blanket apiece, their provisional NCOs being chosen by what they had
done in civilian life. The same Regiment's 11th Battalion:

> turned into a field and found itself without tents, blankets or food. The Colonel and two
> or three officers went into Salisbury and bought what they could, and presently rations
> were being drawn and a tent pitched for every twenty men. The men had been told to
> bring their ordinary clothes. They sweated in these and had no change. To wash, they
> went down to the river, stripped, dipped and ran about to dry.

After weeks of sleeping in the mud, still with one blanket each, and with a
very wet winter setting in, the 11th became discontented and 'serious trouble was
narrowly averted' by an issue of beer and a move to billets in Bournemouth. The
King's Shropshire Light Infantry regimental history recalled that at Codford:

> From October 15 until November 10 it rained in torrents every day. Roads to the camp
> became impassable, and training was suspended. Even route marches were impossible
> . . . the men, of course, had no change of clothing, and no washing accommodation.
> Here was nothing to be done day after day but to lie, in an indescribable state of mud, in
> tents without floorboards, listening to the rain beating on the canvas.

An article by Douglas Macleane, 'Recollections of Salisbury Plain', appeared in the *Saturday Review*, 3rd July 1915. Referring to the Wylye Valley, particularly Codford:

> Thousands of navvies are driving straight roads and crooked railways over hill and over dale, through groves which the nightingale used to read curtain lectures to his spouse. The locality was converted from a haunt of ancient peace into a kind of Californian Aldershot, and seamed in every direction by the spade of the navvy.
>
> —— has become known throughout England, wherever soldiers are found, as 'Mudford'. But what riverside place would not be a sea of slush after four months of continuous rain, with 30,000 men tramping it daily and incessant heavy traction passing over it. When first the troops came in the early autumn they were enchanted with the great, pure, open spaces of the downs and the lucid, azure skies. By Christmas, a bomb dropped from above would have gone almost through to the antipodeans.

Flood on main Salisbury Road, Codford St Mary, January 1915

In 1914 a soldier taking part in manoeuvres was reckoned to need 4,200 calories and was given rations providing between 4,500 and 4,600. During the war the rations and cash allowance aimed at providing a UK soldier with a diet of just over 4,000 calories, though the size of the allowance did not always keep up with the rising price of food. Contemporary accounts give slight variations in the components of rations reflecting local circumstances. Throughout the war adjustments were made several times, the meat ration fell from twenty ounces in August 1914 to eight ounces in May 1918.

In 1915 daily rations for the soldiers were one pound of fresh meat, one-pound bread, two ounces of sugar per man. Jam and cheese were omitted, but the cash allowance to be spent to provide a variety of other food was 5½d. Wilfred

Nevill, a subaltern in the 8th Surreys at Codford in the summer of that year, had been finding it difficult to feed 192 hungry men at the old rate of 4d per man a day to cover butter, cake, jam, flour, cheese, vegetables, sausages, eggs, kippers, and all breakfast dishes. In September general officers commanding were empowered to reduce the daily bread ration to twelve ounces. Terry Crawford notes that Nevill's men seemed to have enjoyed a comparatively good menu.

Cyrus Greenslade was one of the former OTC members who trained at Tidworth Pennings shortly after war was declared. While he was there he was told that, having been a lance corporal in the corps, he had been commissioned into three different battalions of the Devonshire Regiment. He was instructed to join the 10th Battalion being formed at Stockton, to where he rode on his motorcycle. On arrival he was ordered to bring up from Codford station about 1,000 men, mostly in civilian clothing. The divisional commander told all officers and NCOs to take drill books on parade with them and attempt only very limited exercises. Greenslade's platoon included a complete team from Woolwich Arsenal, which won all the football trophies contested during training.

At first the *George Hotel* housed part of the divisional headquarters, hardly encouraging off-duty relaxation there for the rank and file. The bar was open to the troops for an hour at midday and from six until nine in the evening, with an overflow marquee being hastily erected. At Upton Lovell, a mile away, an old shed at the *Prince Leopold Inn* was converted as living quarters for soldiers and workmen.

The YMCA provided a marquee in the centre of Codford that could hold something like 1,000 men; by early 1915 a YMCA refreshment and recreation hut had been built. The Congregational School also offered recreation, books, tea and coffee to off-duty soldiers. Another very early facility was Albany Ward's Picture Palace, one of two cinemas to be opened in the village, with seating for 500. A Red Cross Hospital was set up at St Mary's Church. An early report of enteric in camp stemmed from some men becoming ill after eating horse chestnuts.

When N.M. Hughes-Hallett arrived with the 7th King's Shropshires in early October, he wrote home expressing the hope that chairs would soon replace boxes in the officer's mess – though his battalion had plenty of blankets, and discussions were going on with Harrods about messing.

Until huts were erected, many buildings in Codford were taken over and used as offices by the Army. By September 15th the London City and Midland Bank had a branch in Codford, to be quickly followed by the Capital and Counties Bank.

'The old sleepy village is half filled with horrid booths and shanties, where tobacco, hosiery, and thousands of odds and ends can be bought at an increased cost, for the owner of the property has a week in rent for a glorified cupboard, which now constitutes a shop.'

Tradesmen who rented the Codford shack shops included G. Rogers of Trowbridge, ironmongers and house furnishers; H.G. Stratton, grocer; Cook of Warminster, chemist and manufacturer of mineral water; and S. J. Turner, seller of tobacco and ice cream. W E Chivers and Sons of Devizes erected five veterinary

Codford High Street

hospitals; one was at Codford, the others at Corton, Heytesbury, Warminster and Fovant.

In early October Sir John Jackson's company started to build fifteen hutted camps in Codford, with crowded workers trains leaving Salisbury at 6am and 6.10am Tokens were issued to the men to enable them to travel on the trains. The *Wiltshire Times* reported 33,000 men from Codford and Sherrington going into billets in early November 1915, leaving 2,000 to work on camp construction.

Twice during World War One King George V, the Sailor King, inspected troops in the vicinity. On 25th June 1915 he inspected the 18th Division near Stonehenge, twelve miles from Codford, where most of the Division was based. He then travelled to Sidbury Hill near Tidworth to inspect the 37th Division, which moved to France the next month. On 17th April 1917 the King travelled from Windsor to Bulford by special train in order to inspect the Australian Imperial Force; he rode from Bulford Station on a black charger from Australia. Many Australians marched the fifteen miles from Codford, across the Plain and back again. There were 63,000 men on parade and the march past lasted 1½ hours, from 12.15 to 13.45pm. The King presented some of twenty officers and men with decorations.

In 1917 forty-five acres of land near the camp were planted with vegetables as part of the nationwide efforts to boost food production; bee-keeping was another pursuit soldiers were encouraged to follow. In January that year the *Salisbury Journal* reported that Private Cooper of the New Zealand Regiment was in court for the alleged theft of twenty-two fowls valued at £4 8s., stolen in December from fowl houses on the Down belonging to John Maurice Stratton. It was suggested that he took nine fowls to the cookhouse for Private Jones to cook. Private Jones pointed out that he was in charge of feeding seventy invalided men; he pleaded not guilty of any involvement – saying he had not been absent for more than a quarter-hour of time on the night in question.

The commandeering of farmland for military needs was doubly frustrating to its owners at a time when there was good money to be made from it. The War Office could be a difficult and bureaucratic guest. As A H and E K Collins, the tenants of Manor Farm, Codford St Peter, were serving in the Army it fell to their long-suffering bailiff to deal with damage to gates, fences and crops by corresponding with a succession of army officers. In August 1917 he wrote to Number 13 Training Squadron at Yatesbury claiming £15 after an aeroplane had damaged thirty-two acres of barley. Two months later he complained to the Australians at Codford Camp that 'very serious damage . . . is being done to our Farm by troops digging trenches . . . Great holes are being made on some of the best land . . . it will take a very great amount of labour to fill them in.' In November he feared that the rifle ranges might be extended to include the only area of roots, where 320 sheep were to be 'lambed down'.

Most of his letters are firm but civil, but the bailiff's patience was obviously severely tested in his dealings with the Defence of the Realm Losses Royal Commission in London over delayed payment of rent. He claimed £984 13s. 1d. for almost a year's tenure of farmland by the military, and eventually was awarded £377 2s. 6d., plus £4 4s. towards the cost of preparing the case.

Meanwhile a neighbour, Jack Stratton of East Farm, Codford St Mary, noted in his diary for December 1917: 'War Office to pay £202 per. An. for 107 acres of pasture and 40 acres of arable.' Codford Camps 5, 6 and 7, surrounded the farm itself on three sides.

During the Great War nearly every Wiltshire camp had its own military post office and postmark, with the surprising exception of Codford. The outgoing letters and most parcels received the civilian Codford St Mary date-stamp (though some parcels did receive a simple circular mark bearing the camp name). The camp was among Wiltshire's largest, and one can only wonder how the village postal services were able to cope. In September 1914 Codford post office was extended and an extra pillar box installed, though this could hardly have been sufficient to handle the mail of some 30,000 extra recruits camped locally. In contrast the far smaller camp at Boyton had its own postmark, as did that at Sherrington, which existed for only three months.

After reading *Wiltshire and the Great War* a military postmark collector wrote to the author on a number of points, including the provision of postal services at Codford Camp, and the reason for it not having its own postmark – every other army camp in Wiltshire did! He had speculated that its mail may have been processed by another camp, but after assessing the number of postcards sent from Codford, he agreed that this was unlikely. There must have been post office facilities within the camp to distribute incoming mail for 15,000 soldiers, and Terry Crawford guesses that the camp's proximity to Codford enabled it to use expanded village facilities for outgoing mail. Most of the other camps were some way from civilisation!

By the end of the war, Australian Camp Post Office No 14 is said by one source to have been operating at Codford, though another source says it was No 5; whichever it was, an appropriate 'AIF Camp PO' strike would have applied to outgoing mail.

A Home Office report of January 1918 records POW camps at eight locations in the area, including Codford and Sutton Veny. The American Red Cross appears to have provided a canteen service at 'a large rest camp' in Codford. They also established an 'air service camp' as part of Services and Supply Base Section No 3 in the village on 23rd September 1918.

After the Armistice, with an uncertain civilian life awaiting them, many ANZAC soldiers still in England resented the continuing military discipline. There were some attempts, certainly by the New Zealand authorities at Codford, to provide training in civilian occupations.

[Sources: With the exception of 'Theft of Fowls' story taken from *Salisbury Journal* 20th January 1917 all the material in this chapter is taken from *Wiltshire and the Great War* and additional research by Terry Crawford]

Charge of Inciting Troops to Mutiny at Codford

The Trial of James Edmund Pinder

Supt. Scott said that on Tuesday, at about 1.30, he was at Codford St Mary, when he was called to the guardroom in Codford street, where he saw prisoner (a single man, aged 30, of Chesterton, Cambridge) in the custody of the authorities. They asked witness to take prisoner over on a charge of preaching sedition and of causing dissatisfaction and discontent amongst His Majesty's troops at Codford camps. Witness told prisoner that he would take him into custody, which he did, and brought him to Warminster. Witness had formally cautioned him and charged him, and in the presence of Sergeant Zebedee prisoner replied: 'I admit that I advised the men not to take up arms, as I would not take up arms for the King. I told them to tell their Colonel that they cannot take up arms and love their God.' Witness had the man searched, and 9s. was found upon him. He was placed in the cells.

Supt. Scott added that that was all the evidence he wished to offer. There were a good many witnesses to be called with regard to the case, including four or five men of different regiments and it was necessary to see them beforehand. He also had to communicate with headquarters, and so he asked for a remand of eight days. The matter could then be investigated and laid before the public Prosecutor.

Prisoner said he had nothing to say.

The Clerk You understand the charge?

Supt. Scott The charge has been read over to him again this morning.

Prisoner said that if a man professed to be a Christian and saw he was doing wrong to leave himself in God's hands. He never asked any man to disobey a single order.

The Magistrate's Clerk [Mr H.J. Wakeman] The evidence is that you told them to tell their officer they must not fight.

Mr Gibbings, who was working in the camp in connection with Spurgeon's Tabernacle, said he had been advised by the Rev. F. Smith [Baptist Minister] to offer himself as a witness.

The Clerk We shall not hear any further evidence today.

Mr Lindsay Bury Are you for the prisoner or the prosecution?

Mr Gibbings I simply want to say what I know.

The Clerk If the prosecution want to call you as a witness there is no objection.

Mr Gibbings then said the prisoner had been with him a few times to the camp. They distributed the *Christian Herald* and literature amongst the soldiers. He had on one occasion heard prisoner express his views to a man who the witness thought was a coachman living at Sherrington. The man, however, proved to be one of His Majesty's soldiers, but he was not in full uniform. Prisoner on that occasion expressed views, which he [witness] dissented. He held opposite views to those expressed by prisoner. His only regret was that he was too old to join His Majesty's Army.

The Clerk You wish to disassociate yourself from him?

Witness Yes.

The Chairman I understand that you and the prisoner have been working together, and you now publicly wish to disassociate yourself from his views?

Witness Yes.

The Chairman That's quite all right. We are glad to hear it.

Supt. Scott said it might be necessary to call Mr Gibbings as a witness. The Chairman asked prisoner whether he would like to apply for bail. The prisoner replied that he would, but he did not know who would stand for him. The Chairman said this was a very serious charge and he would have to find two sureties of £25 each.

Supt. Scott said if he obtained bail he should give an assurance that he would not approach any of the men in the camp again. Prisoner said he would give that assurance, and he was then formally remanded in custody. Mr Gibbings added that when the charge was made he was quite four miles away.

The Chairman You are not involved in this case.

The Clerk What you have been doing is creditable, but this is a different thing altogether.

[Source: *Warminster Journal*, 6th November 1914]

Spies at Codford
Recruits in Kitchener's Army

It was announced in Monday's *Daily Telegraph*, on the authority of an Exchange Telegraph Company's correspondent, that two soldiers, a lance corporal and a private, in the Hants Regiment, Kitchener's Army, stationed at Codford, have been proved to be German spies, and have been dealt with by the military authorities. Copies of letters as to the movements and proposed movement of troops were found in their possession.

[Source: *Warminster Journal*, 20th November 1914]

The 10th Essex in Codford
First week in May – late July 1915

Codford St Mary, to which our course was now set, is a quiet little Wiltshire village on the western borders of the Plain. It lies picturesquely in the Wylye valley, and for centuries it has slumbered beneath its thatched roofs under the shelter of the steep slopes above it.

Then, as the books say, came the War. And an Army of Sir John Jackson's workmen descended upon it; and like the mushroom cities of Western America so there sprang up in the twinkling of an eye row after row and camp after camp of corrugated iron huts, sufficient to accommodate the whole of the 18th Division, men, horses and guns, (the latter so far, but for a wooden howitzer, a minus quantity).

Marching from Colchester we billeted for the night successively at Braintree, Bishops Stortford, and Hertford. There was a spell of warmer weather now and the marches were long ones and exhausting. At Hertford some magnificent billets awaited the weary officer, and the champagne of Dr Odell, after the heat and dust of the highway, is still a joyous recollection to some.

Before dawn we were out of bed again and entraining for Salisbury Plain, and the early afternoon saw us marching into our tin huts on the Salisbury Road, south of Codford. John Jackson's mansions were not palatial, nor the pleasantest abodes when a full summer's sun beat down upon their oven-like roofs and sides.

But we were gradually learning the soldierly art of making the best of things, and there were compensations in the shape of shower baths and a running stream at the bottom of the garden which helped towards contentment.

On the whole, however, Codford saw a period of serious business with comparatively scanty time for extraneous occupations. Boots, boots, boots, went slogging up and down day in and day out over Wiltshire until the 18th Division could really lay claim to be able to walk a little bit. Then there was trench digging at Yarnboro' Castle, and manoeuvres at Stony Hill, bomb throwing with Heath-Robinson jam-pot contrivances and gas mask drill with cotton-waste and black crepe, Lewis gun classes in the nullah behind the camp and range finding on the hills above, early morning runs up precipitous slopes, which nearly killed Sergeant Sage and other antediluvian members of our cosmopolitan unit, and night marching lectures conducted by an officer eager to sell his own book on the subject.

And all the time Maxse was hovering over us with the solicitude of a tribal chieftain, telling us what he 'wahnted,' and jolly well seeing that he got it.

True, there were interludes of lighter moments. Several people invested in motor-bikes, which facilitated a run into Salisbury or further afield, and frequently stranded them at midnight on a lonely road or broke their collar-bones when they weren't looking. Others invested in the still more fluctuating stock of matrimony or sported with Amaryllis of Sarum along the shades of the Salisbury Road. Major Wheatley found consolation for his soul in the piscatorial art, and would set off for his fishing haunts in the back of a tradesman's cart in the early hours of a Sunday morning. The inclinations of his subalterns drew them to fish in deeper and more perilous waters further afield.

In July the Division was reviewed by H.M. the King near Stonehenge, and made a brave show as it marched past with bayonets glinting and fixed determination in every heart. We all felt the pregnancy of the moment, and I suppose that many of us had the greeting of the gladiator in our minds. 'Hail to thee, Emperor. Those who are about to die salute thee.'

Before we sailed the King sent to the Division a message of farewell:

> You are about to join your comrades at the Front in bringing to a successful end this relentless war of nearly twelve months duration. Your prompt patriotic answer to the Nation's call to Arms will never be forgotten. The keen exertion of all ranks during the period of training have brought you to a state of efficiency not unworthy of my Regular Army.
>
> I am confident that in the field you will nobly uphold the traditions of the fine regiments whose names you bear. Ever since your enrolment I have closely watched the growth and the steady progress of all units. I shall continue to follow with interest the fortunes of your Division.
>
> In bidding you farewell, I pray that God may bless you all in your undertakings.

To which General Maxse replied: 'I beg you will convey to His Majesty our unalterable devotion to His Person and His Throne and our fixed determination to uphold the best traditions of the British Army in War.'

Packing up days came at last. We had hoped when we moved to Codford during the first week in May that we should be 'out' and 'in it' by mid-June at the latest. But a wise authority decreed some eleven weeks intensive training on the Plain for us, and we were well on in July before our marching orders came. Our camp, which was much ornamented with chalk from the hillside, had many visitors that last week. Relations and friends were to be seen strolling around with their respective heroes at all times of the day. The band put up a good entertainment in the evenings.

Great excitement prevailed in the Officers' Quarters as to what kit should be taken, and what sent home, for everyone during those nine months of training had accumulated kit far in excess of the 35lbs allowed for active service. The enthusiasts had many packings and unpackings; the more dour just threw a few things they were sure they would want in one corner, and stored the rest away. Hudson was a tremendous 'kit wallah,' and had his valise and pack half filled with the latest active service inventions. Among these was an excellent oilskin bivouac. Three weeks later he used it with great success in an orchard at Bouzincourt, while I, covered for the most part by my valise, received the night's rain on my face.

[Extract from *With the 10th Essex in France*, by Thomas Banks, London, 1921]

Soldiers in Trouble
Allegations of Sacrilege and Attempted Arson at Codford St Peter Church
Magisterial Commendation for Constable

At a special sitting of the Warminster Police Court, on Saturday, two privates of the 3/8th Battalion of the Manchester Regiment, named Ralph Frederick Barnes and Edward Ambrose Ryder, were charged with 'breaking and entering Codford St Peter Church during the night of the 25th March, and unlawfully and maliciously doing damage to a certain memorial window in the church' the damage being estimated at upwards of £50. The magistrates present were Mr. G.N. Temple [in the chair] and Mr. E.J. Bradfield.

The case aroused considerable local interest, and the proceedings, although of a formal nature, occupied some time. The manner in which the offenders were brought to book has not been described, but it is understood that the police displayed considerable brilliancy in the achievement, a belief that received endorsement from the appreciative remarks from the Rector of the church.

The first witness, the Reverend Edward Denny, Rector of Codford St Peter Parish Church, gave evidence, as follows:

My attention was drawn to a light in the vestry about 11.15 on Saturday night. I went and opened the vestry door and saw a blaze. Shutting the door I went across the road to my neighbour, Pothecary, and his son came over to the Rectory and we got water.

The Clerk What was on fire?

Witness The floor. We got water and put the fire out. The fire was lit in the corner of the vestry where the roof comes down very low. The door of a cupboard was opened and placed over the flames, and the flames were coming up the door to the roof. We put the fire out and then I noticed that the door into the church from the vestry was open. I went into the vestry with my light and saw the Cross on the altar thrown down and broken. One of the candlesticks was broken, the other had been left alone, and two smaller candlesticks which had had candles in them were now empty. I went into the nave and found the lectern thrown down. The old, ancient bible, 300 years old, had leaves torn out of it in two places. I then went to see where they had got in, and found that they had broken and forced their way in through a stained glass window. I then went back to the vestry and my attention was drawn to smoke issuing from two chests. We put out the fire in both cases. I think the contents of the chest were largely injured and destroyed.

The Deputy Clerk,[Mr T. J. Rushton] What were the contents?

Witness Oh church linen and vestments and clothes for the altar. I estimate the damage done by the fire and covered by insurance at £30, but the other damage – the window, cross and candlesticks – not covered by insurance.

The Chairman Is it the only damage by fire?

Witness The damage by fire is estimated at £30. I am afraid that the Cross is seriously damaged, and I should think it would cost at least £5 to put it right. Apart from the fire, I should think £30 was what it would cost to repair the damage, or £60 altogether.

The Chairman Were the doors of the church locked that night to your knowledge? —Yes because I locked them myself.

—At what time? —At 5.30.

—And you had the keys? —Yes.

—There are three doors are there not? —Yes, there are three doors, the main door, the chancel door and the vestry door.

This concluded the examination of the witness, who added that he would like to say that PC Hillier had taken great pains and proved to be very intelligent in his investigations.

Constable W H Hillier, stationed at Codford, affirmed that on the night in question he was informed that there was a fire at Codford St Peter Church. He arrived at the church about 11.30pm., and on examining the windows found a stained one on the north side had been forced open.

The Chairman In the nave or the chancel?

Rector In the aisle of the nave.

Continuing: witness stated that he had found that the crucifix had been smashed to pieces. There were fires in the vestry which were put out with a few buckets of water. From inquiries made and information received, on March 31st, in company with Captain Broadbent, the Assistant Provost Marshal for the Codford district, he went to No 7 Camp, where he saw the two prisoners. He cautioned them, and Barnes, after some hesitation, said: 'I will make a voluntary statement,' and did so. It was written down, and he signed it. Ryder also made a statement.

The two statements were put in and read as follows:

I, 4070, Private Barnes, R.F., 3/8th Battalion, Manchester Regiment, on advice given me, voluntarily made the statement that I and 4546, Private Ryder, E.A., were responsible for the breaking into of the church at Codford St Peter on Saturday night, March 25th. At the time it was done we were under the influence of drink, and did not realise what we were doing.

Ryder's statement read: 'I have had the above statement read over to me in the presence of Private Barnes, and it is perfectly true what he has stated.'

Supt. Scott asked for a remand. There would be two or three other charges he would have to prefer against the prisoners, but as it would take a considerable time to make enquiries, he would like a remand in custody until Saturday April 8th. In assenting to the application, the Chairman complimented PC Hillier upon his smartness. He quoted the remark of the Reverend E. Denny, and said that the constable looked, 'like a smart officer with prospects of a speedy promotion.'

[Source: *Warminster Journal,* 7th April 1916]

The Resolute, the Young, the Eager and the Whole Hearted

According to *Soldiers Died in the Great War* twenty-seven men enlisted in Codford in World War One, none of them from Wiltshire! Eight of them joined the 13th Battalion Cheshire Regiment, five were Pioneers who joined the Special Brigade Corps of Royal Engineers, three were in the Royal Army Medical Corps, and others enlisted in the Royal Fusiliers [City of London Regiment], the Buffs [East Kent Regt], Royal Army Service Corps, Loyal North Lancashire Regt, Duke of Cambridge's Own [Middlesex Regt], Queens Own [Royal West Kent Regiment], East Surrey's and the Kings [Liverpool Regt].

Twenty-two men died in France and Flanders, one in Italy, one in Egypt and three at home. Seventeen men were killed in action, seven died of wounds, and three just died. All three men who are listed as 'died' were with the Army Medical Corps – Private Lewis Cox at home 9th December 1917, Private Ernest Gilbert at home 11th November 1918 and Private Wesley Lancaster in Italy 14th October 1918. Private Frederick Panton died of wounds in Egypt, 24th October 1918 while serving with the Queen's Own [Royal Kent Regiment] 2/4th Battalion, and Private Fred Smith of the Cheshires died of wounds at home on 17th August 1917. The rest of the soldiers died where they fought, either in the heat of battle or in the aftermath of wounds received.

Of the men who left the two villages in the Great War never to return, eighteen men are recorded. In St Mary's a simple plaque on the wall lists ten men, while in St Peter's a memorial window to eight is dedicated, 'In grateful memory of the gallant men of this parish who fell in the Great War 1914-1918'. But there were others, some perhaps impossible to trace after all this time. The Commonwealth War Graves Commission and *Soldiers Who Died In The Great War* list more men as having local connections.

Alfred Henry Ford's mother lived in Codford St Peter. He was a twenty-year-old member of the Carpenter's Crew, killed in action in the North Sea aboard the battle cruiser *HMS Invincible* during the Battle of Jutland on 31st May 1916.

The Battle of Jutland was one of the largest naval battles in history and the only time in World War One that the German fleet faced the British Navy in open combat. According to Ian Sturton in *All The World's Battleships: 1906 to the Present* during the engagement the *Invincible* disabled the light cruisers *Wiesbaden* and *Pillau* and seriously damaged the battle cruiser *Lutzow*. However the *Derfflinger* hit her five times, the final hit blew the roof off a turret and set fire to the cordite propellant. When the flash reached the magazine the *Invincible* was blown in half by the massive explosion. Only three crew members survived.

The British lost three battle cruisers, three cruisers and eight destroyers with a death toll of 5,069 men. Alfred Ford is remembered on the memorial on Southsea Common overlooking the Promenade, and in Codford St Peter's church.

Ernest George Poolman had been born in Codford, but was residing in Devon when he enlisted in the 2nd Battalion Devonshire Regiment at Newton Abbot. He was killed in action on the Somme on 17th July 1916 and is buried in Cambrin Churchyard Extension, Pas de Calais. This village was only about 800 metres from the front line trenches until the end of World War One.

A young private, just twenty years old, died while a Turkish Prisoner of War in Mesopotamia on 1st August 1916. Charles Frank Singleton was the son of Francis Edward and Elizabeth Ann Singleton of 28 Boyton Cottages, just outside Codford. He was serving with the 1st/4th Battalion, Hampshire Regiment, and is remembered between panel 21 and 63 on the Basra Memorial. Originally sited within the Basra War cemetery, the Memorial was moved by presidential decree in 1997 and has been re-erected in its entirety in the middle of a major battleground during the Gulf War.

Private Henry James Cull of Codford St Peter had originally been in the Wiltshire Regiment, but was serving with the 2nd Battalion Royal Munster Fusiliers at the time of his death. The Royal Munster Fusiliers were formed in 1881 by linking the 101st [Royal Bengal Fusiliers] Regiment and the 104th Bengal Fusiliers, becoming respectively the 1st and 2nd Battalions of the Regiment. They fought in the 3rd Burma War [1885-7] and in South Africa during the Boer War [1899-1902]. Between 1914-18 they fought in the Retreat from Mons and the Ypres battles through France and Flanders, eventually to the Helles and Suvla landings and on to Jerusalem.

Henry Cull was born in Fisherton Delamere, enlisted in Salisbury and was residing in Codford St Peter when he went to war. He died of wounds in France on 16th September 1916, possibly of injuries incurred during the First Battle of the Somme, and is buried in Abbeville Communal Cemetery Extension, Somme.

British casualties in the Third Battle of Ypres between 21st July- 6th November 1917 were 400,000 – among them Sergeant Walter Feltham of 1st Battalion Hampshire Regiment and Private Harold Henry Kitley of 1st Battalion Devonshire Regiment, killed in action on Thursday 4th October 1917. Sergeant Feltham was born in the village but living in Hampshire; Private Kitley was born in the Wiltshire village of Orcheston, but residing in Codford when they enlisted. Their names are recorded on the Tyne Cot Memorial in Belgium, the furthest point reached by the Commonwealth Forces until almost the end of the war. The battles of the Ypres Salient claimed so many lives on both sides that in order to commemorate all the members of the Commonwealth forces with no known grave several sites were needed. The Tyne Cot Memorial bears the names of almost 35,000 officers and men whose bodies lie in unknown graves.

A victim of pneumonia, thirty-one year old Private Percy William Bennett of the 2nd/5th Battalion, Suffolk Regiment, succumbed to the disease in Doncaster, Yorkshire, on 13th February 1917. The son of the Reverend William and Alice Bennett, Percy was born in Codford St Mary, but the family had moved on and his parents were living in St Albans at the time of his death.

Frederick Bertie Price was a married man whose wife Alice Louisa lived in Vine Cottage, Codford St Mary. He was a thirty-seven year old member of the 50th Machine Gun Corps [Inf]. Well-placed single guns could cut great swathes through advancing enemy infantry; co-ordinating barrages and interlocking fields of fire using multiple machine guns were a deadly shield to protect allied troops. By 1918 machine gunners were often placed about 1,000 yards behind the advancing infantry, moving up as the enemy positions were captured. Concentrated fire would sweep the ground behind the front and support positions. Taking out the machine gunners was a priority for attacking forces, the gunners were in a position of clear and present danger at all times in conflict, the MGC was formed as a wartime fighting machine and was disbanded in 1922 when its role was no longer necessary.

Frederick Price possibly died in the Battle of Lys River, also known as Ypres IV. On 11th April a massive German offensive was launched to drive the British into the sea. He died on the day Haig issued an order forbidding further retreat; the British were to 'stand with their backs against the wall.' On 12th April 1918 many men fell where they stood – Frederick Price was one of them. He is remembered on panel 11 of the Ploegstreet Memorial, close to Mesen in Belgium.

A twenty-year-old private in the 1st/15th Battalion, London Regiment [Prince of Wales Own Civil Service Rifles], died thirteen days before the Armistice on 29th October 1918. Private Harold Roy Bowden was born in Codford St Mary but possibly living with his parents in Chippenham when he went to war. He is buried in Hautmont Communal Cemetery, Nord.

Rudyard Kipling wrote: 'They shall not return to us, the resolute, the young, the eager and the whole hearted who we gave.' It is at least eighty-four years since the last of Codfords young men died in what was meant to be 'The war to end all wars.' Their families have passed away, no one remains that can remember their faces or recall their names, but their sacrifice will never be forgotten. In the history of one small Wiltshire village they are remembered.

[Sources: Commonwealth War Graves Commission; Ministry of Defence Admiralty Library; *All the World's Battleships: 1906 to the Present*, edited Ian Sturton, Conway Maritime Press, 1987; *A Register of the Regiments and Corps of the British Army*, edited by Arthur Swinson; National Army Museum, Chelsea; Brassey's Battles, edited John Laffin; *The Oxford Companion to Military History*, edited by Richard Holmes; www.1914-1918.net/mgc.htm (Machine Gun Corps, 1914-1918).]

The Road to Recovery

Codford Hospital was taken over by the New Zealand authorities in July 1916 when it was decided to open a new New Zealand infantry base unit in England. The NZMC took responsibility for a RAMC hospital, which became known as No 3 New Zealand General Hospital. There were just over 300 beds available and by September 1916 it was partly manned by New Zealanders with several RAMC officers temporarily attached.

Situated on Salisbury Plain it was close to New Zealand Command Depot at Codford Camp and the nearby training depot located at Bulford, Sling Camp. 'Command Depots' was a term used to distinguish depots specially devoted to the reception of unfit men from the ordinary Infantry or General Base depots where reinforcements and fit men were in training and readiness to proceed to the Front. The site, locally known as 'The Punchbowl' was in a deep cleft of the downs. It was very damp and drowned in mists during the winter, hot and breathless during summer. The tier-like structure of the hospital on the hillside made the place both uncomfortable and inconvenient for staff and patients alike.

The formation of new medical units that included staffing Codford and Sling Camps drained the New Zealand Medical Corps personnel; at any one time only

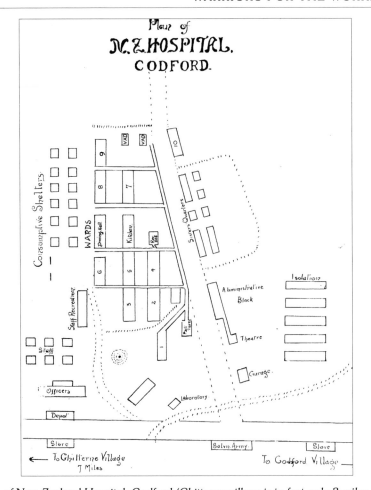

Plan of New Zealand Hospital, Codford (Chitterne village is in fact only 3 miles away)

one general hospital was up to strength. Unlike the other New Zealand Military Hospitals the Codford Camp hospital accepted Imperial and other troops as well as New Zealanders.

In October 1916 there were 4,740 New Zealand sick and wounded in England, casualties of the Somme. By the end of the year there were 12,124 members of the New Zealand Expeditionary Force in England, 3,449 at Codford Command Depot and 3,229 at Sling Camp.

In October a Venereal Diseases Section was formed as a minor part of the Hospital complex at Command Depot. Initially this area had been designated for rations and discipline. Captain, later Major. J. Falconer Brown, who had been wounded on the Somme, took over this work, which he retained until demobilisation. Owing to the policy of the day the Section was regarded as a detention hospital with barbed wire surrounding the perimeter and armed guards patrolling the area. A NZ soldier who had arrived at Codford to undergo 'hardening up' training prior to returning to France, commented:

> On top of the hill is another NZ camp which is out of bounds and ringed with by high barbed wire fences. This is both a hospital (3 NZGH) and a prison combined for those whose relations with the civil population were of undue familiarity. Apparently Venus deprives Mars of many warriors.

Commonly referred to as 'the Pox' Syphilis is from the Greek word meaning 'filthy.' Venereal sores or ulcers appear, usually at first on the genital organs. After the ulcers, according to Virtue's, *A Household Physician- a Twentieth Century Medica* (1924), comes the bubo, a swelling in the groin, followed by further eruptions of the skin. As the disease progressed there was a possibility of body ulcers, agonising pains in the joints, hair loss, blindness, deafness, dementia and eventually death.

Gonorrhoea, 'the Clap', resulted in the inflammation, itching and discharges from the urethra. Early indications were a reddening of the penis and difficulty passing water, followed by a discharge; if treated at this early stage it was easy to cure. Unfortunately before medical attention was sought the symptoms of the next stage were usually present, violent scalding when passing water, painful erections and a discharge of greenish matter often tinged with blood. Later it is possible for the infection to effect the prostate gland, irritating the bladder and because of its proximity to the larger bowel causing a desire to empty the bladder and evacuate the bowels, actions which cause agonising pain not unlike dysentery.

The treatments available to the unfortunates who contracted a sexually transmitted disease during this period were often very painful. Either Arsenic by intravenous injections or Mercury in the form of solutions, syrups, tablets, suppositories, and intramuscular and intravenous injections were used to treat syphilis, by far the most serious of the venereal diseases. Medical advice was that Mercury needed to be continued with occasional intermissions, if side effects such as sore gums or pain while biting occurred, for at least a year after all symptoms had disappeared.

According to Virtues *Household Physician* treatment involved cauterising with either nitrate of silver [stick nitrate], nitric acid, chloride of zinc, potassa with lime and painless caustic. After cauterisation a little vinegar and water was immediately used to neutralise the caustic, then a piece of lint dipped in a solution of watery extract of opium should be laid on, followed by lint soaked in tepid water and the injured member wrapped in oiled silk. The patient should then remain at rest, keeping the penis elevated repeating the opium and the water dressing night and morning. A regular and unstimulating diet, no tobacco or alcohol and daily cold or tepid baths completed the regime.

Gonorrhoea was treated by injections of silver solutions, irrigations and calomel ointments. In the early stage patients were kept quiet, fed for a few days on crackers and water or something equally simple, all meats and stimulating drinks were forbidden. The second stage required thirty drops of a solution of potassa in half a

New Zealand Military Hospital, Codford

tumbler of water two or three times a day, and seeking relief by holding the penis for some time in warm water. For painful erections from one to three camphor and opium tablets a day, thirty drops of laudanum at bedtime, cold applications to the affected part or walking barefoot on a cold floor was thought to offer relief.

During the first half of 1917 of 1,138 cases of VD admitted at Codford Command Depot, 233 patients had contracted the disease in France. Of the other 905 men who acquired the disease in England 50% of those infected could trace the source to London. At the end of the year there were 400 venereal patients and 200 convalescents.

The Curator of the Royal New Zealand Army Medical Corps Museum, Ken Treanor, comments:

> At the time VD was regarded as a misdemeanour, as it was a preventable disease and the loss to the army was in the form of a month to several months while they were being treated. Therefore they were confined in a detention hospital surrounded by barbed wire with a guard at the gate until they were clear. Of the infections 77% was gonorrhoea and 22% syphilis.

The wastage was such that orders were issued that no VD cases were to be evacuated from France to England or to Australia or New Zealand. All cases were to be treated in France until they were fit to return to their units. There were vigorous campaigns to reduce the incidence, ranging from issuing free condoms and personal ablution packets (a sort of 'do it yourself kits'), high-pressure educational programmes and in some areas inspection of brothels and treatment of the women. There was an army regulation creating it an offence if a woman infected a soldier, with a penalty of up to 6 months in prison, but obviously it was a difficult law to enforce.

Lieut. Col. D. Carbery writes in *The New Zealand Medical service in the Great War 1914/1918* that every unit had its own ablutions room, canteens sold prophylactics at a minimal cost and salutary warnings on the dangers of infection and the methods of prevention were given as a matter of course. Approximately 3,600 men of the New Zealand Expeditionary Force per year were infected and needed treatment, about 2% of the men in England and a lesser proportion in France were constantly off the strength due to VD. An estimated £70,000 a year was lost to the State due to this reduction in available manpower.

Given the horrific experience treatment must have been, the story passed down orally from World War One has a certain plausibility. It is said that when the Australian troops were in Codford a prostitute infected them with VD. Some of the soldiers killed her in a rage and dumped her body down one of the wells on Manor Farm. The crime was neither discovered nor reported and there she remains to this day.

The Codford hospital was very well equipped. It dealt with serious medical and occasional surgical cases, rather than men wounded in the trenches and on battlefields of France. Codford was too far away from the coast to accommodate the recently wounded, who were treated at either Brockenhurst or Walton on Thames.

When the New Zealand Expeditionary Forces Headquarters was formed in England Hornchurch was the chosen convalescent hospital for the troops. Once the soldiers were on the way to recovery they were given a period of fourteen days leave before being sent to the Command Depot at Codford to be hardened before an assessment of their capabilities. Initially 467 men were transferred to Codford, the men were divided into three categories – A, B and C. Those judged A1 were fit

One of the wards, New Zealand Military Hospital

for active service; B1 – Able to be made fit by medical treatment; C1– Likely to become fit for service overseas, C2– Permanently unfit for active service but fit for service in New Zealand; and D – Permanently unfit.

On arrival the soldier would be graded B3 and given light work, potato picking and a little digging. The next phase as he became fitter was B2, beginning bayonet practise and a physical exercise regime which included four- to six-mile a day route marches and bayonet practice. When the soldier was categorised as B1 he was given a stiffer course of physical training and bayonet fighting and his route march was prolonged to eight or ten miles a day.

Classification by the medical team was once a week. Once a soldier was able to march fourteen miles a day he was classified as A and sent to a reserve unit as fit. Many men failed to qualify. Their fate was then either to hospital, to headquarters for allotment to duties as 'permanent' or 'temporary unfit', or to Torquay for return to New Zealand. Before this could happen they were 'boarded' by a travelling board of experts. A number of men passing through the depot were found to be unfit to return to the trenches. Many of these men went to France to join the Divisional Employment Company engaging in base duties rather than combat.

For obvious reasons Codford was not a popular camp, as it was the first stage of the return journey to the trenches for many. After the brief respite from the horrors of warfare, men recovering from illness and wounds were well aware of the filth, the exposure, the racket of guns and the possibility of further injuries or probable death that awaited them at the end of their recovery period. The men seldom admitted their fears, they knew their duty and faced the inevitable with determination. Given the mental and physical condition of the soldiers the management of the depot presented a challenge for the officers, and men of a special calibre were needed, able to deal with all ranks with tact and consideration.

Early in 1918 the number of men accommodated in Codford had reached 3,200. To control and administer the depot it required a commanding officer, a second in command and adjutant, a quarter master and supply officer, ten combatant officers, an A.P.M., four medical officers and, as Codford was the centre of dental operations, five dental officers.

The officers were not necessarily convalescents themselves, but were serving a six-month tour of duty away from France, and so one imagines their view of Codford was much more positive. They were men who, besides being able to exercise command and drill troops, could take an interest in and appreciate the value of sports and other recreations on the morale of the men. Military training was naturally the priority, but it was recognised that sports promoted fitness as well as enjoyment. All training was controlled by the commanding officer advised by the senior medical officer and the sergeant major of the Army gymnastic staff. It followed the general routine governing infantry training ; but as the aim was to help men recover from injuries, attention was paid to the practical skills rather than barrack square drill. This system was very effective in preparing the troops for the most strenuous routine of the camp life of the reserve units.

A medical officer was always in attendance at the parade ground, noting any problems, ensuring that men were not taxed beyond their capabilities and that any weakness or injury could be assessed on the spot. At Codford the unusual sight of a medical officer taking part in the daily route marches, declining to ride their horses as a point of honour, was normal practice.

As well as general training, special classes were held periodically in which men with service to their credit, and who showed interest and skill in physical training and bayonet practice, could take a course to become instructors. Twenty-one of the men at Codford trained at Aldershot before returning to New Zealand to assist in training operations in their homeland.

The New Zealand War Contingent Club the Aotea Roa [literally 'Land of the Long White Cloud'– the Maori Name for New Zealand] possessed a library, reading and writing rooms, a large games room with billiard tables, a room with easy chairs where troops could sit in front of a roaring fire, read a book and buy tea, coffee and food. It was in the Club that the soldiers sat down to Christmas Dinner on the opposite side of the world to their families, in an alien and very different climate to the blue skies and sunshine of their antipodean homelands. On Christmas Day 1917 the New Zealand Command Depot menu consisted of a dinner of Roast Turkey, Roast Fowl and Ham, Roast Beef and Yorkshire Pudding, with baked and boiled potatoes, cabbage, carrots and parsnips. This was followed by New Zealand Plum Pudding and Brandy sauce, stewed fruits, then fresh fruit and nuts served with beer and minerals.

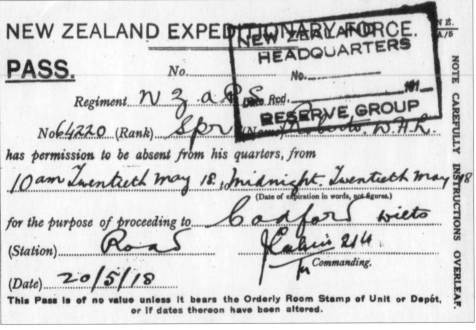

New Zealand Expeditionary Force Pass (courtesy of Owen Pearce)

In the latter stages of the war Codford Hospital was expanded to nearly 1000 beds. By 1918 five new wards were completed and shelters for the accommodation of tuberculosis patients had been erected on the hillside above the hospital. Tuberculosis at the beginning of the twentieth century was a contagious killer disease. Victims were isolated and exposed to a healthy lifestyle, fresh air, warm clothing, lack of stress, good food with plenty of dairy products and cod liver oil after meals. The Punchbowl was certainly a site where fresh air was guaranteed.

INSTRUCTIONS FOR NEW ZEALAND SOLDIERS ON LEAVE.

It is your duty as a New Zealander to at all times endeavour to maintain the honour and good name of the N.Z. Forces by—

  (1) Appearing in public smartly and correctly dressed.
  (2) Saluting all officers.
  (3) Civility and courtesy to all.
  (4) Conducting yourself as a soldier and gentleman.
  (5) Avoiding drink and immorality.
  (6) Readily showing your pass to the police when called upon to do so.
  (7) Not overstaying your leave.

If you require medical aid you should apply to the nearest military hospital and notify your O.C.

Board and lodging in London can be obtained at the New Zealand Hostel, 17, Russell Square, or the N.Z.Y.M.C.A., Shakespeare Hut, near British Museum.

You are warned against risking infection of Venereal Disease and thereby rendering yourself unfit to serve your country.

Should you, in spite of the above warnings, be so foolish as to risk infection, you must report within 12 hours to the N.Z. Medical Orderly, 17, Russell Square, London, or the nearest military hospital.

Those who contract Venereal will be returned to New Zealand for segregation until cured.

Instructions for New Zealand soldiers on leave (courtesy of Owen Pearce)

At the end of hostilities the New Zealanders were demobilised on the principle 'first to join, first to return home' system based on length of service. This caused difficulties as the drafts were mixed units and officers, the comradeship and trust built up during combat were fractured by the separation of established units. In his book *On The Fringe of Hell* Christopher Pugsley quotes:

Codford the last few weeks has been unbearable, discipline has gone to the pack and the troops don't care a damn for officers and NCOs. The big canteens are simply gambling dens. All sorts of games of chance are being conducted and no notice is taken of the orders that say it has to stop. As fast as boats are available, men are despatched but everyone is impatient and as there is no leave issued prior to a boat leaving many men just hire a taxi and decamp for a week. When they come back they find they have to go through the performance of waiting.

The great Spanish flu epidemic, seamen and docker's strikes and lack of shipping added to the general discontent. March 1919 Sling Camp saw canteens and messes raided and vandalised by frustrated South Islanders eager to return to their homes. By June 1919 demobilisation was well under way and 3 NZ General Hospital was closed in July except for the VD Section which stayed open until August when the remaining 200 patients were transferred to the British Military Hospital in Chiseldon. All the remaining equipment and stores were shipped to New Zealand. Ironically some of this equipment was later used to set up medical units at the outbreak of World War Two some 20 years later!

[Sources: *The War Effort of New Zealand*, edited by Lt. H T B Drew, 1923; *The New Zealand Division 1916-1919*, by Col. H Stewart, 1921; *The New Zealand Medical Service in the Great War 1914 / 1918*, by Lieut. Col. A D Carbery, 1924; *On The Fringe of Hell: New Zealanders and Military Discipline in the First World War*, by Christopher Pugsley, 1991; Ken Treanor, Curator RNZAMC Museum.]

New Zealand General Hospital, Codford, Staff List
Ken Treanor

This Staff List contains those that we know were posted to the unit. However there was a lot of movement between medical units during the course of the war. For instance it was not impossible for some of those listed below to have served in all or some of the medical units. This list does not include reinforcements from New Zealand.

Matron Elizabeth Nixon AARC RRC
    Matron from 1916 to 1917
Matron Louisa McNie AARC RRC Matron
    1917 until 1919
Sub Matron Jean Dodds ARRC
Sub Matron Edna Pengelly RRC Later
    Matron
Staff Nurses Ruby Brayshaw
Constance Brigham
Clara Cherry mid (MI D)
Sister Margaret Eady

Staff Nurse Marion Garland New Zealand
    Army Nursing Service (NZANS)
Sisters Florence Hart
Jessie Law
Rose Newdick

NOTE:
    AARC = Associate Royal Red Cross
    MID = Mentioned in Despatches
    RRC = Royal Red Cross

New Zealand Medical Corps (NZMC)
Lt Col PC Fenwick CMG Commanding
    Officer
Lt Col HJ McLean CBE (MID)
    Commanding Officer
Lt Col G Home CBE Commanding Officer
Maj W Aitken MC
Capt VH Barr
Capt FD Barron
Capt JA Berry
Capt DH Beit
Capt JF Brown
Maj F Brown
Maj HM Buchanan DSO, OBE (MID)
Capt AD Clark
Capt AO Evans
Capt JN Keith
Capt EC Lowe
Capt FW Lumsden MC

Capt PG McEvedy
Capt K MacKenzie
Capt HE Owen
Capt AW Owen-Johnston
Capt WJ Reid
Capt SD Rhind MC Plastic Surgeon
Capt TR Ritchie
Capt RJ Rogers
Capt TJ Rowley Dentist
Capt RS Stephenson
Capt GB Sweet
Capt HT Tait MBE
Capt AC Thomson
Capt RWF Wood MBE Quartermaster
Capt AM Wright Bacteriologist

Padre
Ch Cl4 HLB Goertz

Extract from *Hurcombe's Hungry Half Hundred*, a memorial history of the 50th Bn A.I.F. 1916-1919

by R. R. Freeman

Camp In England

The training depots of the A.I.F. were scattered throughout the Salisbury Plain in Wiltshire. The nearest sea-ports were Southampton and Devonport. The 4th Division was stationed at Rollestone Camp and the 13th Brigade at the village of Codford St Mary. The large hill behind the camp at Codford was known as 'The Pimple.' Training on the Pimple remained a vivid memory for all. Leave was taken on foot to the local villages or by train to London.

Private Jack Brooks

At 6.05 we entrained and, after a six-hour train journey, we arrived at Codford Station, Salisbury Plains, Wiltshire. What a miserable night it was, too! A further march of two miles, through slush and mud, brought us to our training camp at Codford. Codford was a typical English village, with its thatched roofs; the charm of these quaint old towns is wonderful. And so, tired and hungry we trudged to our huts, glad to reach our destination after spending an interesting two months at sea and visiting the ports of call.

The morning of 29th December brought good tidings in the shape of numerous letters from loved ones at home in sunny South Australia. What a contrast to the weather we were experiencing; the worst and most intense winter the English people had experienced in forty years.

New Years Day; on guard duty and how cold it was!

On the morning of the 8th January, excitement among the troops was intense. We were preparing to go to London on four days furlough – a privilege granted to all Australian troops on their arrival in England. The boys were early astir, polishing buttons, cleaning boots and performing other necessary duties in order to present a smart appearance to the London people.

We entrained at Codford; 105 miles to London which took two hours. Arrived at Paddington Station at 11am. We set off on a two mile march to Horseferry Road, the Australian Military Headquarters. We were dismissed here and were free to do as we liked for the next four days.

What a revelation were these four days. I visited almost every historic place in London, sometimes in company of other diggers, other times by myself. Y.M.C.A. guides performed excellent service to us in the way of entertainment and showing us things of interest around London. The time passed all too quickly. On Thursday 11th January, we entrained at Paddington and returned to Codford.

The cold weather was again terrible, many deaths occurring among the Aussies in the camp. Well do I remember the hill at Codford [commonly known as The Pimple]. And what a climb it was, too!! This was our training ground; the wind was so keen here it almost cut one's throat! Training in all the various phases of warfare was carried out from 8am – 12.30, and from 2pm – 5pm. It made one fit all right.

Private Joe Scales

It was very cold and bleak at the top of the hill in the early mornings. We could get hot while climbing up, then we would all have to strip most of our clothes off for physical exercises and stand shivering in the cold wind while the instructors explained what we had to do. It was no wonder that we were nearly all dead with colds after a few days. It was enough to kill anybody, especially later on in the depths of winter, it was so bitter cold.

We could get a magnificent view from the top of this hill; the country looked beautiful all around, everything was nice and green and the villages nestling in the valley looked so pretty. There was an old Roman fort on the top of this hill. There were several of them about in a line on the highest hills; it must have been the border line of the country the Romans once held. It seemed strange that men of the young nation of Australia were camped on the same ground as Caesar's legions were many centuries ago.

The next Sunday afternoon another chap and I went for a walk down to the village and I found it pretty lively. The narrow, winding streets were full of soldiers for there were fifteen camps around this village; Australian, English and New Zealand Camps.

Codford High Street

All the shops were open and the pub full of men drinking, cursing, fighting, while further along the street there were several big football matches in progress. It was not much like a Sunday at all, and the thought came to me that if this is the way they carry on in England, desecrating and all the other sin going on, it was no wonder we were not winning the war. Even in the camps the wet canteens were open nearly all day and young fellows were drunk all over the place. It's a shame that this should be allowed; the people in Australia would not have the wet canteens open there and it should not be so here. It was heartbreaking to see so many lads, who had never touched the stuff before, getting blind drunk, rolling in the mud and spewing all over themselves, bringing themselves below the level of the lowest beast.

One could hardly wonder at them going astray as there seems to be such a lot of evil and so very little good. This was the first time a lot of our fellows had been away from home and all good influences, and they seem to let themselves go and do things they would not think of doing at home.

Postscript

When Dr. Roger Freeman gave me permission to use the above chapter from his book, I asked what had become of the two soldiers who had so graphically described their impressions of Codford Camp. 2616 Private John Brooks was a clerk by profession. He lost a limb in the war, on his return home he was a founder of the local [Adelaide] Limbless Soldiers Association. He died on 14th August 1970.

3716 Private Joe Scales also survived, he was a devout Salvationist, which explains his distress at the soldiers' behaviour on the Sabbath and the easy availability of alcohol. Back in civilian life he was a member of the local Salvation Army Band. Joe Scales died on Armistice Day 1964.

[Note: Dr Freeman's book published by Peacock Publications, Norwood, South Australia, 1991]

Australian and New Zealand soldiers outside the George Inn

Chronicles of the N.Z.E.F. 1916

The *Chronicles of the New Zealand Expeditionary Force* was first published on 30th August 1916, edited by Glutha Mackenzie at 11 Southampton Row, London; it cost 6d or 3d to the troops. Its avowed intention was to gather and dispense all interesting information concerning New Zealand soldiers in Europe, and a gazette of New Zealand patriotic efforts in this country. The paper collected material from the High Commissioner's Office, from the New Zealand War Contingent Association and from the men themselves. Letters were regularly published from Codford, Brockenhurst, Walton, Sling, Salisbury, and elsewhere.

These letters will be interspersed with other chapters chronologically throughout the book. The 'Blue Sisters' frequently referred to in the letters are very likely the women of the Voluntary Aid Detachments [VAD]. Ken Treanor of the Royal New Zealand Army Medical Corps Museum explains, 'Women who were not trained nurses but wanted to help the war effort joined the VAD. They helped in and around the hospitals as cleaners, kitchen-hands and nursing duties. The New Zealand nurses wore grey uniforms, but the nursing VAD wore a working uniform of blue with fine white stripes, with a walking out navy blue uniform. So there are your 'Blue Sisters.' Of course working on the wards for some time they must have picked up considerable nursing skills, enough for the soldier patients to confuse them with the registered staff and call them 'Sisters.'

Codford Letters

September 15th 1916
The club has been opened just about three weeks now, and is going strong. Every night we seem to have more and more men in, and the clubroom is full of talk and men reading, writing or playing draughts; at intervals the piano and gramophone are kept busy, and the place is becoming very popular. I think it must have been the free supper that started the ball rolling. The buffet was packed that night from end to end, four deep, each man asking for four plates of fruit salad for his pals – rows of faces trying to catch an eye before the other man, while we, behind the buffet, dashed to and fro madly with plates, cups of tea, scones, etc., etc., till 10pm, when everything had vanished, not one of the heaped-up trays remained, clean sweep and a bare counter. Since then we have found the favourite cakes, scones and sandwiches, and when we are at our busiest it is funny to listen to the mixture of orders: '2 cups of tea, a date scone and a box of matches.' 'Three CHRONICLES,

a glass of Horlicks and book me a game of billiards,' or a voice from one of the 'Blue Sisters' saying, 'I'm so sorry but the fried man has gone off with your poached eggs,' all to the accompaniment of clinking pennies, cups, and the sharp click of billiard balls from the next room. Then there is the library going and books to be entered, and perhaps in one corner there is a committee meeting going on for the next concert, which is in its chrysalis stage; So and So can't sing because he's off to Sling and its no use wearing those dresses until we get the stage lights. Then suddenly 48 wicker chairs arrive and have to be unpacked. A fatigue party sets to work and in the usual Colonial way have it done before one can look around, and there are so many that at first it is difficult to find a spot to put each one. The billiard tables are a great success and are going all day. Mrs Wilder is interviewed all day by various people, butchers, bakers, eggmen and so forth, each one of the staff has her special department, or rather takes charge of whatever happens to be going, and always has plenty of volunteers to run anything special.

October 3rd 1916
The days go by pretty rapidly here, I can tell you. Thursday evening entertainments have been the greatest success, and many thanks are due to Miss Dobie, and the rest of the Committee for their efforts. The week before last they gave us a most excellent programme starting with an opera selection by our band, most ably conducted, and here I want to record our appreciation of their playing, and also say how they improve day by day.

We are very lucky to have so much talent amongst us. Gunner Braithwaite is an artist at the piano, and his delightful playing often helps us through the somewhat monotonous but necessary employment known as 'washing up.' Private Westhead is an artist with another instrument – the violin – and his numbers are always vociferously encored. Corporal Murphy, with his musical monologues and humorous recitations, Private W. Steed also recites and we have songs from Trooper Brown, Signaller Manning and numerous others – all most enthusiastically received by the audience.

The hall is usually full to overflowing, and the business of the buffet is now stopped during the performance as the tintillating of teaspoons and the clinking of china are rather disturbing to those taking part in the concert. One Thursday Col. Fenwick kindly allowed the hospital patients to attend, and the club was therefore placed within bounds for the occasion. During the second half of the programme a Maori Haka was given, and it being heartily applauded and encored, was performed again. This was too much for one of the Maori brothers in blue; he hopped up on the platform and joined in his native dance with a will, the unrehearsed effort bringing the house down.

This last Thursday our entertainment was varied by a farce entitled 'The Area Belle.' The cast was:

Penelope [the area belle]	Miss Dobie
Mrs Croker	Sergeant Prain

Tosser [a policeman]   Sergeant Fisher
Pitcher [a guardsman]   Corporal Kennedy
Chalks [a milkman]   Private MacKenzie

It was a thrilling moment when Mrs Croker fished for his matches in his trouser pockets, and again, when Chalk hugged the area belle, he was not a very backward milkman, though such a plain man. Penelope was very saucy in golden hair. All parts of the club were crowded, even the windows, and the interval was lively by the audience singing its own favourite songs and choruses at its own sweet will.

The concert was given again the following night at the hospital, but unfortunately the actors were unable to repeat the farce owing to stage deficiencies.

The worse part of living in a camp of this description is that one morning one is awakened in the semi-darkness by the strains of the band, to remember with a pang some of our friends are marching away from us. Our best wishes, needless to say go with them, but we miss them sadly at the club.

This week there has been a great influx of Australians, and on Sunday night it was not easy to cope with the numbers; the food disappeared from the buffet in an amazingly short time. The usual frequenters of the club were very good, and took a back seat to permit their hungry brethren, who were just come from a long sea voyage, being fed.

Chronicles of the N.Z.E.F. find a ready sale, as indeed they should, for it is a very successful publication, and the information about sick and wounded at the hospitals is very useful.

It is quite inspiring to hear a voice calling through the evening mists, 'Chron-i-cles' and the rest dying away in a mysterious and inviting murmur. It is quite a good idea to hand some of the numbers to be sold in this way, though I was told by the small lad to whom I entrusted the sale last week that 'Some of these newspaper chaps aren't honest.' I hope this is only the exception that proves the rule, and I don't feel seriously alarmed.

Overheard in the buffet during the Australian rush:
Australian, buying sandwiches: 'Why, this lot ought to be half the price.'
Blue Sister ' Well, if you know a cheaper hole, go to it.'
                                    AOTEAROA.

November 10th 1916
I am writing this to the accompaniment of pelting rain, which on this iron roof sounds rather like a thousand banjos playing different war dances at the same time! All the same things could be worse and we manage to keep fairly comfortable with the stoves going, etc, in the hall. We know the mud will be pretty thick in the morning [inside the room as well as out], but we keep on smiling, for what does it matter, our linoleum washes, and as long as the room is occupied, writing tables in use, games going, etc, we are contented, and feel that we are needed far more in weather like this than at other times.

We have had some very good entertainments, and are looking forward to a conjuror this week, as well as a concert. We are most fortunate in our talent, and the last 'local' concert was a great success – it's very pleasant just to sit still and be played and sung to occasionally.

Funny things happen here sometimes; for instance the other day coffee was 'off' for a considerable time, the ultimate explanation being that the boiling water necessary for its production had been used by the ladies to dye their blue veils – dismay on the part of the culprits can be better imagined than described.

We pride ourselves on the absolute cleanliness and purity of our buffet counter, and to let you into a trade secret we use 'Vim' [I think the Vim Company should give us a handsome donation for our club]. One of our sisters, in her zeal to effect a fine polish, sprinkled the counter vigorously with what she thought was the 'Vim' tin – only to be seized with a violent fit of sneezing, and discover that white pepper was the medium she had employed.

If our clocks do not always keep Greenwich time, we remind each other sadly that our special clock winder has been moved on to Sling, and so the clocks run down.

It is very pleasing to get letters from friends who have gone on to France from here, and the last few days we have had news from several of them. We hope many others will write and tell us how they are getting on, as we don't forget them, and news of their well-being will always be welcome.

I fear I am an irregular correspondent, but please do not be hard on me. We lead quite strenuous lives I assure you; and though nothing gives me greater pleasure than writing to you, I cannot al ways indulge myself- perhaps when our quarters are moved down into the club we shall have more leisure. We shall miss the Supply Depot next door; or, rather, I should say, the administrators of the supplies; and we shall feel very lonely when they take their departure. I had no idea that a Supply Depot was such an interesting place, and I can commend it to any person who is a student of the human race. I have learned a great many useful lessons from just 'looking on.'

AOTEAROA.

Codford Hospital
Visited by Miss D.H.Barren:
The following men are doing well: – Bennett H.A., 25/593; Cruttenden, S., 23/1024; White, R.J., 23/641; Neill, A.A., 12456; Moore, H.E.J., 2/2033; Hampton, F,. 10/ 1832; Summerfield, G.T., 12949; Collins,T., 14758; Phillips, F.T., 6/3130; Page A.M., 8/3378; Davis, T.P., 24/1637; Nelson, C.C., 13081; Langford, A., 8/ 3309; Wyatt, L., 8/3443; Tabling, A,. 2/1155; Greenwood, A.C., 13546; Hogan,G., 12402; Winjeich, A.C., 23273; Winter,H.,12/867; Mark, J.V.,8/2050; Boore, R.D., 26/291.

Banks, A.L., 4/1730; strain; getting on slowly. Peard, R., 12/429; gastritis and appendicitis. Mcauliffe,J.H.,7/78; suffering from the effects of a crush received in Gallipoli ; probably returning to N.Z. Burrell, P., 25/1677; wounded in right shoulder;

leaving on furlough. Findlay, H.A., 23/421; wounded in right foot. Coxhead, H.B., 6/3289; wounded in left leg; leaving for N.Z. Robbins, R.A., 7/113; ingrowing toenails. MacDonald, J., 26/613; removing shrapnel from elbow. Graydon S., 12/1027; septic throat rheumatism; not feeling very fit. Strode, W.E., 8/3774; dislocated shoulder. Davey, H.E., 18631; anaemic. Russell, D., 13104; cold in chest. McDonald, T.M., 10/3006; amputation of right arm; operated again; doing fairly well. Blackholme, B.A., 15125; pleurisy. Dorrien, W., 25/383; injured knee.

Note: Findlay's wounded right foot gained him a place on the S.S. Rotorua listed in Departures from 3rd N.Z.G.H. Codford in 29th November 1916 copy of the Chronicles.

November 23rd 1916

Just a line to let you know we are still alive after our snow storm, which was walked into the club and melted with a mixture of mud into a vast sea, with the chairs and tables dotted about in rows of islands, and men steaming around the stoves in tight groups.

Codford in winter

We have been frightfully busy for the last four days, our staff being reduced to half. On payday we ran the buffet with the help of some of our army sergeants. We had one pouring out tea, another cutting up beetroot and two making sandwiches. A sergeant-major volunteered to serve out sausage and mash at the 4.30 rush, which he did most efficiently, wearing one of the staff's little spotted aprons. With two large steaming bowls in front of him, one mashed potatoes and one of shiny sausages, rows of plates were dealt out smartly to an accompaniment of respectful chaff from the waiting men. We had men in to help all day making fruit salad and buttering scones; the pantry was a seething hive of workers. The only accident of the day was a sequel to the cleaning of the counter with pepper; one of the men peppered his potatoes with Vim, and was rescued just in time by a 'blue sister.' We had a shortage in sugar, which caused a good deal of conversation while it lasted, most of the men answering the 'no sugar' statement by replying, 'Oh there must be a war on somewhere.' But they were all very cheerful about it, and the washers-up scored over the teaspoons. Another helper distinguished himself by dripping kerosene into the milk jug when he filled the lamps under the urns, which didn't improve the tea; he declared he 'didn't sleep a wink all night, thinking about it – all that milk wasted and everything.' Another excitement was the bowl of butter put to melt on the heater, which accidentally upset over the pantry floor, causing much commotion. Then we discovered that the remainder of the bowl was full of enamel chips, so the whole lot had to be melted down and put through a hair sieve. These events keep us amused and busy, so that we haven't time to remember the snow outside and the mud which is always with us.

P.S. – Three of the staff are in hospital, one with trench fever.

AOTEAROA.

December 7th 1916
Codford is just as quiet as ever but much drier, as the last week or so there has been very little rain and the sun has ventured forth at times, and dried the ground up wonderfully. No.8, the detail camp, is the driest of all, so the wet canteen has been closed there. Our navvy team have been very busy lately, digging drains and putting down new 'duck walks' before the wet weather sets in, so we should be pretty comfortable this winter.

Chris Read is here on the staff, but we see very little of him, as he is kept busy, but you will hear from him later on, when he gets settled down. A French class has been formed in our local YMCA, and is fairly well patronised by the boys, some of whom are making great progress.

The YMCA and Ao-Tea-Roa have been kept busy lately, and in the mornings one invariably finds these buildings packed with men who are dodging parade to get a cup of tea or soup. The fatigues for these huts are supplied by the different camps, and we have no trouble to get volunteers as there is always a cup of 'Baksheesh' [tea] when the job is done.

I believe Christmas dinner is going to be a 'fair dinkum' one this year, and I hear the menu has already been approved of by the G.O.C., so we are looking forward to a good time.

There are a fair number of P.M.s in the camp now, among whom is Gunner Joe Mars, of Invercargill, well known in athletic circles. He has been gassed and is waiting for the next New Zealand boat. Jimmy Gallon, of tailoring fame, is also here and expects to return to Big Island shortly.

PADDY.

27th December 1916

AN ODE TO CODFORD

Codford, we love thee more and more,
We soldiers from a far-off shore
Thy sunny clime and clear blue skies
Are at a premium, I surmise,
But memories of our stay down here
Will ever be to us most dear.
      Thy frosts cut like a fine steel blade,
The glass shows nothing in the shade.
Of fogs thou hast just one or two-
We like them not – 'tween me and you.
But all the same, we think you fine –
You're far more cosy than the Line.
      We have within our boundaries
   here
Many an institution dear –
'Aotea-Roa Hut' comes in
For praises high – an easy win,
A smile – good food – a cosy spot –
Ladies, d'you know, it helps a lot?
      The canteen is some place too,
To judge by noise and eager crew,
Who bide their time before the door

Till they may drink their fill – or more.
The history of this place of fame?
The conduct sheets will show the same.
      'YMCA's' are relished too –
We get home news both old and new,
'Tis mostly old we must admit.
That matters not one little bit.
And officers, my, how hard they work
   here,
They love not to leave you, that is clear.
      To cap our joy down here with thee
We get a monthly – three pence the fee.
The N.Z. Chronicle it is named –
For faithful records it is famed.
Through it, while here with thee we stay,
We trace our comrades day by day.
      Now farewell, Codford – we away
To join the old boys in the fray.
We know just what we're going to –
Perchance sometimes we'll think of you,
Some things men want you sure do lack,
But fare thee well, till we get back.

December 27th 1916

BATTALION ORDERS by Kernal Bert Frost, Commanding N.Z.Submarine*Lancers*, Codford

    REVEILLE PARADE, 3am – Battalion will parade with bare feet and helmets, when they will proceed to the beach, and dive off Southampton Lighthouse. Anyone found wandering at the bottom looking for promotion will receive his discharge on coming to the surface. All submarines found will be handed in to the Q.M.'s stores.

    ROUTE MARCH: There will be a route march as far as Russia, headed by the band, which will play the great march, 'Here We Suffer Grief and Pain.' In case of frost bite being prevalent in the ranks, every man will be provided with a box of sunstroke ointment and crutches.

    CAMEL PARADE, 7.22am – Camel parade before proceeding to Egypt. All humps to be polished and chins shaded. N.C.O.'s will be provided with goats. Anyone turning out rusty will be handcuffed to a ghost.

SPECIAL RATIONS: This being the Kernal's birthday every man will receive: 2 boiled mackerel, 1 glass rum, and half a cocoanut.

SPORT: Sports will be held in the quarry, admission by tram ticket. The great draw will be a juggling exhibition by Sergeant Brown, who will juggle with split peas and 2 rashers of bacon.

TRAINING: There will be a night attack on the nearest pub with grubbers. A fatigue party will be told off to carry the empties away.

SICK: All men with corns will parade at the Q.M. stores for sandpaper. There will be an inspection by Major Gorton, of the Jerusalem Light Horse, who will operate by moonlight on urgent cases. Special arrangements have been made by the War Office for Colonel Peerlot to cure the following complaints: Cancer, consumption, flat feet, overlapping toenails, varicose veins.

DEFAULTERS: In future defaulters will stuff palliasses with hedgehogs. Major Nicholson will give lectures on parts of a grubber, and how to make holes with a square shovel.

LEAVE: Leave will be granted annually for the purpose of having a bath and a change of clothing. Special leave will be granted for those able to promise they are snuffing it.

FIRE ALARM: Upon this sounding men must lay perfectly still until carried to a place of safety.

PROMOTION: The O.C. is pleased to make the following promotions: Private Harry Spencer to be a temporary private, unpaid. Field Marshall M. Paget to be a temporary Sanitary Corporal. The above men will be attached to Tea Company for groceries and pay.

PUNISHMENT: the following punishments have been awarded to Private Oke Galloff: 5 years C.B. for refusing to eat his rations. Private Kego Paul 756 days C.B. for refusing to whitewash the last post.

[signed] G.W. WATTY, Adjt.

Codford Command Depot, November 5th 1916

Fred Thomas

Frederick William Thomas was born on 1st July 1890, and between 1906 and 1910 he served in the Royal Navy Voluntary Reserve. Fred originally went to New Zealand to look for his half brother Albert, whom he found married with two children in Rotorua. Fred signed up on 14th August 1914 at the outbreak of hostilities, and because of his four years naval service he was assigned to *HMS Torch*, a depot ship for *HMS Philomel*, New Zealand's only battleship. Within a

Fred Thomas pictured with his mates in the Ao-Tea-Roa Club at Codford – nearest to the camera in row of three.

month *HMS Torch* was de-commissioned, so while he was awaiting his next posting Fred worked for John Court Limited, a large clothing and haberdashery store in Auckland.

In March 1915 he appears to have volunteered his service to the New Zealand Army and had been given a job as an ambulance driver in the New Zealand Medical Corps. In November that year he was shipped via Alexandria, Egypt to Marseilles and on to the Western Front. His grandson Jeremy Unsworth-Joss believes that during the Battle of the Somme, 23rd September 1916, Fred was shelled and gassed near La Sars while advancing with the No. 2 NZ Machine Gun Corps. He was discovered barely alive, buried in the mud. He was dug out and was taken as a stretcher case to the hospital at Rouen.

Fred was transported across the channel by the hospital ship *HMS Asturias* to the port at Southampton, recovering at No 1 NZ Hospital at Brockenhurst. He worked as a medical orderly at Hornchurch and Codford for the remainder of the war, reaching the rank of Staff Sergeant.

In 1919 he returned to Rotorua and persuaded his half brother to return to the UK with his family. They arrived home aboard the liner *SS Ruahine* [pronounced Roo-Ah-He-Knee] on 3rd September 1920. Fred joined the Territorial Army in 1925, serving for twelve years with 162nd Royal Artillery in London until 1937.

[With thanks to Jeremy Unsworth-Joss]

The Badge on Misery Hill

W iltshire has a chalk landscape, and beneath the grassland of Salisbury Plain lies the evidence that during the Cretaceous period, 65 million years ago, this area was beneath the sea. The soft limestone is a result of calcium carbonate deposits from the shells of marine organisms that existed at the same time as the dinosaurs. Hill figures carved into the Downs, gleaming white chalk against the undulating greensward of the high places, have featured throughout our history.

During World War One, with troops stationed all over the Plain, a plethora of military badges appeared. At Fovant, between Salisbury and Shaftesbury, a collection of Regimental Badges, which include a map of Australia, were carved along the length of the Down.

The Codford Badge is locally known as either the Australian Badge or the Rising Sun. In its original form it was meant to depict a Trophy of Arms – the badge of the Australian Imperial Force. The 175 by 150 foot badge was begun in 1916 and

The Badge on Misery Hill

cut into a steep hillside at the eastern end of Codford facing southward towards the Wylye Valley. Its history is as follows: the then Australian Brigade Commander of the Australian Garrison could look on to the hill from the reading room of the HQ at Stockton House, and he came up with the idea that defaulters should be made as their punishment to carve the badge in the most prominent position in Codford. The soldiers, not unnaturally given the steepness of the hill and the fact that they had to march up and down it wearing full kit, and climb up for physical exercises in bitter conditions, nicknamed it 'Misery Hill.' Another name bestowed on the hill, in common use with the soldiers, was 'The Pimple.'

The Badge today

The badge is on Josh Stratton's pasture, on Lamb Down, and figures on a website as the Lamb Down Badge. This is a name of recent origin bestowed by someone who looked at a map for a reference, and it has no real historical significance – locals have never, to my knowledge, referred to the badge by that name.

The initial work was begun by the 13th Training Battalion, Australian Imperial Forces, and it was embedded with green, brown and clear beer bottles that would gleam in the sunlight, suggesting the bronze badge worn by the AIF on their uniforms. During World War Two it was covered over to prevent the Luftwaffe using it as a navigational aid. After hostilities when it was uncovered most of the glass had been washed away or sunk into the chalk.

The present outline is less intricate and pristine than the original – through the years after World War Two local groups worked to maintain the badge. In recent years, thanks to the work of Captains Dave Killcullen, Tony Egan and Craig Shortt, Australian Liaison Officers based in Warminster, each year in late spring or early summer members of Operation Long Look, Australian and New Zealand military personnel spend a day in Codford to clean the Badge. Farmer Josh Stratton, farm manager Mike Read and Tom Thornton have been instrumental in organising materials for the refurbishment. The Australian Veterans Association have made monies available to re-fence the badge, to fund a pamphlet recording the history of the ANZACs in Codford and for two explanation boards to be sited in the War Grave Cemetery and at a view point in Stockton. There is now a Badge Committee composed of the current Australian Liaison Officer, members of the military and the Parish Council, committed to protecting and preserving the Codford Badge for posterity. The men who toiled up Misery Hill with full packs and curses, in dreadful conditions, have left a legacy that outlasted their lifetimes.

'Members of a Suicide Club'

On 23rd November 1916 Corporal Button was killed in a training accident. The details given in the records list only surname, initials, rank, number, regiment and date of death – it is thanks to research by Terry Crawford, author of *Wiltshire and the Great War*, that I accessed the facts from a local newspaper. The 1st December edition of the *Warminster Journal* reports:

SERIOUS ACCIDENT AT CODFORD
Corporal Killed and Ten Men Wounded – Dangers of Bombing

At the Codford Military Hospital, on Saturday, Mr F A P Sylvester, Coroner for the District, conducted an Inquiry relative to the death of Albert James Button, aged 23, a corporal in the 51st [Reinforcement] Battalion of the Australian Imperial Forces, who was killed on the previous Thursday though the explosion of a bomb, which resulted in injuries, though of a minor character, to ten other men. Mr W. Comins was the foreman of the jury.

Second-Lieut. Swann, of the AIF stated that he was bombing officer in 'D' Group at No.2 Camp, Codford and was in charge of the bombing practice which took place on the 23rd inst., when a serious accident happened, resulting in the death of Corporal Button. The accident occurred at twenty past four in the afternoon. Lance-Sergeant Brown was acting as instructor at the time, and Private Taylor, of the 51st Battalion, threw a bomb against the parapet of the throwing bay and to the rear of the thrower. Taylor held the bomb too long, and, not throwing it correctly, it curled along the parapet about three feet and entered the next bay, in which were about 20 men who were awaiting their turn to throw. Men waiting to practice were never allowed in the same bay as the thrower, the bays being divided by a sandbag partition nearly five feet high. The bomb thrown by Taylor went out fully a foot, but the spin on the grenade, resembling the twist on a cricket ball, brought it back.

In reply to the Coroner, witness explained that there was a wire netting above the sandbag partition, making a total height of eight feet. The bomb did not touch the netting, but went in front of the far edge, and then fell into the adjoining bay, at about three feet from the inside edge of the partition. Witness, who was in the observation pulpit ten yards in the rear, immediately shouted out to the men in the waiting bay, 'For God's sake get out of the bay,' and, with the exception of the deceased, they immediately ran. Corporal Button did not stir. He seemed to be paralysed with fear.

The Coroner Could he hear well?

Witness Yes; quite well. He seemed to be absolutely paralysed, and stayed in the bay until the bomb exploded. Witness found deceased lying across the sandbags in the rear of the bay, his head being just out of the bay and his feet inside. Deceased was alive, but very badly wounded. Witness sent for an ambulance, upon which the deceased was taken to hospital. A number of other men were wounded. Had they dropped flat instead of running none of them would probably have been wounded at all. Deceased, however, was the only man who lost his presence of mind. The other men merely had leg wounds. They stooped down as they ran.

The Coroner Would there be any difficulty in making it impossible for a bomb to go from one bay to another?

Witness It is almost impossible. Bomb throwing always will be dangerous. A bombing officer is practically a member of a suicide club.

The Coroner said it appeared to him that a five- foot parapet was extremely low. Witness pointed out that if the parapet were higher the bomb would be repeatedly hitting the top and coming back into the bay, and there would be a great many more casualties. Witness added that he never thought it possible that the spin on the grenade would cause it to go out and come in again.

The Coroner Do you know of any objection to the protecting bay, where the young men are waiting, being further away than it is from the throwing bay?

Witness They are perfectly safe.

The Coroner That's not the point. What I want to know is whether there would be any objection, from the point of view of training, to the men being, say, 50 yards apart?

Witness In this respect – you could not control them, could you?

Coroner Not at 50 yards?

Witness No, not very well.

Coroner What is a safe range?

Witness 200 yards.

The Coroner And the throwing bay and the waiting bay actually adjoin?

Witness Yes, but it is perfectly safe. The men are instructed to get round to the other side of the sandbags. That is clearly laid down.

The Coroner And were they?

Witness Unfortunately they did not do that. They lose their heads at a time of stress like this. That is why so many got wounded.

The Coroner You mean if anything like this happens?

Witness Yes, and it happens fairly often. Bombs are very dangerous things.

In reply to further questions, witness said the man practised with dummy grenades before being allowed to throw live bombs. The grenade thrown on the occasion in question was a Mills No. 5, which had a safety pin and lever and was recognised as the safest and best bomb in the British Army. The bomb thrown by Private Taylor exploded rather prematurely, viz . . . in about three seconds rather than four and a half seconds. Bombs were not all exactly the same, as they varied in manufacture. Witness added that deceased was moved to the hospital on a stretcher from about half-an-hour to three-quarters of an hour after the accident, the other men being removed by ambulance at seven o'clock.

Lance-Sergeant Brown, 16th Battalion, Australian Imperial Forces, stated that he was the instructor on the occasion when the accident occurred, and was in the throwing bay with Private Taylor. Taylor had gone through a course of dummy practice, but on the occasion in question it was the first live bomb he had thrown.

The Coroner Did he appear to be cool about it?

Witness I should say he was a bit nervous. Describing how the accident happened, witness said Taylor threw the bomb with a round-arm motion, and, not releasing it, his hand practically completed a half circle, with the result that the grenade hit the top of the parapet and twisted back into the next bay.

The Coroner Do you think he held it too long?

Witness Yes, far too long. Instead of throwing with a straight over-arm motion, Private Taylor swung his arm round.

The Coroner How much do the bombs weigh?

Witness One and a half pounds. Witness heard Lieut. Swann call out to the men in the waiting bay to get out, and he also shouted to them.

The Coroner Do you see any objection to the waiting bay being further apart?

Witness The best way I know is to have the men waiting in a special bay further back, say about ten yards behind the throwing bay, and let each man advance into the throwing bay when it is his turn to throw.

Lieut.-Colonel Fenwick, New Zealand Medical Corps, the officer in charge of the hospital, said the deceased was dead when he reached the hospital. A bullet had passed completely through his brain, death being due to fracture of the skull. Deceased had a few wounds on his legs, but they were quite slight. The Coroner commented on the fact that the hospital staff displayed considerable skill in getting the ambulance up to the scene of the lamentable affair. Lieut.-Colonel Fenwick stated that the injuries received by the other men were of a minor character, and they would all recover.

The Coroner remarked that the circumstances attending the accident had been very carefully explained by Lieut. Swann, who was in the observing pulpit and was therefore in a position to describe what occurred. It appeared that owing to some unaccountable reason – for Private Taylor did not know exactly what happened – the bomb was improperly thrown, and, going in a wrong direction and pitching on the parapet, it fell close to a large number of men. Fortunately all except Corporal Button were able to get out of the way, and only the deceased was seriously injured. It was, of course, difficult for a court like that to say anything about the arrangements for instructing men in bomb throwing, because it was a thing they knew nothing about, but it occurred to him that there should be no difficulty in placing the waiting bay in a different position. The waiting bay might surely be placed in such a position that whatever happened the men waiting to throw should run no unnecessary risks. The men would run risks soon enough at the front. He was sure everything was done to protect those practising bomb throwing, but he could not imagine that there should be the slightest difficulty in avoiding any risks to the waiting men, for there ought to be no risks.

The Coroner added that the jury would join with him in an expression of condolence with the relatives of the deceased and sympathy with them upon Corporal Button's unfortunate death on this side of the water. The jury returned a verdict of 'Accidental Death.'

[Ironically given the casualties while training and Second Lieut. Swann's comments that 'Bomb throwing always will be dangerous. A bombing officer is practically a member of a suicide club,' grenades were only responsible for 2% of the British casualties in World War One. Mortar bombs and shells accounted for 58.7%, bullets 39% and bayonets 0.3%.]

[Sources: *Warminster Journal*, 1st December 1916; *The Faber Book of War Poetry*, edited by Kenneth Baker, 1996]

The Hottest Place this Side of Hell
The Codford Diary of a War Poet

One of the finest and most influential war poets of the First World War spent the first month of 1917 in Codford. [Philip] Edward Thomas was the son of Welsh parents, born in Lambeth on 3rd March 1878. He was a freelance journalist,

professional reviewer, editor and
author who had studied at Oxford
after winning a history scholarship.
He began writing poetry in the latter
part of his all too short life, after
meeting Robert Frost, who was to
become one of his closest friends.
Between December 1914 and his
death in April 1917 he wrote 142
poems, many echoing his enduring
love of nature and the countryside,
others encompassing his wartime
experiences, some reflecting both
themes:

A Private
This ploughman dead in battle slept out
     of doors
Many a frozen night, and merrily
Answered staid drinkers, good bedmen,
     and all bores:
'At Mrs. Greenland's Hawthorn Bush,'
     said he,
'I slept.' None knew which bush. Above
     the town,

Edward Thomas

Beyond 'The Drover', a hundred spot the down
In Wiltshire. And where now at last he sleeps
More sound in France- that, too, he secret keeps.

Married to Helen Noble while still an undergraduate, the father of two children,
in July 1915 at the age of thirty-seven he enlisted in the Artists Rifles. The following
year, in 1916 he was commissioned in the Royal Artillery and volunteered for service
overseas. In January 1917 he arrived in Codford before being shipped to France.

Edward Thomas said his goodbyes to family and friends, wrote cheques for
the next six months and visited the dentist between 8th and 12th January 1917. His
diary takes up the story:

January 13th. Nothing to do but test compass which never gives same results. Walk
and tea with Flawn. Cold drizzle. Horton and the battery left early for Codford. Even
wrote verses. Early to bed.

14th. A Sunday and no letters as I am supposed to be at Codford. A cold bright day.
Walked with Flawn through Old Romney and Ivychurch. Flawn to tea with me. Packing.

15th. Up at 6. Packing. Left Lydd at 9 with Q.M.S. [Quartermaster Sergeant] and
Grier and 3 men. Light snow and red sun. 4 hours to spare in London but could only see
T. Clayton and D. [A. Duncan] Williams: could not find J. Freeman. Then to Codford in

the dark, writing to Helen and beginning 'A Sentimental Journey'. Arrived too late for dinner.

16th. Took route march to Wigtye [Wylye?], Stockton, Sherrington, and had great luck in short cuts and byeroads over the river. A frosty, clear day: men singing 'Dixie', 'There's a long long trail of winding to the land of my dreams', and 'We're here because we're here' to the tune of Auld Lang Syne. Only Smith and I and Capt. Fenner left of the 6 officers. Afternoon walked with Smith to Chitterne and had tea there. Evening dined together and talked about practical education – pronunciation of 'girl', 'soot' and 'historian' – and about rhymes to eye.

17th. Light snow in night; hard frost. Men on fatigues or drawing overseas clothes etc. Office full of boot, blankets, pails, axes, shovels, dixies, stretchers etc.

Route march to Tytherington, Heytesbury and Knook. Afternoon walked over Downs by Stockton Wood to Chilmark with Smith: tea at inn and Smith played ragtime etc. A cloudy clear frosty day. Back over the downs on a dark night, but only went astray 200 yards.

18th. To Warminster to the bank. Still frosty. Afternoon lectured on map reading. Orderly officer for the camp from 6.pm Indoors all evening, talking to Smith about marching songs.

19th. Morning orderly officer – latrines etc – lectured on maps – paid Battery. Afternoon learnt to ride motorcycle. Mild and drizzly. Guns are due to arrive. A cake from Mother. Shakespeare's sonnets from Helen. Capt. Fenner talks of having to take sick leave.

20th. Mild snowy. Arranging stores. Guns arriving. Smith to Bath. So I had to see to unloading and parking the guns till dark. No use walking after dark. The roads are pitch dark and crowded with men going to cinemas, darkness worse from blaze of motor lamps and electric light in camps nearby. Long queues waiting outside cinema at 5.30. Tested battery compass. Talk with Fenner about martens in Ireland, badgers, plovers, barrows etc.

21st. No church parade for me. 9.30- 1.30 walked over Stockton Down, the Bake, and under Grovely Wood to Barford St Martin, Burcombe, and to lunch at Netherhampton House with Newbolts. Freezing drizzle – freezes on the ground, white grass and icy roads. 2 families of vagrants in a green road roasting a corpse of something by a slow wood fire. Beautiful Downs, with one or two isolated thatched barns, ivied ash trees, and derelict threshing machine. Old milestones lichened as with battered gold and silver nails. Back by train at 5.

Guns in line out on parade square. Smith back. Talk with Fenner after dinner about fishing- river and sea.

22nd. Set men branding and sorting stores. Left at 10.30 for Gloster to see Haines. Still

Badge of the Artists Rifles

frosty and dull. Gloster at 2.50. Sat til 12.15 gossiping about Frost, de la Mare, and the army, marching songs etc. Haines gave me Frost's 'Mountain Interval.'

23rd. With Mrs Haines and Robin most of the morning. 3.30 left Gloster via Mangotsfield and Bath for Codford. Read 'Mountain Interval.' Horton, Rubin and Thorburn back. Fenner merry; he is probably going on sick leave. He and Rubin returned late and had a noisy parting from 2 others. Thorburn had a screaming nightmare.

24th. All men on fatigues. A short walk with Thorburn to test compasses. Parcel of medicines etc from Helen, cigars from Harry. Walked in afternoon with Thorburn to Chilmark for tea, and back over frosty Downs with new moon and all stars. But my ankles chaffed by new boots lame me.

25th. Resting my sore ankles. Dial sights tested and stores arranged for packing tomorrow. Guns leave on 27th and Battery on 29th. Fenner is to go to hospital and Horton to take charge. Very cold with East wind. Capt. Lushington is to be our new o/c [Officer Commanding 244 Battery (Acting Major Lushington)] and to take us out.

26th. Loading lorries and attaching guns to 4 wheel drives- standing out in dusty icy East wind doing nothing but getting cold and dirty. I sleep badly too. Also I have taken charge of mess and mess accounts. Thorburn is on my nerves – he had a nightmare lately – asking 'Can you tell me how much 55lbs is?' – the weight of officer's luggage. I feel useless. Am still in slacks and shoes on account of bad ankles. Thorburn and I dining alone, the others with Capt. Lushington in the village – our mess kit being packed. Can't even walk far enough to get warm. Thorburn goes tomorrow with guns. Dined with him and then talked about philosophy and poetry, and Yes and Perhaps, and the lyric and the Bible. I have a cold. The frost is worse tonight.

27th. A clear windy frosty dawn, the sun like a bright coin between the knuckles of opposite hills seen from sidelong. A fox. A little office work. Telegram to say Baba was at Ransome's, so I walked over the Downs by Chicklade Bottom and the Fonthills to Hatch, and blistered both feet badly. House full of ice and big fires. Sat up with Ivy till 12 and slept till 8.

28th. Slept late. Rested my feet, talking to the children or Ivy cooking with Kitty Gurd. Hired a bicycle to save walking. Such a beautiful ride after joining the Mere and Amesbury Road at Fonthill Bishop- hedgeless roads over long sloping downs with woods and sprinkled thorns, carved with old tracks which junipers line – an owl and many rabbits – a clear pale sky and but a faint sunset- a long twilight lasting till 6. We are to move at 6.30am tomorrow. Horton and Smith and I dined together laughing at imbecile jests and at Smith's own laughing. Had to change in order to send home my soiled things. Letters. Mess accounts and cheques to tradesmen.

29th. Up at 5. Very cold. Off at 6.30, men marching in frosty dark to station singing 'Pack up your troubles in your old kitbag'. The rotten song in the still dark brought one tear. No food or tea- Freezing carriage. Southampton at 9.30 and there had to wait till dusk, walking up and down, watching ice scattered water, gulls and dark wood beyond, or London Scottish playing improved Rugger, or men dancing to concertina, in a great shed between railway and water. Smith and I got off for lunch after Horton and Capt. Lushington returned from theirs. Letter to Helen from 'South Western Hotel', where sea-captains were talking of the 'Black Adder' and of 'The Black Ball Line' that used to go to Australia. Hung about till dark – the seagulls as light failed nearly all floated instead of flying- then sailed at 7. Thorburn turned up. Now I'm in 2nd officers' cabin with Capt and Horton, the men outside laughing and joking and saying fucking. Q.W.R's [Queens Westmorland Rifles] and Scottish and a Field Battery and 236 S.B. [Siege Battery], also on 'The Mona Queen'. Remember the entirely serious and decorous writing in urinal whitewash – name, address, unit and date of sailing. A tumbled crossing but rested.

30th. Arrived Le Havre 4am. Light of stars and windows of tall pale houses and electric arcs on the quay. March through bales of cotton in sun to camp. The snow first emptying its castor of finest white. Tents. Mess full of subalterns censoring letters. Breakfast at 9.45am on arrival. Afternoon in Havre, which Thorburn likes because it is French. Mess unendurably hot and stuffy, tent unendurably cold till I got into my blankets. Slept well in fug. Snow at night.

31st. Had to shift our lines in the snow. 12 to a tent with 2 blankets each. Ankles bad. Nearly all water frozen in taps and basins. Mess crowded – some standing. Censoring letters about the crossing and the children and ailments etc at home. Had to make a speech explaining that men need not be shy about writing familiar letters home. At 'Nouvel Hotel,' Havre, while we had tea, waitress kissing a Capt. and arranging for another visit. 4 f. for 2 teas. Battery had to be specially warned about venereal in Havre. Read sonnets in evening: to bed at 9 to escape hot stuff room. Officers coming and going. Some faces you just see, drinking once and never again. More fine snow like sago.

February in France that year was bitterly cold. Edward Thomas continued to have problems with his ankle, new field boots added to his discomfort and attempts to get shoes from Ordnance proved fruitless, eventually he bought low soft boots in Le Havre. His time was spent censoring letters, overhauling guns and rearranging stores, his evening discussions with fellow officers returned to literary, philosophical, moral and practical topics. On 4th February the men and guns moved out towards the Front. On 24th February Edward Thomas wrote:

Why do Huns not retaliate on Arras guns? Some day this will be one of the hottest places this side of Hell, if it is this side. Dined with the 244. Walked back to Arras in dark with Thorburn, challenged by *only 2 sentries* who were content with 'Friend' though they could not see a yard among the ruins. Owls on Daneville Road. Machine guns and hanging lights above No Man's Land. New moon – *last* as I walked from Hatch to Codford.

The diary is filled with descriptions of life on the Front interspersed with observations about the natural world, a nature oblivious to the horrors of wartime in the burgeoning spring.

Beautiful clear cloudless morning and no firing between daybreak and 8. Linnets and chaffinches sing in waste trenched ground with trees and water tanks between us and Arras. Magpies over No Man's Land in pairs. The old green [grey] track crossing No Man's Land- once a country way to Arras. The water green and clear [like Silent Pool] of the Moat of the Citadel with skeletons of whole trees lying there.

Comments about his own fears are brief and factual:

More shells came in the afternoon. The fire is warm but the room is cold. Shelling started at 5.30- I don't like it. I wonder where I shall be hit as in bed I wonder if it is better to be on the window or the outer side of the room or on the chimney on inner side, whether better to be upstairs where you may fall or on the ground floor where you may be worse crushed.

On Easter Monday, 9th April 1917 Second Lieutenant Philip Edward Thomas of the 244th Siege Battery, Royal Garrison Artillery was killed in the Battle of Arras, just over a month after his 39th birthday. Five days earlier, on 4th April Sir Douglas Haig ordered a massive artillery bombardment, using 2,800 guns including gas, along a twenty mile front. On the 9th April Haig sent his Infantry into combat, they gained just three and a half miles of territory but were unable to make any impression on the strongly reinforced German lines.

Edward Thomas was among the first of the 84,000 British casualties who fell during the month long Battle of Arras which ended on 3rd May 1917. He was killed at an Observation Post during the opening barrage of the Battle, at 7.36am, while directing the fire of 244 Battery. He is buried in Agny Military Cemetery, Pas de Calais, south of Arras. The Military Cemetery was begun by French troops and used by British units and Field Ambulances from March 1916 to June 1917, with two further burials were made in April of 1918. According to the Commonwealth War Graves Commission graves were brought from the battlefields east of Arras in 1923-24. The initial forty French graves have been removed, and the cemetery, covering 3,572 square metres, now commemorates over 400 casualties from the 1914-18 war, more than 100 are unidentified.

Rain, midnight rain, nothing but the wild rain
On this bleak hut, and solitude, and me
Remembering again that I shall die
And neither hear the rain nor give it thanks
For washing me cleaner than I have been
Since I was born into this solitude.
Blessed are the dead that the rain rains upon:
But here I pray that none whom I once loved
Is dying tonight or lying still awake
Solitary, listening to the rain,
Either in pain or thus in sympathy
Helpless among the living and the dead,
Like a cold water among broken reeds,
Myriads of broken reeds all still and stiff,
Like me who have no love which this wild rain
Has not dissolved except the love of death,
If love it be towards what is perfect and
Cannot, the tempest tells me, disappoint.

Edward Thomas's great friend Eleanor Farjeon wrote:

EASTER MONDAY (In Memoriam E.T.)
In the last letter that I had from France
You thanked me for the silver Easter egg
Which I had hidden in the box of apples
You liked to munch beyond all other fruit.
You found the egg the Monday before Easter,
And said, 'I will praise Easter Monday now –
It was such a lovely morning.' Then you spoke
Of the coming battle and said, 'This is the eve.
Goodbye. And may I have a letter soon.'
    That Easter Monday was a day for praise,
It was such a lovely morning. In our garden
We sowed our earliest seeds, and in the orchard
The apple-bud was ripe. It was the eve.
There are three letters that you will not get.
    April 9th 1917

    In Memoriam Easter 1915
    The flowers left thick at nightfall in the wood
This Eastertide call into the mind of men,
Now far from home, who, with their sweethearts, should
Have gathered them and will do never again
                    (Edward Thomas 1878-1917)

[Sources: *The Collected Poems of Edward Thomas* edited by R George Thomas, 1978 [some
passages have been omitted or abbreviated]; *Men who March Away: Poems of the First World
War*, edited by I M Parsons, 1978; *Scars Upon My Heart: Women's Poetry and Verse of the First
World War*, selected by Catherine Reilly; *Brassey's Battles*, by John Laffin, 1995; Commonwealth
War Graves Commission; *The Richmond Review*]

Chronicles of the N.Z.E.F. 1917

January 5th 1917
CHRISTMAS AT CODFORD CAMP: Ao-Tea-Roa Club
Well, on the whole, Christmas week was a great success. To begin with, the sun
almost smiled, for once, anyway, we were not enveloped in fog as per usual, and
our dear old companion the mud, that is forever with us, was frozen stiff and for
once was kept in its proper place.

Decorating was a serious business. Weighty were the discussions and many the views aired on colour schemes to be each in turn squashed by a ruthless sergeant who had view of his own.

Six mess rooms entered for a competition, the prize being a huge cake made at Ao-Tea-Roa. Big bundles of coloured tissue paper were sent down from the N.Z.W.C.A., but many of the messes must have spent huge sums on streamers and lanterns, etc. and some of the results of their labours really were ripping. Snow covered foliage [cotton wool and greenery] looked very pretty, and showed a sort of compliment to the country we are in. We would never think of decorating at Christmas time in dear old NZ with sham snow, would we? Each mess room was sure of winning the prize.

On Christmas day five of the Blue Staff from Ao-Tea-Roa motored round and judged all the mess rooms, and a very difficult job it was too. At first the voting was for the Details Mess-room and the Maories, but finally Auckland and Canterbury ran in the lead, both very different, and excelling in its own way. It was decided a tie- they must toss for the cake. However, a better solution was thought of, and a football match was arranged. Well, they nearly killed Tiny, [who played for Canterbury]. He is at present our cook's best factotum– wee thing fourteen stone or so. He appeared the next day with the most fearsome black eye and three bruised ribs. I can swear to the former, a vision that sort of hit you in the eye, as it were; the latter he didn't offer to show me. Auckland won and 'took the cake'. So much for the camp decoration.

Now about ours. Miss Mair, with a voluntary fatigue party of sergeants, worked hard stringing the rafters of the clubroom of Ao-Tea-Roa with mauve and pink, some sweet cocoanut ice colours draped the kettle globes and the result was delightful, although it did not come up to some of the companies messes. These sergeants worked like Trojans and were chaffed unmercifully by the men, who all swore they had never seen them work before. The buffet was a bower of peach blossom and a rare [entirely new species] of gorgeous lotus flower. When finished a man who wandered in remarked tentatively: 'Was he in Heaven?'

Christmas Eve being Sunday, we held the concert on Saturday night. Mrs Leedham Crow's party came from London and stayed over the week-end, which enabled them to give concerts at the hospital as well. During the interval in Saturday's concert, Captain McKay, on behalf of the men, presented to the YMCA ladies at their two huts in the camp, two silver tea-sets, and the Ao-Tea-Roa ladies with a lovely china dinner service, a cutlery set [a most splendid present], and a dozen silver table napkin rings, one of the latter to be kept by each of us in memory of the Christmas at Codford. Needless to say it was a great surprise, and Miss Dobie, who received the present in Mrs Wilder's absence, was too overwhelmed to make a speech, and could only say 'Thank you, boys, very much. It is too good of you.'

On Christmas Eve Ao-Tea-Roa gave a free supper. Oh, my! It took some preparing, as we expected many hundreds to partake of it. The buffet was piled high with cakes, mince pies, sandwiches, biscuits, oranges and apples in basketfuls, and nuts. Overhead was a garland of crackers. The fruit salad was in such quantities that it had to have a buffet of its own – a sort of sideshow exhibit.

All the evening the 'wash up fatigue' worked at fever pitch and with the aid of some of the members of the concert party who 'dried,' kept enormous supplies of cups and plates going.

The evening finished by all 'hands and the cook' going up to the stage and singing 'Auld Lang Syne,' and the pulling of an immense cracker presented by Miss Mackenzie. The Maories decked themselves in the paper fancy dress costumes that had been inside it, and danced a haka. Much applause.

On Christmas Day there was a great weight of turkey and duck consumed by the men in various messes. They were waited on by the sergeants, and pretty busy it kept them too. I understand everyone of them had as much as he could eat – and DRINK. After dinner, sports were intended, but they fell through, and I believe everyone slept. Anyway, the camp was very quiet.

The Maories gave a special dinner of their own at 2 o'clock, at which Col. Mackenzie, Lieut. Macpherson [Adjutant], Lieut. Seddon, and Capt. Dobson, and two of the Blue Staff were invited. It was a huge success. The hosts did everything in their power to honour and amuse their guests. They sang and danced hakas of welcome throughout. Speeches were made and compliments exchanged, in which the 'Blue Sisters' of the Ao-Tea-Roa came in for a share.

In the evening, as everyone had enjoyed the dinner so much, they reassembled for a dance. The officers' mess and sergeants' mess also gave dinner parties.

We had a small impromptu party at the Ao-Tea-Roa, and saw in the New Year. On New Years Night the sergeants' mess of No 8 Camp had its official opening, and gave a most successful dinner. Seven of the Blue Staff went and had a splendid evening, which finished up with games, songs and a dance. And here concludes a sketchy account of how we spent Christmas at Codford camp.

Yours,

'BEHIND THE BUFFET'

31st January 1917

CODFORD COMMAND DEPOT NEWS: Despite the cold and the wet, and the snow, and the coughs and colds, and other complaints that soldiers are heir to, the camp has gone on cheerfully and well. From physical drill there is no respite, and the number of Huns killed daily at bayonet fighting would wipe out that race of vipers.

The entertainments have been splendid. The YMCA and the Ao-tea-roa folk last week provided great surprises for the soldiers. At the YMCA hut the famous hunter, Captain Seton Carr, adorned in a long black coat, with fur collar and cap, and underneath a navy blue uniform, told in silvery tones, of his adventures by field and flood and wild beasts. His lantern slides of his big game shooting in Africa were wonderful.

'The Goods' came and conquered. These entertainers, from the 28th Division, provided a wonderful show, every item being splendid. The 'star' turn was Gladys

Cooper, who came straight from London to amuse the boys. Her elegant figure, winsome manner, and the lure she had for the lads on the stage and off, were remarkable. When, in the last scene of this strange performance, she took off her golden curls, the roars of laughter were deafening from the ones 'in the know,' only to be measured by groans of disappointment and sighs of disgust. It was the most startling performance we have yet had at Codford.

CODFORD 'SOCIETY' NOTES   Since there seems to be some controversy about Princess Mary's future husband, what's the matter with the 'Crown Prince of Codford?'

Since the publication of the January Birthday Honours quite a few distinguished visitors here are writing 'C.B.' after their names. It is an honour not much sought but very much run after.

Miss Johnson has been appointed Buffet Commandant of the Ao-Tea-Roa Battalion ['The Blues'], and is ably assisted in her arduous duties by Sergeant-Major Whettan, Quartermaster Winder, and Sergeant-Cook Ross.

Owing to having their morning slumbers disturbed by the sound of the guns at Lark Hill, the Artillery have reluctantly removed to Aldershot.

Quite a nobby invention in this season's fashion for soldiers is the wearing of embroidered chevrons on the sleeves, I have noticed quite a considerable number with one, two, and even three chevrons. If this fashion becomes the vogue I shall expect to see no unadorned sleeves shortly.

Another very pretty idea is the wearing of coloured ribbons on the shoulder straps, the prevailing colours being yellow, green, blue, and red, red being the most fashionable.

The new Government is making great strides. It has already discovered that a week consists of two weekend leaves: viz., Saturday and Sunday, and any other vacant day.

Medical authorities have discovered that men requiring further treatment at the Rotorua Sanatorium can obtain mud baths equally as efficient here in Codford.

Can any reader define the meaning of the phase 'Light Duties'? Does it mean handling sacks of potatoes, boxes of fish, metalling roads, or emptying sacks of coal?

The Misses Machine Gun, being unable to withstand the inclemency of the Codford weather, have gone to Grantham for further treatment.

It is rumoured here that 'Colonel' Frost is to proceed to France to take over the official duties of Sir Douglas Haig, F.M., whom, we hear, is to have a few weeks rest.

'WAHUD WALLAH'

January 31st 1917
[When the 3rd NZ General Hospital was visited by Miss E.Guiness she reported that: Three patients had rheumatism, two bronchitis and were improving, one had bronchial catarrh, another pleurisy, Smith was suffering with influenza and laryngitis,

Wilson had chest trouble, Mallett was suffering with haemorrhoids and Pilkinton had a hammer toe, getting better.]

February 14th 1917
CODFORD COMMAND DEPOT NEWS Before the snow came our principle occupation was digging potato patches. Yes, it was grand work in the cold mornings, slogging in at the frozen ground where there wasn't even a frigid worm to be discovered. When the summer comes and we have gone won't the gardens between the huts present a homely sight? Now the boys are talking of 'early kidneys' and other varieties. The suggestion about growing peas and beans has not met with a favourable reception! Can you imagine raids on the Chinese garden of P.U. Company by the Huns of Y Company? The farmers among the workers are doubtful of a large yield unless some fertiliser is added. Well, even that may be remedied, and intense cultivation followed.

On Sunday the snow fell upon the just and the unjust – soft feathery flakes that glistened in the moonlight. All hands and the cook took to snow-balling and stiff-necked NCOs ducked and dodged and were thoroughly dowsed by the devoted full privates. The officers also indulged in the old fashioned pastime. At the hospital those who were well enough pelted the orderlies, and the orderlies pelted the VADs,

'A quiet spot at Codford'

who retaliated with vim and determination. It was a merry time. Some nurses, who usually look so trim and neat in their uniforms and caps, looked bedraggled and dishevelled as they joined the cheery throng for a few moments. Some Australians and Tommies made snowmen with varying degrees of success. Sunday will be a long time remembered day at Codford.

February 28th 1917
CUTS FROM CODFORD CAMP Ao-Tea-Roa flourishes. Along the window sills the spring bulbs are pushing up their green heads. But, cold and rain, snow or sleet, it is always springtime in Ao-Tea-Roa. Everyone gets a cheery welcome. Miss Dineen has taken charge. Miss Johnson, who worked very hard, left for her home. She will be very much missed. Miss Dineen is very busy raising her standard all around, and at present has spread the alarming report that the tearooms are below the level of the road. Fears of a flood of mud terrifies the inmates of the Convent. The Mother Superior ought really to be less alarming. Miss Moore is away. Not being able to get a word in with the rest of the chattering sisterhood, her jaws swelled for want of practice. She has not got 'mumps!'

The Railway Battalion proceed today for – an unknown destination. We shall be sorry to see them go. The Battalion is regarded as a Codford production, the officers and men being called principally from this Depot. Captain Roger Dancey is in charge. They will, with their greasers, drivers, shunters etc., do well. The whole Depot wishes them the best of luck, and we all hope for a free ride behind their 'Puffing Billy.'

A big draft of P.U.s left last week. Our band escorted them all off to the strains of 'Pack up your troubles in your old kit bag.' They went off smiling and cheery, some limping but all happy, with the prospect of seeing soon home and beauty.

March 14th 1917
CODFORD TO HORNCHURCH Codford has learned from the CHRONICLES that their comrades at Hornchurch are employing their spare time in planting five thousand bulbs. As the boys at Codford have been very busy converting all their spare ground into vegetable gardens, this news has caused a Codford poet to burst into rhyme:

We've been lost in contemplation, at the struggles of our nation,
[And although we are not absolutely fit]
Still, privations to diminish, and this bally war to finish,
We've been thinking how to do our little bit.
Now old Fritz has got us thinking, for too many ships he's sinking,
Though, of course, our Navy's got him well in hand,
So at Codford we're commencing, with the aid of spades and fencing,
To make a Chinese garden of the land.
Hornchurch at us is mocking, in a manner something shocking,
For their energies take quite a different line;
We are feeling most dejected, such a thing we ne're suspected,
For we thought that our idea was rather fine,
They've been wrapped in contemplation on the subject – cultivation –
With their energies they've made all England ring,
To our queries they are lofty, 'What! Plant cabbages! you softy,
Why WE could not even think of such a thing!'

    'No! We're planting Melba roses, and how anyone supposes,
That we'd spoil OUR view with cabbage, pea, or bean,
Is beyond our comprehension, though, of course, we'd like to mention
That on daffodils and violets we are keen.
Whilst mid vegetables you're moping, in the coming Spring we're hoping,
To wander at our leisure and our ease,
When your carrots you are weeding, 'neath our roses we'll be reading,
Or be chasing butterflies from our sweet peas.'
        Now then all you Hornchurch sinners, what about your Sunday dinners?
Are you going to live on scent and honey-dew?
Do you think your 'rose leaf trifle,' will assist to slope a rifle
Quite as quickly as our vegetable stew?
When you come to do your training, you'll want something more sustaining
Than a Candied rose or violets lovely smell;
Though advice is hard to swallow, Codford's lead you'd better follow,
And plant some useful VEGETABLES as well.
                                B.B.W.M.

CODFORD Y.M.C.A. My record this week must be of disappointments and pleasure.
Disappointments first, if you like. Our weekly 'Boys Own' Concert, into which Miss
Vidler throws so much energy, was duly announced, and ready to start, but many of
those on the programme failed to appear. That worry of camp life – Mumps – and
Measles – had wrought havoc with the boys, who were to have charmed and thrilled us.
        'Private Dunn,' called the Chairman – an ominous silence – then that answer
that is all too well known: 'Isolated, Sir!' One after another failed to respond to the
roll-calls. There must have been a game lot of singers in the Isolation Hut. One
hopes they were able to have a singsong on their own.
        Now for the pleasures. Our Y.M.C.A. headquarters do us finely in the way of
speakers and lecturers. On Wednesday and Thursday we had a visit from Canon
Perkins, of Westminster Abbey. Chaplain Dobson introduced the Canon, whose
subject was: 'Westminster Abbey.' We were glad to see such a fine crowd of the
boys and as they listened to the story of the abbey, so finely told, and saw the
beauties of our old Empire Church on the screen, by the aid of lantern slides, one
felt that the better the subject the better it is enjoyed.
        On Thursday night the Canon told the story of the Cinque Ports, and the rise
of the British Navy. It was a fascinating story of the part played in the history of
England by the Cinque Ports, and told in a way that fixed itself on the mind.

March 28th 1917
A Reply To 'Codford To Hornchurch,' In The Last Issue Of *The Chronicle*

    Hornchurch boys are lost in wonder at poor Codford's stupid blunder,
In imagining a thing that's purely vain:

Codford seems to take for granted, bulbs are ALL that Hornchurch planted,
And this error gives us here the greatest pain.
     Now, I never was a poet, and I'm glad to say I know it,
But this insult to our camp has raised my ire.
Don't you know that we have acres richly sown with seed 'pertaters,'
And at *digging* Hornchurch boys will never tire?
     Yes! Its true we are artistic, and they say we take the biscuit
For Revue and Pantomime and all such shows.
But, although perhaps exotic, we're distinctly patriotic,
And we're out to help old England with our hoes.
     With our ploughs and patent barrows we're preparing for the marrows,
And the cabbage and the cauliflowers, too.
And our poultry farm will knock you – with our new laid eggs we'll mock you;
Poultry farmers now are all our boys in blue.
     We have white Leghorns, and black 'uns, so get ready all you slack 'uns,
Who complain that Salisbury Plain is rather damp;
Though you call us Hornchurch 'sinners,' we will prove to be the winners
Of the prizes for the produce grown in camp.
GISBORNE

CODFORD NOTES At Codford it has been a week of farewells. A 'P.U.' convoy of cheery souls has left us for the Blighty of the Southern Seas, their troubles packed up in their old kit bags, and their heads full of memories of doughty deeds and happy experiences. We are to lose the rest of the 'P.U.' band of brethren, who are no longer going to shed their lustre on this quiet spot, but are to bask in the sunshine of Torquay.

     For entertainment we have been very fortunate. The 'local' talent concert was a great success and all the efforts were loudly applauded. Miss Wyld sang very sweetly 'The Last Rose Of Summer.' The *piece de resistance* was the 'Maori Haka' – it was real, it was earnest, it was meant! There was no apologetic war dance. The tattooing design was not quite what the Ngapuhi or Ngatiporou would call classic, but it was up-to-date. Hone Mahupuku was lightly clad and heavily tattooed with 'le dernier cri' in tattooing, and bore with brazen effrontery on his bounding bosom the strange device 'No bonne.' Another brave displayed shamelessly on his heaving breast the words 'Lead swinger,' for which the Maori tongue has no equivalent. One warrior with a shrill suggestive Scottish scream swung his tiahia like a claymore. Corporal Keepa was clad somewhat like Lady Godiva, his clinging garment being mostly a gracious grin. It was a great performance, and left the crowd demanding more and more until the warriors were only left with a gasp and a gurgle.

     Padre Cruikshank is a prime favourite. Whether he recites something from the 'Sentimental Bloke' or one of Kipling's the boys yell for more. The house rocked with the Padres interpretation of 'The Intro.,' and they liked very much indeed the version the Padre gave of 'Boots.' An Australian who hypnotised a comrade will have great opportunities of practising on Fritz. Fancy, if you could hypnotise a battalion at a time instead of one man- there would be decorations galore for hypnotic glancers!

Our gardening has gone apace. At dewy eve 'the ploughmen homeward plod their weary way,' and talk in the huts of long furrows, crows, twitch grass, and spuds. Our soldier farmers are doing great work, and already the aspect of the camp has changed. Never Roman nor Greek made war in the air, on the earth, in the waters under the earth, and underground like we are doing. The spade has proved a great weapon in this campaign, for with it trenches have been dug; but wait until you see the fruits of our labour – the 'murphies' that will sprout in the trenches of Codford!

Ao-Tea-Roa has a garden! 'Oh the roses round the door make me –' well, never mind. The roses are not yet in bloom, but we have hopes. The crocuses are out, and the fuchsias are scenting the air, and the colour is just creeping into the hyacinths. Why, the place is just like home, but the hours are unfriendly and inconvenient,; no food sold until six in the evening.

Three of our buffet ladies went away. Change of air and a diet of Devonshire cream and delicious honey and odious ozone have worked wonders. One has mumps; another arrived back safe and sound and smiling, and the other is lost – shell shock is feared.

May 2nd 1917
CODFORD HOSPITAL NOTES EHOA,– Easter came in glorious sunshine – with a promise of a good summer to come. Unfortunately, our hopes were not realised, for since Sunday, it has been bitterly cold, with lots of snow, hail, sleet, rain, and hard frosts.

On Good Friday a concert party from Bristol very kindly gave an entertainment in the Patient's Dining Hall, and their efforts were very much appreciated. On Easter Monday night we had an excellent concert arranged by Padre Cruikshank. These Monday concerts are now quite an institution, and the padre is a great organiser.

On Monday and Wednesday afternoons, the motorbus excursions are run to Salisbury, and twenty-five patients are entertained by the New Zealand Club there. Frequent spring showers have not spoiled the enjoyment of these trips. Captain Evans, one of our best-known medical officers, left last Saturday for the Officers Convalescent Home, at Brighton.

On Tuesday, April 10th, the hospital was visited by our High Commissioner, Sir Thomas Mackenzie, who was accompanied by Mrs and Miss Douglas. Sir Thomas arrived on one of the coldest days we have had. Small notebooks, full of useful inform-ation, were distributed among the patients. After going through the wards, the visitors were entertained at tea by the Matron. They left immediately afterwards for London.

May 2nd 1917
CODFORD-ON-THE-SLUSH
Black were the streets in the saddened light,
Wet was the wet which gripped the night,

Cold was the chill of Blighty's blight,
When I arrived at Codford.

I have changed my habitation. The sanctuary which knew me in Southampton Row for five joyous months will know me no more forever, unless of course, I am shifted back again. Now alas I am located down a bye-way, which wallows in mud, and which does not breathe peace to a tired soul. The Medical Board is responsible for sending me here – the fact is they pinched my blue ribbon when I was not looking. No more do I wear the ribbon of blue that matched the colour of my eyes so perfectly, the lapels on my tunic, are no longer adorned with pretty colours, now, alas, they are bare, bare as a new born baby's cranium.

Our camp is situated in the midst of rich pasture land [?] Not exactly verdant fields, just an odd green patch here and there where a fatigue party spilt some paint. All those who seek me will find me in an ancient bye-way running off the road opposite the canteen. I am tenanted in an edifice which is not very palatial when compared with my previous whereabouts. A decrepit door which will not close is the first striking object to be met with. The name is not on the door, in fact my abode is branded with a number. But we have another sign so that the wanderer should not go astray, and those seeking us will find the following information very useful should they get into difficulties or wander into the wet canteen.

Although there is only one direction to proceed after coming through the gate, yet we have made the way easier by having this sign board on which the arrow in painted, pointing the way to our hut. At the end of this alley, another bold sign announcing our exact situation greets the pilgrim. It is in plain black and white, and is without embellishment. The colours denote our poverty, and the lack of embellishment denotes our fed-up-ness. On this sign is printed these words:

HUT
PALACE OF VARIETIES
CHANGE OF PROGRAMME
NIGHTLY
ADMISSION FREE. TAX 1/-

On our door we have tacked the invitation 'walk right in.' It is an invitation to all except those to whom we owe money, and to the Orderly Sergeant. Having a keen eye to eventualities we always keep the near door open, as through it we can make a hurried exit, should the Orderly Corporal make a call and catch us unawares for a fatigue party.

We have a number of windows on which are scratched various inscriptions done by some of our more – or less artistic inmates. These are extremely interesting, owing to the fact that we defy anyone to tell us what they represent.

Upon entering our portals, the first thing to attract your attention will be the stove. This leaks furiously as all good stoves should, as the smoke from good quality army coal helps to keep the rats and mosquitoes away, a commendable point in favour of smoky stoves. It is a known fact that not a single mosquito has been seen in our hut, all through the winter months. One night a chap did see snakes, crocodiles and various other insects, but we cannot blame the stove for that. Despite this fact, however, it has one great drawback. The stove uses so much coal that we have to get up very early in the morning, in order to replenish our stock, before the man in charge is out of bed. In other words we have to 'catch him napping,' so that we can pinch it.

One advantage which my new quarters hold over the old, lies in the fact that we have a very good big back yard. This, I take it, is forethought on the part of the Military Authorities, and despite the fact that the majority of it has been commandeered for the purpose of raising 'Spuds,' ample room is provided for the purpose of settling arguments.

My abode is on an elevated position, on the side of a hill, and admittance is gained by a few thousand wooden steps soaring heaven-wards, and commonly known as the 'Duck Walk.' The visitor, however, may find it more convenient to crawl up on hands and knees.

Another accessory which pleases me in my new abode, is my lovely hard bed. This consists of three wooden planks and a palliasse. The straw with which this last is stuffed is very conspicuous by its absence. During the long watches of the night, I turn over about every half-hour in order to give my other side a chance of getting the cramp. Oft-times my slumbers are rudely awakened by a big tame rat making a meal off my big toe nail.

Sleeping next to me is a mysterious party. I have never seen him. At night I hear him, and judging by the fact that he only drops one boot on the floor, as he prepares for his night's repose, I conclude that he has a wooden leg. Some day I hope to meet him in the daylight.

Should I be out when you call you will probably find me on an adjacent paddock, with tunic and puttees off, trying to put my kneecaps where my face is, to please an Instructor who has Physical Jerk Mania. If you fail to find me there, you will in all probability see me with a full pack and a rifle chasing up and down a hill like a bloomin' rabbit, or pricking a stuffed sack in the region of the heart with my 'Tin Opener.' I am here night and day – call and see me – I shall be pleased to see you –

I am a soldier once more. My term of 'Pushing a pen Parapit' has all come to an end.

No more Records!
Betty's or Maude's!
All that were dear to me!
I have spoken.

G. Edgar Maylett, 10/2702, 1st W.I.R., Codford

August 8th 1917
CODFORD NOTES Miss Dinneen has left us, and we are all lamenting her departure. Ao-Tea-Roa loss is France's gain. Troubles never come singly. Col. McKenzie, our

C.O., has been confined to bed for three weeks on account of an accident. He has gone to Brighton for further treatment.

A team of Tommies beat the Depot boys at cricket last week by many runs; but on Saturday we had our revenge by a good win, Q.M. Roberts being our star performer.

Our band has made great strides. Accompanied by Chaplain Captain Winton and a Maori Haka party it took Torquay by storm. The Mayor of Torquay and a large assemblage of citizens welcomed the visitors from this depot. The band performed on the pier, and the Haka party, under Q.M. Roberts, charmed a large crowd the same day at 5pm, and danced again at 7.30pm before an audience of 4,000.

The wet weather did not permit the carrying out in its entirety of the programme arranged for the pleasure of the party by Chaplain Garner, [who did so much to make the day enjoyable.]

On Saturday afternoon the Sisters, Ossies, and Tommies at Oldway, the beautiful hospital maintained by the American women, were entertained by our men, and the visitors received every kindness from the delighted audience. The same evening the Pavilion was packed, and again the show was rapturously received.

The band took part in the Church Parade at our Discharge Depot on the Sunday morning, and played on the lawn at Daison during the afternoon.

Major Kay and all our compatriots at St Marychurch treated the Codfordites splendidly throughout their stay. The party returned to the Tin City of the Plains on Monday evening.

The Salvation Army Hut is now open. It is an up-to-date establishment, of which you shall hear more anon.

W.S.W.

August 22nd 1917
CODFORD CAMP AND HOSPITAL NOTES *Place aux dames*: We record with regret the departure of Sisters Abbott, Miller, Brown, Munro, Brayshaw and Seager from our hospital. Sister Brown's ward [no 10] garden secured Colonel Fenwick's prize, Sister Brayshaw being runner up. Matron Plowman has been succeeded by Matron McNee, late of 'Mahenc' and 'Marama.'

Padre Cruikshank has greatly benefited by his visit to the waters of Bath. Father Daly has arrived and taken up his duties, and talking of duties reminds me that Defaulters has just blown. Taihoa . . . Saieeda. Thank goodness that little lot is nearly disposed of.

The tennis court is in great demand and Maori Jimmy is as keen a judge of a game as he is of a horse, and a crown and anchor.

Our depot garden looks splendid. We have murphies and greens galore, and the flower beds at the officers mess will repay Padre Winton's and the corporal's attentions.

We have many devotees to cricket. Pte Mallick, a Canterbury representative, took 5 wickets for 13 in a recent match, and Kavanagh's googlies are the bewilderment of many batsmen.

Lieuts. Hewitt and Cornaga took a party of men to the Southern Commercial Sports at Tidworth on July 28th, and did very well. After pulling in the tug-of-war the Maoris danced a Haka.

To our regret Padre Winton reports that our O.C. Col. McKenzie is far from well. In addition to other injuries his hand has become paralysed. We hope to hear of a change for the better.

KIA ORA KATOA

N.Z. SPORTS AT CODFORD The value of sports as a means of providing a certain amount of training and arousing a healthy interest is particularly noticeable in a command depot, where the majority of the men are not fit for full military training and time is apt to hang heavy. The attention given to organising sports here has been well worth while. If individual performances at the second athletic sports meeting were not startling, the large number of competitors showed clearly that the effort is not confined to a few experts. In one event [120 yards flat] there were no fewer than ninety starters.

The Military Sports, held on July 11th and comprising, physical drill, competition, bomb throwing, obstacle race, boxing and wrestling, though in some cases rather slow for the spectators, was quite strenuous enough for the competitors.

Inter company cricket matches have provided some interesting games, and the Depot team, though handicapped by the frequent changes in its members, has given a good account of itself in outside matches.

The two new tennis courts will soon be in good order, so that everyone in camp will have the opportunity for working off superfluous energy in some kind of sport with which he is familiar.

'Onlooker'

September 5th 1917
NO 3 N.Z. GENERAL HOSPITAL We have once again to thank the Y.M.C.A. for a very delightful outing. About sixty patients and eight of the nursing staff left No 3 N.Z.G.H., Codford, last Thursday morning, and despite the heavy showers which prevailed, reached Lady Morrison's picturesque old home near Tisbury in the best of spirits. House and grounds were thrown open to us, and the exquisite old china, as well as books and pictures, were very much admired. A sumptuous luncheon was set in the upper gallery, and music added to the quiet charm. Boats were available on the lake, and the boys quickly took to that always fascinating recreation.

Later we drove another six miles to the home of Lord Arundell. The pictures here were a keen delight. There are many works by the great masters amongst them. We tramped another mile to the ruins of Wardour Castle, built in the reign of Richard II. It is of great interest, having been captured and retaken during the civil war. Lady Blanche Arundell held the castle for five days, and was then compelled to surrender. Sir Edward Hungerford and his troops laid waste the whole place with frantic zeal. Then Lord Arundell made several attempts to retake the castle, but without success. Finally despairing, he had a mine sprung which shattered the walls and did so much damage that the garrison, under the command of Colonel Edmund Ludlow, was forced to capitulate. Thus the castle again passed back into the hands of the Arundells, but shorn of all its chief ornaments and its walls battered and disfigured. With all their pathetic history the ruins still stand upon high ground overlooking a small lake, and surrounded by many beautiful old trees. We returned to Codford at 8pm., after a very enjoyable day.

CODFORD NOTES We have had a visit from Colonel Acland, President of the Travelling Medical Board, who, with the assistance of the local medical officers: Major Berneau, Captain Bowie and Lieutenant McMillan, has examined many men, and caused quite a migration to Torquay.

King Mud holds sway, and Codford again justifies its sinister reputation. A cricket match was played on Saturday – Headquarters versus Rifle Brigade – when the former scored a creditable win.

We are glad to welcome back Captain McKenzie, our C.O.: Though not yet quite fit he is well on the way to recovery.

The Codford Farm is in splendid order, and the bean patch is a marvel. From a plot of ground 42 by 185 feet, three tons of beans were secured; which reflects great credit on Lieutenant Hewitt and his staff. Padre Roberts has returned after a short holiday all the better for the change.

The brethren of the Masonic Association had a splendid gathering last Wednesday. S.-M. Lowry gave an excellent address, and received a special vote of thanks. The meetings will be held on Wednesday in future.

Pte. Dick Sawyer now ably assists Padre Winton in the Salvation Army.

19th September 1917
N.Z. SPORTS AT CODFORD The third depot sports meting was held on August 22nd, and again splendid weather smiled on us. Competition was very keen and the close finishes spoke well for the handicapping. In the hundred yards there was barely a yard between the winner and the fourth. The three mile Road Race, a new event for us, brought out some good distance men, particularly among the instructors. A Maori Tug-of-War team – or rather a series of teams, for inhabitants of Codford are birds of passage – has done very well in winning open events at Stockton and Bournemouth, and in coming second to an instructional staff team from Sling at Tidworth. Lt. Cornage upheld our honour by winning the Officers 100 Yards Championship.

Boxing is rather strenuous for most of the men here, with the exception of the instructors, but we managed to get a good team of five to meet Australians at Tidworth on August 24th. Spearman won easily, but the others were given all they wanted. McFarlane's match with Pope of Western Australia was a very fine exhibition, and though our man was nearly knocked out twice early in the fight, his speed and condition gave him a decisive win on points by the time the ten rounds were over.

Fletcher won after a very willing go. Lt. Reeve's opponent pulled out in the fourth round. Dickson's opponent, in spite of giving way a good deal in weight, won by his superior speed.

The cricket team finished the season on September 8th by winning against a team of R.F.A. players at Boyton by three wickets, chiefly owing to the excellent bowling of Nelson and Fogarty. This was the R.F.A. team's first loss on its own ground.

We hope to start the football season soon, and with several members of last season's trench team in camp, we have the nucleus of a good team.

ONLOOKER

NO. 3 N.Z. GENERAL HOSPITAL,CODFORD On the evening of August 27th the large concert hall of the No.3 General Hospital [New Zealand] at Codford was thronged to its uttermost complement. The patients, in their picturesque 'blues,' composed the bulk of the audience, whilst officers, sisters, and nurses of the hospital and visitors, both military and civilian, from the surrounding camps and districts packed the hall long before 7.30pm.

At 7.30 sharp the curtain was raised on a sketch by Captain Chaplain Cruikshank and Nurse MacIntosh, entitled 'The Codford Lunatics.' This was a delightfully farcical, localised adaption presenting both in the role of the hapless visitors to the hospital on the occasion of a dance. Misled into believing it a lunatic asylum, and each independently deciding to try not to look out of place, their dialogue, spiced with distinctly local gags and hits, and supported by the business of a quaint and eccentric character, carried through a difficult sketch with a naturalness as if to the manner born, to the shrieking delight of the keenly appreciative audience.

The *piece de resistance* turned up in a sketch of 'The Court Jester' by Nurse McIntosh, who, in the dilapidated trappings and slouch hat of the poor old 'obo', told in a wonderfully droll manner of the trials and troubles of the average soldier in hospital. Her experiences of misfits in clothing issued, with ludicrous samples produced, the quips and gags upon current topics and local happenings, and scathing criticism of the 'quacks' and 'heads,' kept the house in continual uproar. The performance of this clever little lady was distinctly above the amateur standards, and would be considered an acquisition to many professional bills.

As a suitable conclusion, in his 'A,B,C,' to the tune of 'marching on to Glory,' Padre Cruikshank hit out right and left at everyone from the C.O. down to the hospital orderlies, sparing none, in his inimitable satire, and making all tremblingly expectant. The supply of secret information re the habits and the customs of 'the heads,' which the Padre loosed upon a delighted audience caused blushes and shrieks all over the house. His delivery was superb, and he did ample justice to his own compositions. When he'd finished, one could actually hear the sigh of relief from those whom he had either missed or spared.

Yours faithfully,
'General'

November 14th 1917

CODFORD NOTES There is not a great deal to record in the doings of our ever moving population. We see something of old friends for a few days or a few weeks, and then they leave our peaceful home – it's quiet down here – for the activities of Sling and Brockton or the delights of Torquay, en route to New Zealand.

Among the friends who have left us lately is Mrs Shellshear and several of her assistants, who for so long made Ao Tea Roa something to be remembered as a fragment of home in the midst of the monotony of camp life. Before they went as many men as could squeeze into the building expressed in no half-hearted fashion their thanks for the untiring energy and never-failing sympathy that these ladies have shown. In presenting to each a small gift by way of remembrance and thanks, the C.O. gave official expression to our universal feeling of gratitude and regard. We wish them the best of luck in their new work with the N.Z.W.C.A. at Salisbury and Hornchurch. At the same time, we warmly welcome Miss Hay and her staff, who have taken over Aotea Roa.

There have been changes at No.11 Y.M.C.A. as well, and what has been said above appklies no less to Miss March and the ladies who have helped her. Their departure, too, was preceded by a gathering, which expressed its appreciation in the making of speeches and the giving of gifts. We extend a hearty welcome to Mrs. McHugh and her helpers who have filled the vacancy.

Now that the winter has come football is once more the centre of interest in the camp. As yet the Rugby team, which promises well, has played no outside matches, but the Association team has played five, of which four were won and one was drawn. Will other teams looking for games write with regard to Rugger to Lieut. Cornaga and with regard to Soccer to Lieut. Crooks.

A nine hole golf course, with Padre Roberts as instructor and enthusiast-in-chief, affords exercise and enjoyment to the initiated, and still more exercise with a corresponding amount of vexation to those who think it looks easy to smack the wee ba' wi' a bit of stick. No doubt inhabitants on the far side of the plains are blaming the weather controller for the thunder and lightning that come eastward from Codford's windswept hill.

Boxing is naturally almost a monopoly of the physical aristocrats on the staff jobs, the common herd of B1 and B2 may kick a football about, but must be content to gaze from afar on the prowess of the pug. At a war charity show at Bristol on November 3rd the Depot had three representatives, and two, McFarlane and Spearman, were successful. Spearman's opponent was Phillips, a bantam ex-champion of Wales. A short time ago these same two beat two Canadians at the National Sporting Club.

Good luck, Eoha, from Codford-in-the-Mud, whose inhabitants don't forget – though these notes might give the impression – that there is a war on, and that they have mates in 'Sunny' France, to whom greetings.

ONLOOKER

[NOTE: a few passages have been omitted or abbreviated]

The Men of St Mary's

Ten of the men who marched away to war from Codford St Mary have a local memorial; their names are on a plaque in St Mary's Church. The Commonwealth War Graves Commission have helped trace all but one, Private G. Penny. The records show three named G. Penny and four G. + Penny, but none with connections to either Codford or any Wiltshire Regiment. Two of the men are possible candidates. The first, perhaps the more likely, is Private G. Penny with the 1st Battalion, the King's [Liverpool Regiment] who died on 23rd August 1918 during the period of the Battle of Amiens [8th August–3rd September]. Apart from his burial place Ficheux, close to Arras, there is no further information about him, no mention of age, next of kin or place of residence.

The second Private Penny, George, was with the Royal Army Service Corps [Canteens] who died, aged forty-four, on Thursday 30th January 1919. His parents Joseph and Emily had a south Wiltshire connection, since they lived at Tollard Royal. The marital home was in Chelsea, where his wife Alice was living in Walton Street in 1919. George Penny had been the wine steward at the Hyde Park Hotel for twenty years. He is remembered at Mikra British Cemetery, Kalamaria, Greece, eight kilometres south of Thessaloniki. The Commonwealth War Grave Record of Commemoration states that the Mikra Memorial commemorates almost 500 nurses, officers and men of the Commonwealth forces who died when troop ships and transports were lost in the Mediterranean, and who have no grave but the sea. Others who went down in the same vessels were washed ashore and identified, and are now buried at Thessaloniki.

In some instances information is scanty, in others, thanks to regimental historians, there is at least an outline of the actions in which the soldiers died. Although we may not be certain of the exact circumstances, we do know what was happening around them.

Pte 23129 A.F. Ward was the first and the youngest listed to fall in battle. He was twenty-one at the time of his death on 25th September 1915. He was in the 10th Battalion Gloucester Regiment, and on the day he died there was a Battalion attack on a German trench line in the Noyelles–Hulluch–Puits area of France. The entire Battalion had only 130 survivors, many of the casualties, including Private Ward, were unlisted. He is buried in Grave 2, Row F, Plot 12 in St Mary's A.D.S. Cemetery, Haisnes, France. At the time of his death his father, Ernest Joseph Ward was living at 26 Chitterne Road.

Pte 152634 G. Grant was with the 50th Battalion Machine Gun Corps [INF]. At the beginning of the war in 1914 all infantry battalions were equipped with a machine-gun section of two guns, which was increased to four in February 1915. As the Army expanded, weapon production was unable to satisfy the insatiable demands of the British Expeditionary Force. The infantry battalions were equipped initially with a Maxim machine-gun, with a maximum rate of fire of 500 rounds, the equivalent of 40 well trained riflemen. However the Vickers machine-gun proved more efficient, fired from a tripod and cooled by a water filled jacket against the barrel. Bullets were assembled into a canvas belt which held 250 rounds, 30 seconds of fire power at the rate of 500 rounds a minute. The Vickers Company was struggling to produce 200 machine guns a week, so contracts to provide weapons under licenses were given to firms in America.

In November 1914 the British Expeditionary Force established the first Machine Gun Training School at Wisques, to train officers and men in the special techniques and tactics of the weapon. There was urgent need for more machine gunners and to replace those killed in the conflict to date. A Machine Gun Training Centre was also established at Grantham.

On 2nd September 1915 the War Office proposed the formation of a single machine-gun Company for every Brigade, and withdrew the guns from the Battalions, replacing them with Lewis guns. The Machine Gun Corps was created by Royal Warrant on 14th October 1915. The MGC would consist of infantry machine-gun companies, cavalry machine-gun Squadrons and Motor machine-gun Batteries. The pace of reorganisation depended on the available supply of Lewis guns, which were available in sufficient numbers by the battle of the Somme.

Private Grant would have been part of a six man detachment. Two men were necessary to carry the equipment, since the gun and tripod together weighed forty eight and a half pounds and the water another ten pounds. Two more men were needed to carry the ammunition, leaving two spare men.

The officers and men of the Machine Gun Corps and the regimental machine-gunners were nicknamed 'The Suicide Club', as they were the target of every enemy weapon. In all, 170,500 officers and men served in the MGC – 62,049 of them became casualties. Private Grant was one of them – he died on 23rd October 1918. He is buried in Grave 2, Row C, Quietiste Military Cemetery, Le Cateau, France.

Pte 45197 Herbert Poolman was born and residing in Codford; he enlisted seven miles away from home in Warminster. His mother and wife lived in the village, his wife at 53 Codford St Mary. Herbert served with the 2nd Battalion Durham Light Infantry and died on 27th August 1918 aged thirty-one. He is recorded as buried in Le Quesnoy Communal Cemetery Extension and is remembered on the P.O.W. Special Memorial at Valenciennes [St Roch] Communal Cemetery, Nord.

Valenciennes was in German hands from the early days of the war until 1st/2nd November 1918, when it was entered and cleared by the Canadian Corps. The Prisoner of War Memorial was erected to 19 soldiers from the U.K. who died as POWs, nine are buried in Valenciennes and ten at Le Quesnoy. None could be identified so they are remembered in both places. Private Poolman's grave is therefore a matter for speculation rather than a reality.

Rifleman R/2784 Arthur Francis Simper's unit was the 12th Battalion King's Royal Rifle Corps. His parents George and Eliza lived at 8 Riverside. He died 13th

February 1916, and his name is between panels 115 and 119 on the Menin Gate Memorial in Belgium.

Cpl. 14131 Albert Edgar Read's unit was 'D' Battery, 71st Brigade Royal Field Artillery. He was born and enlisted in Salisbury and was killed in action either in France or Flanders. The 71st Brigade RFA was a Kitchener's New Army unit raised late in 1914. It formed part of 15 [Scottish] Division, a Kitchener's New Army Division. The Division went to France in July 1915 and remained in action on the Western Front for the rest of the War.

In April 1917, the Division and 71st Brigade were in action in the battle of Arras – first battle of the Scarpe. In April 1918, they were again in action in the Arras area – the first of the 1918 Battles of the Somme. There seems to be some confusion over the date and year Albert Read died. The Commonwealth War Graves Commission trace submission form lists his death as 29th April 1917, while the Royal Artillery Historical Trust lists his date of death as 19th April 1918. As he is commemorated on the Arras Memorial, France MR 20 Bay 1 and as in April 1917 and 1918 there were battles in the area of Arras I have yet to establish the correct date. What is certain is that Albert Read was one of the 50,000 members of the Royal Artillery killed in the First World War.

Cpl 456041 William John Arthur Davis was the son of Mr. J.A. and Mrs H. Davis of 31 Chitterne Road. He was born in Westbury, Wiltshire, and enrolled in 231st Field Ambulance Royal Army Medical Corps in Frome, Somerset. The 231st Field Ambulance was a result of an amalgamation on 14th January 1917, between the Welsh Border Mounted Brigade Field Ambulance and the 2nd South Western Mounted Brigade Field Ambulance, both of the Territorial Force, serving at the time in Palestine. William Davis was possibly a member of the 2nd South Western Mounted Brigade.

Codford was one of the RAMC's Training establishments from April 1915 until it joined the rest of the various training centres at one large Depot in Blackpool at the beginning of 1917. Unfortunately the daily working of these establishments in the Home Service Organization has gone unrecorded. What is known is that some of the third-line Territorial Force units were posted to either the 1st, 2nd, 3rd or 4th RAMC Training Battalions at Codford. What happened to them afterwards is unknown.

After the battle of Tell 'Asur between 8th and 12th March 1918 the 74th [Yeomanry] Division to which they belonged was made part of the Western Frontier Force, and they were concentrated around Rue, in France, by the 18th May. The battles and engagements of the Division in France were:

The Advance to Victory-
The Second Battles of the Somme:

2nd-3rd September	the Second Battle of Bapaume
12th-24th September	the battles of the Hindenburg Line:
18th September	the Battle of Epehy
3rd October- 11th November	the Final Advance in Artois and Flanders

William Davis died of his wounds, aged twenty-seven on 31st October 1918, eleven days before the Armistice. He could have been wounded at any time after his arrival in France, but presumably after 2nd September and possibly in the final advance. The 74th [Yeomanry] Divisions entered Tournai on 8th November 1918. William Davis is buried in Grave 7, Row H, Plot 5 in Tournai Communal Cemetery, Allied Extension, Hainaut, Belgium.

Pt. 6558 Arthur Charles Pond was with the 11th Battalion, 21st Reinforcement Australian Imperial Force. He was born sometime in July 1890 at Sutton Parva, the son of William and Marie Pond. At the time of his death his parents lived at Middle Farm, Codford St Mary. Arthur was brought up a Baptist, he went to Emwell House Private School in Warminster, serving for three years with the Wiltshire Yeomanry in England before emigrating to Australia at the age of twenty-two. He settled in Perth, Western Australia, working as a farm labourer. He was brown haired, grey eyed and fresh complexioned, and appears to have been a slight young man, five feet six and a half inches tall, ten stone in weight, with a chest measurement of less than thirty eight inches.

Arthur enlisted on 13th June 1916. On 10th October his unit embarked from Freemantle, arriving at Portsmouth [marching in from Australia] on 2nd December1916. On 23rd December he made an unwitnessed will leaving all his money and anything he owned to his sister, Dorothy M. Pond, youngest daughter of William Pond, Codford St Mary. Early February 1917 Arthur set sail from Folkestone aboard the SS Victoria, and two days later he rejoined a Base Depot at Etaple. He is listed as joining the Battalion in the field in France on 23rd January. On 26th March the 45th Casualty Clearing Station admitted him to hospital with bronchitis, and he was released to a convalescent depot on 14th April. On 21st April Arthur went back to the field, rejoined the Battalion. Just fifteen days later, on 6th May, he was briefly reported missing in action before it was discovered he had in fact been wounded, suffering a bullet wound to the right arm. By mid-May Arthur was back at a Base Depot, returning to the field on 15th June.

The following year, on 27th May 1918, Arthur was back in hospital, this time with influenza. He was discharged to duty on 5th June and killed by a bullet in action on 10th August 1918. Arthur was twenty-eight when he died, according to his military records Lieut. P. Carrington recorded that he was buried by his comrades at location X 24A Sheet 62D about 2,500 yards south of Herleville. Arthur was one of 10,885 Australians killed in France with no known grave, but is remembered on panel 63, Roll of Honour, Australian National Memorial, Villiers- Bretonneaux, 15 kilometres east of Amiens, in France.

Pt. 265988 Archie Arthur Portingale was in the 7th Battalion Somerset Light Infantry. He was born in Monkton Deverill in Wiltshire, and enlisted into the Army at Warminster, originally serving with the Wiltshire Regiment. At the time of his death his parents Edmond and Elizabeth lived at 33 Cheapside, Codford. Archie was the youngest son and he didn't want to go to war. He had only been in France for two to three weeks before he was killed on 16th August 1917, the very first day the 7th Battalion engaged in the Battle for Langemark, one of the Ypres battles.

Statement of Service of No. *6558* Name *Arthur Charles Pond*

Unit in which served.	Promotions, Reductions, Casualties, etc.	Period of Service in each Rank		Remarks.
		From—	To—	
73 Depot *21/11*	*Private*	*13/6/16* *22/9/16*	*C.o. 790* *C.o. 826*	
	Taken on strength of 11 Btn from 21st Rfts & posted to C Coy	*France* *18/1/17*	*p-ee 13/790 5/3/17*	
	To Hospital Sick	*26·3·17*	*A.IV 19/2366.* *9·4·17.*	
	M'ched In to 3rdTng.Bn. Eng 7/12/16. From Australia. E.R.2809		*P.II 5/113/E 24/1/17*	
	Proceeded Oseas to France ex Eng Bath per SC Victoria. Folkestone.	*4·2·17*	*P.IV 7/1558 E ER 9373 7·2·17.*	
X	*Reported MISSING*	*France* *6·5·17*	*AuBL 1417. Do 28/3479 18/6/17*	
11 Bn.	*Now rep. Wnded in Fld*		*AuBL 1438.*	
X Corrigendum	*Ref. Do 39 Intspara 3479 "missing in action 6/5/17" Delte whole & in lieu thereof read "Wounded in action 6/5/17."*	*France*	*Do 39/3703 29/5/17*	
	(Pte) Rejoined Bn. from Hosp.	*"* *15/6/17*	*19/034/4351 26/6/17*	
	Paid 29·4·18. 5/7610	*France*	*Form A/10.*	
	Pte/ Dich : to Unit wef 7 M. Unit (Sick)	*France* *5·6·18*	*Do46 2019. 12·6·18*	
11 d Bn.	*Pte Re Sick to Hospital*	*France* *27·5·18*	*Do49/3123. 29/6/18*	
11 93.	*KILLED IN ACTION*	*France*	*9.B.555 29/8/18*	

CR 2521/5/30 .... 10·8·18 ...... 621BL 2496
I have examined the above details, and find them correct in every respect. 19/068/4841 28/4/18

Memorial Cross
Re Buried Heath Cemetery Sh: 62d Q. 29. d.5.4.
Ref. "A." Sheet 133.

Arthur Charles Pond, statement of service

In the early hours A and D Companies formed the first wave, crossing a flooded stream with banks boggy and slippery with slimy mud. The Companies were forging through limited space, with an enemy machine gun nest on the right flank. The enemy were shelling the Langemarck- Pilkem road using 5.9 shells. Despite casualties the companies, bathed in the glow of Very lights, dug themselves into their allotted positions, all the while in danger from machine gun and rifle fire. B Company, part of the second wave, captured its objective but as the attacking troops advanced they were checked by deplorable muddy conditions on the ground and withering machine gun fire from a line of pillboxes. The Somersets were checked for about fifteen minutes; during this time they took heavy casualties. The battle had not lasted an hour; the Somerset's were encountering heavy machine gun fire and were under attack from snipers. By 7.15am all objectives allotted to the Battalion had been reached

Although the battle was deemed a success for the Battalion, it suffered severe casualties, over 40 members of the Battalion lost their lives, 148 were wounded and 18 other ranks were missing. Archie Portingale was just twenty-two years old when he died. He is remembered in the Golden Book of Remembrance in Wells Cathedral and on panel 41-42 of the Tyne Cot Memorial, Passchendaele, Belgium.

Pt 200495 W. George Portingale died thirteen months after his younger brother, in Palestine on 19th September 1918, and is buried in grave 29, Row L, Ramleh War Cemetery. Like Archie he was born in Monkton Deverill, and he was a married man living in Trowbridge when he enlisted in Warminster. The next of kin details list him as the husband of Mrs Maclean [formerly Portingale] of 4 Carpenters Arms Yard, Trowbridge. He was serving with the 1st/4th Battalion Wiltshire Regiment.

George Portingale fell during the capture of El Tireh. The 1st / 4th Wilts were in the front line with the 2nd/ 3rd Gurkhas on 19th September 1918 and were to be followed by one section of a Trench Mortar Battery ordered to give all the support possible. We don't know at what stage of the battle George was killed; we do know the circumstances in which he went into combat. The Battalion History takes up the story.

> During the night final preparations were completed. As we lay about we could hear our Artillery bringing their guns up to the front. Later they took up a position close to us. The night seemed unusually quiet, though now and again one solitary report from an enemy gun and the screech of a lonely shell would break the silence. There was also the occasional pop of an enemy rifle, and the swish of a bullet would be heard flying over our heads. We were unfortunate in losing one of our NCOs, wounded by one of these stray shots.
>
> At 0315 hours on the morning of the 19th September, the Battalion 'fell in' to await orders to move off by Companies through the gaps which had already been made in our wire, to take up a position on a white tape which had already been laid out by the Second in Command, assisted by the Battalion Scouts, some 50 yards in front. This preliminary move took place without a hitch. We had practiced it so many times during our intensive training at Deir Tureif.

Archie Portingale

We lay down on reaching our position and waited for Zero hour. Those minutes appeared as long as hours. It seemed so uncanny, a weird silence broken now and again by the solitary report of an enemy gun or rifle fire. A glance to our rear, and we could discern through the darkness the figures of the Punjabis taking up their position in support of us. On our left, already in position, were our little friends the Gurkhas.

At 0425 we began to cross 'No Man's Land,' and five minutes later Zero hour arrived. Those of us who were fortunate enough to get through that action will never forget 4.30am on 19th September 1918. At that moment every gun on our side was fired as though by pressing an electric button. This was the commencement of the barrage which was to play on the enemy's line and wire for the period of fifteen minutes prior to the attack of our Infantry. The noise which took place was truly indescribable. To us it seemed as though Hell was let loose, but what it seemed like to the enemy, goodness only knows. At the appointed time the barrage lifted, orders were shouted and the Infantry rose and advanced towards what had been a few minutes previously the undisturbed position of the enemy's defences, but was now an infernal mass of fire and smoke. We first over ran a small detached post, F26. As was to be expected we found the enemy absolutely panic-stricken from the bombardment which they had received. In the front line we captured a number of dazed prisoners and some smoking machine guns. Our barrage crept on in front of us as we advanced. We soon reached the enemy's support trenches, and by this time it was fully daylight. We could plainly see the enemy retreating in great disorder in front of us. They had been completely surprised and everything was going in our favour. We advanced on an on, always keeping just a safe distance behind our barrage, and being led, as was always the case in action, by our Little Colonel.

Up to this time our casualties had been few, the enemy only just beginning to realise what was happening. It appeared that now and again some of his high explosives were coming over accompanied by shells from his field guns, but it was as nothing compared to the barrage which had been put down by our Artillery and Machine- gunners.

As the line advanced, one could not help thinking of the contrast between this Action and that of the previous April when we set out to attack Sheikh Subih Ridge. On that occasion we experienced the greatest resistance by the enemy, both from his artillery and rifles. His position in the hills, too, made it easy for him to stop our advance over the hard going of the hill-sides and wadis. But now we were advancing once again over the plains, only stopping here and there to deal with a few stragglers of the retreating enemy. The farther we advanced the more obvious were the traces of the completeness of the surprise. We found machine-guns, trench mortars, ammunition dumps untouched, stores of every kind overturned and disordered. We also came across field kitchens in which breakfast was being prepared.

A glance to the rear revealed a wonderful sight; we were being closely followed by our supports, and further, as soon as our artillery finished firing in one position, they could be seen dashing forward at the gallop to take up fresh position. Lieut. Doddrell, with No. 14 Platoon and others, were sent into the village of Miskeh on our left. Here our men surprised and took prisoner nearly one hundred Turks, some of whom had only just been awakened from sleep, and the personnel of a Field Ambulance, complete with patients.

Our next objective was the village of El Tireh, some two miles further on. As we advanced we got a certain amount of cover for a short distance, from a ridge which ran in the direction on this objective. As we made progress we could see that the village was flanked with cactus gardens, but of the village itself we could see little. By this time our barrage had stopped, and from the resistance that was being put up by the enemy we realized he was recovering from the surprise we had given him.

For some reason our right had become unprotected by any troops, and in consequence we suffered a few casualties from the enemy's machine-gun fire. The Colonel at once sent a Company to cover this flank, and shortly afterwards we had the assistance of armoured cars and cavalry.

The remainder of the Battalion still went on with the advancing line, but we were compelled to halt and occupy a deep trench which had been used by the enemy, about 400 yards south of the village of El Tireh. It was certain that to our front the village had held in strength, to the right flank the Turkish machine-guns were firing fiercely, whilst on a hill to our left appeared a large number of Turkish cavalry, who suffered some casualties from the fire of our Lewis guns. The enemy held the village stubbornly against our attack, and in consequence of this and also through our flanks becoming somewhat unprotected, we began to suffer many losses. It was a most serious time for the Battalion, for at this time we had the misfortune to lose our Commanding Officer, who was badly wounded and died within a few hours. Immediately after the

George Portingale (right of photograph)

Colonel was hit, we lost Captain R.H.Knight, who was shot through the head and died instantaneously. Officers and men fell fast, and the only thing to do was to hang on and wait until our flanks were covered and supports arrived.

We had not long to wait; the 3rd Kashmir Rifles soon came up to strengthen our line, and at the same time a much needed supply of ammunition was brought up. On our left, the Gurkhas by their heavy rifle fire had the Turkish cavalry on the run, and things in general began to look healthier for us.

In the village of El Tireh there was a lull in the enemy's firing, and on the orders received from G.O.C. Brigade [Brigadier General H.J. Huddleston, DSO], who, with his Staff, was in a position immediately behind the firing line, the Battalion pushed forwards once more. A few minutes later El Tireh was captured and this eventually proved to be the final objective of the 1/4th Wiltshire Regiment.

The Battalion then took up position on the north side of the village and got what cover it could from the long-range fire of the enemy. Soon afterwards our Cavalry and Armoured Cars pushed forward and attacked the Turks who were retreating on Tul Keram. During the latter part of the afternoon everything became quiet in and around El Tireh, and only in the distance to the north could we hear the booming of our guns.

Our casualties in this action were: Three Officers killed [Lieut.-Colonel A.Armstrong, D.S.O.; Captain R.H.Knight and 2nd Lieut. K.C. Doddrell].Six Officers wounded [Captain J.T. Bretherton, M.C.; Lieuts A.E.Kimm, and S.W. Stevenson (died of wounds the following day); 2nd Lieuts. S.J.Bessant, W. Hardman and E.D.Jackson]. Sixteen N.C.O.'s and men were killed and sixty-two wounded.

The World War One memorial in St Mary's Church makes no mention of nine other men who died from Codford St Mary, such as George Sparey of 1st Battalion Wiltshire Regiment, whose story is told in *The Wiltshire's War in France*, below. In St Peter's church there is a tablet commemorating the World War Two dead of both villages, and a memorial window remembering Percy Brown, Henry Cull, Alfred Henry Ford, Charles Singleton, Frederick Sparey, Edward Thomas (not the war poet – Albert Edward Thomas lived at Ivy Cottages), Frederick Whatley and Henry C. White. Codford in general has, as far as I can tell, 37 men with local connections who died in the Great War. The memorials in the two churches suggest 18 of these men were villagers at the time of their deaths. Presumably the others had moved elsewhere or were only temporary residents of the two settlements. The only man I cannot trace is Henry White.

[Information on: Albert Read supplied by Brig. K.A. Timbers, Historical Secretary for the Royal Artillery Historical Trust; William Davis and the 231st Field Ambulance Corps supplied by R.L. Barrett-Cross, M.R.S.H. the RAMC Historian; A.F. Ward supplied by Colonel [Retired] D.E.Whatmore, Regiments of Gloucestershire Museum; Charles Arthur Pond supplied by Australian Archives Service Records from World War One and University College, Australian Defence Force Academy, Canberra, Australia; Archie Portingale supplied by Brigadier A.I.H. Fyfe DL, Regimental Secretary for the Somerset Light Infantry and from Ron Sutton; George Portingale supplied by Major P.J. Ball [Retired] on behalf of Royal Gloucestershire, Berkshire and Wiltshire Regiment

Museum, Salisbury. Quotation from G. Blick, *The 1/4th Batallion the Wiltshire Regiment, 1914-19*, 1933; other information from Ron Sutton.]

The Wiltshires' War in France

Up to around 1908 the Army's reserve force for home defence was the Militia, and the Wiltshire Regiment had a 3rd (Militia) Battalion. In 1908 the Territorial Force Battalion (T.F. Battalion), comprising committed soldiers, rather like the late Territorial Army (T.A.) of today, was formed. At the outbreak of World War One all the reservists were called up. These were men who had been regular soldiers and were committed to being recalled to the Colours in the event of an emergency. A similar, but lower key, call up took place at the time of the Boer War. The reservists joined the 4th (Territorial Force) Battalion of the Wiltshire Regiment. They had so many soldiers it was decided to split the Battalion in two, the 1/4th and the 2/4th. Both of these Battalions were sent to India to guard the Raj. Later the 1/4th were sent to the Middle East.

Queen Victoria's second son was Prince Alfred, Duke of Edinburgh and Saxe-Coburg-Gotha. In the mid-19th century the Prince was so impressed with the 99th (Lanarkshire) Regiment that he asked for the Regiment to take his name. So, in 1874 it became the 99th (Duke of Edinburgh's) Regiment. In 1881 the 99th was amalgamated with the 62nd (Wiltshire) Regiment, to become the Duke of Edinburgh's Wiltshire Regiment. In 1920 the title changed to the Wiltshire Regiment (Duke of Edinburgh's).

In August 1914 the 1st Battalion were in Tidworth on Salisbury Plain. The 2nd Battalion were in Gibraltar, but they returned to England, landing at Southampton on 3rd September. The 3rd (Reserve) Battalion were in Devizes; they remained in the United Kingdom throughout the war.

The 1/4th Battalion T.F. were in Trowbridge and were part of the South-Western Brigade, Wessex Division. On 9th October they sailed from Southampton to Bombay, landing on 9th November. The Division (later renamed the 43rd) was broken up on arrival in India. In September 1917 it moved to Egypt, where it remained. On 25th September it was attached to the 233rd Brigade, transferred to 232nd on 3rd May 1918.

The 2/4th Battalion T.F. was formed in Trowbridge in October 1914, becoming part of 2nd South-Western (135th) Brigade, 2 Wessex Division. They moved to India on 12th December 1914 and landed in Bombay in January 1915. The Division was broken up on arrival in India; the Battalion remained through the war.

The 5th and 6th (Service) Battalions were formed at Devizes August 1914. In September 1917 the 6th amalgamated with the Wiltshire Yeomanry, to become the

6th (Royal Wiltshire Yeomanry) Battalion. On 16th June 1918 they were transferred to the 42nd Brigade, 14th (Light) Division. They were reconstituted on 18th June with the 9th Battalion, the Dorsets.

The Regimental History for World War One takes up the history of the 1st Battalion.

> On 27th July 1914, the officers of the 1st Battalion at Tidworth were to dine with those of the 4th in camp at Bulford. About 7.15pm. just as the Commanding Officer, Lieut. Col. Hasted, was setting off for Bulford with his Adjutant, Captain Rowan, word came from the Orderly Room in Jellalabad Barracks that one or the other was wanted on the telephone by Command Headquarters, Salisbury. War was at hand, and this started the chain of events that led to the 1st Battalion embarking at Southampton on 13th August for France.
>
> At the mouth of the River Seine instructions were received from Havre to go on up the river to Rouen. As the ship drew alongside the quay the sound of the *Marseillaise* came out of the darkness, sung as only Frenchmen can.

Disembarking at Rouen with his comrades on 14th August 1914 was 34-year-old private George Sparey. His widowed mother Clara Ann Sparey lived at 78 High Street, Codford St Mary. Ten days after leaving England, as part of the 7th Brigade in the 3rd Division,they were digging in south of Mons, in Belgium. This was the right flank of the 2nd Army's position, on which during the 23rd August the full might of the German attack in the First Battle of Mons was concentrated. Fierce resistance and concentrated rifle fire held off the outnumbering Germans initially, but sheer weight of numbers pushed the British back. The 7th Brigade acted as a rearguard to the Division, the Wiltshires and the South Lancashires held all day and half the night, then did the same next day at Caudry, at the Battle of Le Cateau.

On 26th August 170,000 Germans with overwhelming artillery were held all day by the 30,000 of the 2nd Army. Pressure was especially severe on the British centre around Caudry. The Wiltshires suffered heavily in this long battle, before leaving St Quentin, 20 miles south of Le Cateau, on 27th August.

There was rearguard action and night fighting in the withdrawal that followed. The 1st Battalion were with the 3rd Division in the long retreat across the Marne. On 6th September the withdrawal halted and the enemy were driven back. Again the Wiltshires were in the thick of the fighting. The next day the Battalion were the first troops across the Grand Morin, a tributary of the Marne, pursuing the retreating Germans. On 14 September the Wiltshires occupied the high ground north of Vailly, and during the week-long shelling and attacking which followed they lost 160 all ranks.

In October the Battalion were back in the north, arriving at Abbeville, on the river Somme between Amiens and the sea, on 6th October. A week later they were driving the enemy back across the River Loisne, and advancing to Neuve Chapelle west of Lille. They fought in this area for nearly a fortnight, and although often outnumbered and partially surrounded the Wiltshires restored the line on two occasions. On 25th when the 7th Brigade was being heavily attacked at Neuve

Chapelle, George Sparey was killed in action. He has no known grave but is remembered on Le Touret Memorial, Pas de Calais. By 30th October, after ten weeks of fighting, the 1st Wiltshires had lost 26 officers and 1,000 men, more than the equivalent of a whole Battalion. Between 14th October and 11th November 1914 in the First Battle of Ypres, the British lost 2,368 officers and 55,787 men. The French lost 50,000, the Belgians 32,000 and the Germans 130,000.

Another likely casualty of Ypres, Albert Edward Thomas was born in Codford St Peter. His father, listed as next of kin, lived at 133 Ivy Cottages. Albert Thomas enlisted on 9th May 1912 according to the records of the Wiltshire Regiment, and embarked with the 2nd Wilts Battalion from Southampton on 5th October 1914. He was reported missing on 24th October 1914, at the age of twenty-four, but was not officially reported as dead until 19th July 1915.

On 4th January 1915 twenty-one year old Sidney Walter Randall disembarked at Havre. The young private was born in Islington and enlisted in Hampstead, London, but his parents John and Mary Randall were living at 13, Stockton when he died. When he set sail for France and Flanders, he was listed as residing in Codford St Mary, perhaps because this was the largest settlement in the area, compared to the much smaller village of Stockton. He was killed in action nineteen days after his arrival, on 23rd January 1915, and is buried in Wytschaete Military Cemetery 7 kilometres from Ieper, formerly Ypres town centre.

Arthur John Johnson's parents lived at Netherhampton, near his place of enlistment, which was Salisbury. He was living at Codford St Mary when he set off to fight. He was twenty-one when he arrived in France on 21st January, joining the 1st Battalion in the field six days later. A month later, on 27th February 1915 he was killed in action. When Arthur Johnson and Sidney Randall were killed the Battalion was engaged in trench warfare at Messines.

Lance Corporal George Smith was with the 2nd Battalion, embarking at Southampton with 20th Reinforcements on 27th July 1915. He was born at Odstock just outside Salisbury, had enlisted at Westleigh and was living in Codford in 1915. On 31st July he joined the Battalion. His death is listed as killed in action 25th September 1915 according to *Soldiers Died in the Great War*, in which case he was probably one of the first casualties of Loos [Artois III], one of the bloodiest battles of World War One. The battle, between 25th September and 8th October 1915 claimed 60,000 British, 190,000 French and 178,000 German casualties.

A lone Welshman, Charles Edward Jones, born in Newport, Monmouthshire, was among the residents of Codford St Mary to die in the 1st Wilts. He enlisted in Devizes, and embarked on 31st May 1916, joining the Battalion on 12th June. By July the Battalion had moved farther south still to the River Somme. On 4th July came the great Allied offensive in which the Battalion attacked at Thiepval. The fighting was heavy and their losses great, including the Commanding Officer, Lieut. Col. W.S. Brown, who was killed. Twice more they were to assault at Thiepval. Captain S.S. Ogilvie took command. He had joined up at the beginning of the war as a private soldier.

Private Jones is listed as having died of wounds on 7th July 1916 according to *Soldiers Died in the Great War*. The regimental source states 'To be regarded for official purposes as having died on or since 7/7/16.' On that same day he is listed 'Wounded and Missing. C. List.' The 1st Battle of the Somme between 24th June and 18th November 1916 gained just 125 square miles, at a cost of 420,000 British, 195,000 French and 650,000 German casualties. *Brassey's Battles* describe it as 'One of the bloodiest and most futile battles of history.'

Another victim of the Somme had been with the 1st Battalion from the very beginning. Sergeant Hector James Down was a Bournemouth man, who had enlisted in Devizes and was living in Codford. He had sailed as a Lance Corporal with the Battalion when they first left England, disembarking at Rouen on 14th August 1914. Hector Down was with the Battalion at the First Battle of Mons, fighting at Le Cateau, the retreat to the Marne, Ypres I, Neuve Chapelle, Hooge and Messines.

In March [1915] the British Army mounted an offensive at Neuve Chapelle and the 1st Wiltshires played a prominent part in a supporting attack at Spanbroek-Molen. April and May were spent in the trenches in the Dickebusch area, south-west of Ypres. In June the Battalion moved east of Ypres, and twice took part in attacks on the German trench system round Hooge Chateau, where the fighting was most severe. With the rest of the 3rd Division the Wiltshire's were now in the 3rd Army under General Allenby.

In July the Battalion were in trenches near Ypres where they remained for three months. Most of the period was spent at Hooge, alternating with rest periods in the ramparts at Ypres, itself under shell fire. On 30th July Hector Down was wounded in action, on 1st August he was admitted to the 9th Field Ambulance with a gunshot wound to the left hand. He rejoined the Battalion on 5th August.

On 17th October the 1st Battalion, with the rest of the 7th Brigade, left the trenches at Zillebeeke, near Ypres, to join the 25th Division. The 25th was a New Army Formation, recently arrived from England and had suffered heavily at Loos. General Haldane bid the Wiltshires 'Goodbye' in warm and complimentary words, saying they had seen more fighting than any other Battalion in the Division. They marched away south to Bailleul, and, on 1st November, relieved the 5th Loyal North Lancashires in Ploegsteert Wood, north of Armentieres.

On 4th December 1915 Hector Down was wounded in action for the second time, and he was admitted to the 76 Field Ambulance with shrapnel wounds. He returned to duty on 12th December, but was readmitted to the 76 Field Ambulance, this time suffering from rheumatism. Presumably he was still receiving treatment when the troops ate their Christmas dinner on 1st January 1916. They had been in the Ploegsteert trenches for three months. Hector returned to duty from the Casualty Clearing Station on 8th January 1916, he was wounded in action again on 6th July 1916 on the Somme, this time with a severe gunshot wound to the right thigh. He was sent back to England from Stad Antwerpen to 3C General Hospital on 9th July.

The trench warfare in the Thiepval area continued until October when the 25th Division went north, detraining at Bailleul, near the Belgian border south of

Ypres. At Christmas 1916 the regiment were out of the line at Pont De Nieppe.

The New Year saw the Battalion still in the Ploegsteert area. In the middle of January the Battalion came out of the line for a fortnight's hard training. Trench warfare had by now developed many techniques. It was even possible to tell, through long experience, from what part of Germany the opposing Regiment in the line came, by the change of attitude after a relief.

Late in February the 1st Battalion and the rest of the 7th Brigade were relieved by the New Zealanders, and spent six weeks training. The chief point of interest was the reorganisation of all Battalions. Each Platoon became a separate fighting unit with its own Lewis gunners, bombers and rifle flame throwers, as well as its old sections of riflemen. This signified a more mobile outlook, as, in completely static trench warfare, it was easy to have little groups of specialists working on their own.

In April, the 7th Brigade relieved some Australians, the Wiltshires taking over south of Ploegsteert Wood near the River Lys, with the 8th Loyal North Lancashires in support, the 10th Cheshires in reserve, and other old friends the 3rd Worcestershires nearby.

Between 7th-14th June 1917 the Wiltshires were in action at Messines Ridge, the British break-out into enemy held territory after thirty months of containment. By 11th June they had taken their objectives, and captured 148 prisoners plus 7 machine guns. Their total casualties were 140, of whom 29 were killed or died of wounds. The Allied casualties as a whole totalled 108, 882.

The Battalion moved north to Ypres, to fight around Westhoek Ridge and back into the trenches in the Givenchy sector. In December 1917 the 25th division were transferred from the 1st to the 3rd Army.

Hector Down, now a Sergeant, was to be killed in action on the first day of the Battle of Bapaume, on 21st March 1918. Early on the morning of 21st March a great German offensive started. Heavy shelling caused casualties to the Battalion in reserve at Achiet-Le -Grand. By evening they were in position in front of Fremicourt, a village two miles east of Bapaume on the road to Cambrai. The Germans had carried the Corps line ahead of them by assault.

Hector Down is buried 19 kilometres south of Arras in Achiet-Le-Grand Communal Cemetery Extension, Pas de Calais. The town was occupied by 7th Bedfords on 17th March 1917, lost on 25th March 1918 after a defence by the 1st/ 6th Manchesters, and recaptured on 23rd August 1918. From April 1917 – March 1918 the village was occupied by the 45th and 49th Casualty Clearing Stations and Achiet Station was a British railhead. At the time of Hector Down's death, the village was still in British hands and the British medical units used the cemetery extension.

Percy Charles Brown was a 23-year-old private in the 1st Battalion Wiltshire Regiment, whose parents Alfred and Harriet Brown lived at French Horn, Codford St Peter. On 21st March 1918 71 German Divisions launched a massive assault after a bombardment of 6,000 guns and gas on the British lines along a fifty-mile front south of Arras. The British with only fifteen Divisions, heavily outnumbered, fell back across the Somme river. Percy Brown died of wounds on 26th March 1918, and he was buried 13 kilometres east of Arras in Bac-Du-Sud Cemetery, Bailleulval, Pas de Calais. The days before his death are recorded in the Regimental History:

> On the 24th March, the German artillery, directed by aeroplanes unmolested by our own, shelled the Battalion trenches. British guns retaliated, but increased the casualties by firing short. An intense bombardment in the afternoon was followed by a German assault at 4pm. Fighting was in progress, but the attack on the Wiltshires front was failing, when the Commanding officer was ordered over the telephone to retire at once. As the Companies received these instructions the two Battalions on the right came back in a hurry,. This left the flank completely exposed, and the Wiltshires were practically exterminated by machine gun fire as they withdrew. That night three officers and fifty-four other ranks reassembled at Achiet-Le-Petit in rear, all that was left of a Battalion that had suffered over four hundred casualties in four days.
>
> Next morning, the 25th March, the remains of the Battalion and of the rest of the Brigade were ordered to dig in north-west of Achiet-Le-Grand, this forward sector being commanded by Lieut. Col. S.S. Ogilvie. After fairly heavy shelling the Brigades on either flank withdrew in the evening, but Lieut. Col. Ogilvie received no orders at all. He, therefore withdrew his force about five miles west, to Puisieux. From there they went a further four miles north-west to Gommecourt, arriving at 6am after a night of marching. Here the Battalion was ordered to occupy a wood to meet an attack, which did not materialize.

The 1st Battalion fought a magnificent defence in April during the Battle of Lys, where for the second time in under a month they were reduced to three officers and about one hundred men.

On 23rd April a new Commanding officer, Lieut. Col. A.G.C. Cade, D.S.O., M.C., and 21 other officers and 760 men, many from the disbanded 6th Wiltshires, had been posted to the Battalion. All the new officers came from the Durham Light Infantry and were very young, three of the four Company Commanders being Second Lieutenants. Two days later preparations were made for the 25th Division to counter-attack Kemmel village on Messines Ridge, in conjunction with the French.

Very early in the morning on 26th April the attack went in. Complete surprise was achieved and 7th Brigade soon captured the village and 200 Germans. Shortly afterwards the Brigade withdrew as the French on their right had not been able to advance. The Wiltshires casualties were fairly light, but their new Commanding Officer was killed. The Battalion remained in the trenches in the same area till 4th May, for part of the time under the French. There were frequent enemy bombardments with gas shells.

The Wiltshires were in the Fismes area when the German breakthrough to the Marne occurred. On 27th May the Germans attacked in force with strong artillery support. The Battalion were ordered forward to cover the withdrawal of the troops of the 8th Division, and early that evening the enemy attacked them in great strength in front of Boufignereux. The Wiltshires were pushed back, splitting into small parties, fighting rear guard actions all the way. Their Brigade came under the orders of the 8th Division and detachments were sent up to plug the line. The Commanding

Officer died of wounds and losses were heavy. This marked the beginning of three weeks of fighting as the Germans broke between Soissons and Rheims, and crossed the River Marne.

On 17th June they were relieved by an Italian Regiment. Major J.V. Bridges, D.S.O., of the Worcestershires, took temporary command of the Wiltshires. The 25th Division had now suffered so many casualties from continuous heavy fighting that it had to be broken up. The 1st Wiltshires left this sector to join the 110th Brigade in the 21st Division, north of the Somme. They returned to the trenches at Acheux near Thiepval on 20th July 1918, and were now more than up to strength with 40 officers and over 900 other ranks. Earlier that month Colonel G.B.C. Ward, D.S.O., of the South Wales Borderers, had taken over command.

By the middle of August there were signs of an enemy withdrawal on the Brigade front. The Wiltshires were now in the final phase of their war. They deployed on 24th August in support of the 64th Brigade at Miraumont Ridge, five days later they led an advance towards Beaulencourt, south of Bapaume. The village was captured after severe close quarter fighting on 1st September, at a cost of 60 casualties but a gain of over one hundred prisoners. By 11th September the Wiltshires were in the front line near Epechy, where they beat off a heavy counter-attack. On the 18th they attacked and captured over 200 Germans. Their own losses were heavy, being nearly 100, mostly wounded.

On 5th October the Battalion crossed the canal at Bantouzelle, south of Cambrai, and occupied part of the Hindenburg Line. A successful attack followed on the Beaurevoir Line. The Wiltshires took all their objectives with about 100 casualties, again mostly wounded. On 5th November the 1st Wiltshires moved through Fort Du Monnal, about ten miles north of Le Cateau, in support of a British advance. Berlaimont was captured and the River Sambre crossed.

Early next morning the 6th Leicesters and the Wiltshires crossed the river under heavy fire to attack the village of Aulnoye. Further movement was impossible for some time, but later in the morning the troops on the right managed to get forward. This enabled the Wiltshires to outflank and capture the village, and establish themselves on the high ground beyond it. Next day they made a further advance under heavy fire. That night their Division was relieved when the 17th Division went through to further objectives.

The 1st Battalion had fought their last action of the war. When hostilities ceased at 11am on 11th November 1918 they were at Berlaimont on the Sambre. Their few days of fighting in this, last month of the war, added to the long list of awards for gallantry, six M.C.s, four D.C.M.s and nine M.M.s.

In all it appears four local men from the 2nd and 6th Battalions died in France and Flanders, Private Thomas and Lance Corporal Smith with 2nd Battalion in 1914 and 1915 respectively, Lance Corporal Pretty on 18th October 1916 and Private Pike on 31st May 1918.

Lance Corporal George Pretty had embarked from Southampton with 11th Reinforcements as a private on 1st April 1915, joining the 2nd Battalion on 5th. He was born in Stockton and although he is recorded as living in Codford St Mary, men living in neighbouring smaller villages were sometimes listed as 'living in Codford.' He enlisted in Salisbury at the beginning of the war, on 1st September 1914, six months before he went to the Western Front. George Pretty was in 'C' Company and had been made up to Lance Corporal by the time he went missing on 18th October 1916. He is buried in Warlencourt British Cemetery. The village and its neighbouring community of Eaucourt L'Abbaye, was the in the thick of fierce fighting in early October 1916 and was not taken until the end of February the following year.

Percy Pike was twenty-eight when he was killed in action on Friday 31st May 1918. He lived with his wife Ellen at Hill View, Shrewton Road, Chitterne – again the main village of residence is given, erroneously, as Codford. Percy was formerly with the 2011 Royal Wiltshire Yeomanry. One source has him killed with the 2nd Battalion, but on 20th September 1917 the Wiltshire Yeomanry amalgamated with the Duke of Edinburgh's (Wiltshire Regiment) to become the 6th Royal Wiltshire Yeomanry Battalion. David Chilton, the Curator of the Royal Gloucestershire, Berkshire and Wiltshire Regiment, has Percy Pike with the 6th Battalion for an unspecified time.

Most of the local men joined the Wiltshire Regiment. Nineteen of them lost their lives – eleven of them died in France and Flanders, four in Mesopotamia and one each in India, Gallipoli and Palestine. The Regimental History is the backdrop against which the lives of the Wiltshire men who fought can be measured. Some men returned to their homes, many died on the battlefield. Some of the soldiers have identified graves, others disappeared in the melée of conflict, and lie in unknown and forgotten resting places. All of the men who left Codford faced the horror of warfare on a scale never before imagined. The Great War, the War to end all Wars, that took a generation of hopeful, young men, and sent them against the barbed wire, the shells, the machine guns, the gas and overwhelming odds, into Flanders fields. The pity of it, and the pride too, must never be forgotten.

[Special thanks to David Chilton, Curator, The Royal Gloucestershire, Berkshire and Wiltshire Regiment Museum, The Wardrobe, Salisbury. Other Sources: N C E Kenrick, *The History of the Wiltshire Regiment in World War I*; The Commonwealth War Graves Commission; *Soldiers Died in the Great War*; John Laffin, *Brassey's Battles*; Richard Holmes, *The Oxford Companion to Military History*.]

The Swallows on the Somme
Robin Selby and the Taranaki Rifles

Several years ago a copy of a faded letter, discovered amid a trunk full of documents bought at a car boot sale, found its way into my possession. So began a detective story through military records and letters to newspapers on the other side of the world, to discover the history of one man, Warrant Officer Robin Selby.

Codford 12/4/17.

Dear Mr McGovern,

I still have before me your letter of 15/2/17- and have neglected to answer it till now.

Am still in Blighty as you can see by the address – and date of leaving for France has not yet been fixed. I am now in a new Brigade which has just been formed and we are delayed by having to wait for its completion. We are only half strength and only today were issued with rifles – first time I have handled one for just six months, so feel a trifle awkward. This forms New Zealand's 4th Brigade of Infantry – while we have a Mounted Brigade in Egypt – or should I say Palestine – and of course we have our own Artillery in France – Field Guns and Howitzers – so are a very complete little army in a way. To date New Zealand has sent out just on 80,000 men out of a population of just over 1,000,000.

Things seem to be moving the way they should – in France just now, and the weather is so bad that you can hardly call it a spring push – but we can hardly hope for better results than are eventuating these days.

We have had snow this last three nights and it looks as if we shall see snow in May alright, and I haven't seen a swallow yet. I shall never forget the swallows in France – in Sept – just as we were going into the Somme – we saw them gradually collecting in flocks and then one day they were gone. We have none in N.Z. and consequently our fellows were very interested in them.

By the way I was looking through the old Roll book the other day and I see one of our fellow's people came from Huddersfield; had I known when I was up there I should have called to see them. His name was W. Booth and his next of kin was his Mother Mrs M. H. Booth Coalpit Lane – Mt Longwood – Huddersfield, England. There is just a remote chance that one of your staff might have known him as they would be schoolboy contemporaries. He was killed last June, I never wrote Mrs Booth but I know some of our fellows did.

Well if you are reading this at the Office I must be boring you – Many thanks for your kind invitation to visit you again – though I'm afraid that will not be till I've been to France once more. Also many thanks for your kind thoughts re Colne Vale – it certainly is worth consideration – and I'll be up to see you again before I leave for New Zealand.

With very best wishes to Mrs McGovern and family and remembrance to your staff

Yours sincerely

Robin Selby

10/3731

Taranaki Company,

3rd Wellington Batt

4th Brigade N.Z. Forces

The passage referring to the snow and the swallows on the Somme was very poetic; it conjured up a romantic picture of the writer, and posed unanswered questions. It was likely that Robin Selby had been wounded in France, and obvious he would soon be returning to the battlefield. I wanted to know what had happened to him on the Somme and whether he survived the carnage of War.

Robin's father, Edwin Selby, was born in Wareham, Dorset on 18th February 1853. In 1874 he applied for the Vogel Immigration Scheme to New Zealand. He was accepted and on 24th June that year he set sail aboard the steel-built sailing ship *The Cartvale*. The crossing to Wellington took 110 days, and the £14.10s. fare was paid by the New Zealand Government. Edwin landed on 11th October 1874, labouring at a variety of jobs around Wellington province before becoming a carpenter.

Although they were not to meet until some years later in Masterton, Edwin's future wife arrived with her family in Wellington eleven days after him. Thirteen-year-old Mercy Gardner had been born in Putney, London on 19th August 1864. Together with her eleven-year-old sister Ruth, she had travelled in single woman's quarters aboard the *Douglas*. Mercy was the eldest surviving child in a family of three girls (her youngest sister Rachel was eight) and two boys (nine-year-old Frederick and Alfred aged four) when the Gardners landed in New Zealand on 22nd October. A baby brother, Arthur, had died during the long sea voyage. Thomas and Charlotte Gardner settled in the bush, in the town of Masterton, opening a small cobblers shop in the front of their house. They had one more son, Herbert, born in 1877.

Edwin was twenty-six and Mercy seventeen when they married in 1879. Robin Selby was born in 1891. He was the youngest of their first six children – George, Harry, Alice, Thomas and Edwin had arrived at two-year intervals since 1880. Edwin Senior continued as a carpenter and builder, and he also specialised as foreman of bridge building gangs, work that took him away from home for long periods. He worked on many of the old wooden bridges around Manawatu and Wairarapa.

In 1893 Edwin acquired a small farm at Scarborough, Mangamutu, about two miles from Pahiatua . Life was tough, living in a cottage in the bush on land that had to be cleared and burnt. Later a large handsome house was built, but this burnt down in 1923. Between 1896 and 1904 there were three more children, James, Nellie and Florence.

Robin was only two years old when he moved to the bush where he grew up part of a large family. His pre-war occupation was as an accountant, employed by F. Wise of Eketahuna. He was a handsome young man of twenty-four, blue eyed, brown haired and fresh complexioned, five foot seven inches tall, weighing ten stone eight and a half pounds when he enlisted on 18th October 1915. He joined B. Company 9th Reinforcement Wellington Infantry Regiment, registering for compulsory military training under the Defence Act of 1909. He listed his previous military experience as in Wellington, two years with D. Battery and three years with Civil Service Rifles.

The final question on the Attestation Form which Robin signed read: Are you willing to serve in the Expeditionary Force in or beyond the Dominion of New Zealand under the following conditions, providing your services should so long be required: For the term of the present European war and for such further period as is necessary to bring the Expeditionary Force back to New Zealand and to disband it?

Robin named his father Edwin, then living at 6 George Street, Masterton, as

Robin Selby, Convalescent at Hornchurch, 1917

next of kin before setting off to fight. He was to remain in Europe after hostilities, returning to his native shores almost a year after the Armistice.

Robin served exactly the length of time it took his parents to cross the ocean, 110 days, in New Zealand before being sent overseas for 3 years and 352 days. His first theatre of operations was in Egypt during 1916. On 17th March 1916 Robin was promoted to Corporal, on 9th April he embarked aboard the Llandovery Castle from Alexandria, en route for France and the Western Front. During the first Battle of the Somme, on 1st July, Robin was appointed a Lance Sergeant, and three months later, on 1st October, he was wounded in action. He was admitted to the General Hospital at Etaple with a gunshot wound to the buttock, and on 5th October he embarked for England, first hospitalised in Oxford, then to the N.Z. General Hospital at Brockenhurst on 10th November. Five days later Robin arrived for the first time at Hornchurch for a period of convalescence.

On 29th March 1917 he was transferred to 3rd Battalion Wellington Infantry Regiment, given a new regimental number 15/161 and sent to Codford. On 2nd April he was taken on the strength of the 11th (Taranaki Rifles) Regiment, and he returned to France on 27th May 1917. Eighteen days later he was appointed temporary QMS in the field, and the permanent promotion was confirmed on the 11th July. On 23rd July he received his second gunshot wound to the buttock while in action. A week later Robin embarked once again for England, this time to the 2nd NZ General Hospital at Walton. On 23rd August he was transferred to Hornchurch and on 6th October 1917 was once again attached to the strength at Codford. Robin spent the next three and a half months in the Command Depot, the autumn in Wiltshire seems to have been stormy, with thunder and lightning and bitter east winds. He no doubt spent Christmas in Codford-on-the-Mud, perhaps attending the concerts, the soccer and rugby matches, watching the boxing matches and enjoying the nine-hole golf course. All too soon the brief, wintry respite in England was over, Robin returned to the trenches, marching into camp at Etaple on 28th January 1918. Between 16th and 29th August he was on leave in Paris, on 31st August he transferred to 1st Battalion Wellington Regiment in the Field.

Robin was promoted to Warrant Officer Class II on 27th September 1918 and on 16th March 1919 was mentioned in a Despatch by Field Marshal Sir Douglas Haig for gallant and distinguished services in the Field. The signatory on the certificate

Ben Doyle (left) and Robin Selby (right) outside their farm living quarters

was Winston S. Churchill, the then Secretary of State for War. Robin's nephew John Selby believes the reason for the 'Mentioned in Dispatches' could have been for the final battle fought by New Zealanders, the capture of Le Quesnoy. Given the date this was awarded, during the clean-up process after hostilities had ceased, it could also have been in recognition of Robin's services as Regimental Sergeant Major over a period rather than for any particular act of bravery. In later life one of the locals who knew Robin said that the part he hated most in the war were the bayonet charges where as a Warrant Officer he had to lead his men.

In all four Selby brothers served in the War, Harry, Ted [Edwin] and Jim [James] fought together with their two more or less adopted brothers, Jack and Ben Doyle. Jack Doyle was killed at the Somme, Harry Selby was a fitter with the New Zealand Field Artillery; he died on 5th October 1917. Family history papers list Harry's dates as 1882–1917. Robin's niece Joyce Dodd thinks Harry was killed at Passchendaele, where the Allied casualty rate in the quagmire of mud was 25%. The majority of the troops in the first two battles of Passchendaele were the New Zealanders and the Australians, joined in the third and final battle by the Canadians.

John Selby says that Harry received a posthumous Military Medal for helping to remove burning ammunition boxes, thus preventing the explosion of an ammunition dump near Neuve Eglise on 5th June 1916.

Robin Selby sailed for New Zealand on 3rd November 1919. Together with his foster brother and partner Ben Doyle, he returned to the bush in 1921, taking advantage of the opportunity of a Returned Serviceman's Rehabilitation Farm block in the Moki [Maori name] /Mount Damper area some sixty miles east of Stratford in Eastern Taranaki. The Government of the day made land available, but it was not easily assessible or cleared; in some cases the only way in was a mud track through the bush.

Robin's farm was in sheep and cattle country, his beloved dogs were his companions and co-workers. He worked a relatively remote, rugged, steep and broken landscape given to landslides in wet weather. The settlers had to clear thick forest and establish farms with little more than axes, saws and shovels in a completely undeveloped area of high rainfall, no shingle for road work and only horse transport, far from the nearest town with shops. There was a house cow, milked in the open as required, with a calf using the surplus milk, and large numbers of wild pigs and goats in the forest providing extra food for the men and dogs.

The farm four-roomed living quarters Robin moved into was made of split timber slabs made from the native New Zealand totara tree. It consisted of a large living room, with a big open fireplace in which all the cooking was done with the aid of camp ovens and large pots hanging from hooks over the fire. There were two bedrooms and a combined kitchen and laundry with a stove that was never used. Baths were taken in a tin bath in the open air and the laundry was done in a primitive manner in the fine weather otherwise in front of the fire.

Selby family gathering, April 1944: (from left) Florence, Ted, Alice, George, Edwin (sen.), Tom, Nellie, Robin, Jim

During the 1930s depression because of the difficult access and low productivity returns most of the land was abandoned. The settlers simply walked out with what they could carry. Robin was able to buy two neighbouring farms, when one of the farmers died and the other was accidentally killed. The additional land increased his income and enabled him to become relatively well off. About this time he turned a farm shed into a garage for his Essex Tourer motorcar, which could make it over the clay roads with the help of chains. Robin farmed his land and carried out fencing and shearing in the local area until around 1960, when he sold up and moved to Alfredton near Pahiatua in the Wakakapa District.

Robin loved to travel, and by the late 1930s he had become sufficiently established to set up a pattern that would last for the rest of his life. He would work the farm for a period of a year or eighteen months, then employ a manager and take off to see the world. His journeys took him to Australia, Canada, America, India, Manchuria and China. He was in Shanghai when the Japanese attacked China and was interned in Japan at the beginning of World War Two, taking some time to return to New Zealand. Despite staying at the best hotels on his travels, he always returned to the spartan life of the bush.

Joyce Dodd has fond memories of 'Uncle Rob' during the 1920s and 1930s. The family saw him often, always with a bag of sweets for the children. He was a great favourite with his nieces and nephews who remember him as a most interesting person. They knew he was wounded in the Great War but he laughingly told them he wasn't proud of it, being hit in the backside. His sister Nell wrote this poem after his death:

THE FARMER

Rob died last June: The gorse reigns gold.
The hills slip away,   Sheep on the slopes
Rain dribbles down   Grow shaggy and bold.
Over wounded clay.   The pack of black pig dogs
The house hangs open   Took to the hills,
To the drifting day.   The gun lies rusting
  They gave him the land   The notched row of kills.
Soon after the war.   Deep down gullies
A Rehab. Loan   The shingle spills.
Paid off the score   A tidy investment,
Of all those years   The lawyer said.
He died and swore.   Wool cheques pulled the farm
  The Trustees wait   Out of the red;
For the land to be sold;   Land values rise,
Bracken chokes the valleys,   But the farmer is dead.

Robin Selby died of throat cancer at the age of seventy-eight on 3rd September 1969, and is buried in the Soldiers Cemetery at Pahiatua along with his old partner Ben Doyle who predeceased him in 1963.

[Note: The 11th (Taranaki Rifles) Regiment was formed on 17th March 1911, with a change of title of the 4th Battalion Wellington (Taranaki) Rifles. It had consisted of Taranaki Rifle Volunteers, the Taranaki Guards Rifle Volunteers and six other regional volunteer units. It supplied Service Companies during World War One and these saw service in Egypt on Gallipoli and in France as part of the 'Wellington' Regiment. The Regiment saw battle in the Somme (1916-1918), France and Flanders (1916-1918) Hindenburg Line, Messines (1917), Ypes (1917) Bapaume (1918) Gallipoli (1915), and Egypt (1915-1916). In 1921 it became the Taranaki Regiment, later becoming the only NZ Regiment to be awarded the battle honour 'New Zealand.' After World War Two it amalgamated with the Wellington West Coast Regiment to become the Wellington, West Coast and Taranaki Regiment. In 1964 it became the 5th Battalion Royal New Zealand Infantry Regiment.

Information supplied by Fran McGowan, of the Defence Library, New Zealand Military. Military Records supplied by New Zealand Defence Force. For personal information and photosthanks to John Selby, Joyce Dodd, Derek Morris and Clem Hill. For Robin's letter thanks to Peter Ranger.]

Tumult in the Clouds

Major Benjamin Stevens Jordan was a thirty-four year old married man who came from Christchurch, NZ. He was in the Canterbury Regiment N.Z.E.F. and at the time of his death in a plane crash was second in command of the New Zealand Command Depot at Codford. The R.A.F. pilot on the fatal flight was a New Yorker, 2nd Lieut. Joseph J. Daly, who was based at No. 8 Training Depot Station at Netheravon in 4th Wing, No.7 Group, Training Division. This was formed on 1st April 1918 and was one of two Training Depot Stations responsible for basic and advanced training.

On Friday 24th May 1918 Major Jordan was the passenger on an Airco DH6 C6518, which crashed at Codford. The aircraft had completed a loop and a dive to 1000 feet, on pulling out it began to break up, followed by the collapse of the outer port wings. Before the crash site could be secured parts of the wreckage disappeared, so that when the accident investigators arrived at the site later, they were unable to conduct a conclusive examination to determine the cause. This was very shortly after the No. 8 Training Depot was formed, and its first fatality. Major Jordan is one of the 66 New Zealanders buried in the ANZAC Cemetery.

> Nor law, nor duty bade me fight,
> Nor public men, nor cheering crowds
> A lonely impulse of delight
> Drove to this tumult in the clouds.
> From: 'An Irish Airman Foresees His Death', by W.B. Yeats

[Sources: *The War Dead of the Commonwealth*, Rod Priddle, and *For Your Tomorrows* by E. Martin (Christopher Green)]

The Wiltshires in the East

The Great War was fought on five Fronts – the Western [France and Flanders], the Eastern [Russia against Germany], the Italian, the Balkan and the Middle East [Britain and the Empire against Turkey.] The majority of local men fought the Germans on the Western Front, others were fighting the Turks. Seven Codford men died in the Middle East, four in Mesopotamia and one each in Palestine, Gallipoli and India.

The casualties were with the 1/4th, 2/4th, and 5th Battalions of the Wiltshire Regiment. The 1/4th were sent to India in October 1914, moving to Egypt in September 1917. Lance Sergeant Frederick Charles Whatley was the son of Codford's last drowner (water-meadow bailiff), William Whatley, and his wife Mary. William had been born in Upton Lovell, just across the Codford boundary of Manor Farm, where he worked for more than fifty years, retiring in the 1930s. Young Fred Whatley had been born in Codford St Peter. He exchanged the green fields of Wiltshire for the deserts of Mesopotamia in modern day Iraq. He was only twenty-one at the time of his death on Sunday 16th July 1916 and is buried in Baghdad [North Gate] War Cemetery. In 1914 Baghdad was the headquarters of the Turkish Army in Mesopotamia, and the supreme objective of the Indian Expeditionary Force 'D' – it was captured by General Maude on 11th March 1917. Baghdad became the Expeditionary Force's advanced base, with two stationary hospitals and three casualty-clearing stations. The North Gate Cemetery was begun in April 1917, and the Commonwealth War Graves Commission notes it has been greatly enlarged since the end of World War One by graves brought in from other burial grounds in Baghdad and northern Iraq. Fred Whatley may have been moved from elsewhere, as there is no indication as to how or where he died. It does not appear he was killed in action or died of wounds; it may be that he succumbed to one of the many diseases rife in the Middle East, or that he was a prisoner at the time of his death.

George Portingale was also a member of the 1/4th, but as his name is on the memorial in St Mary's Church his story is told in *The Men of St Mary's*, above. His parents lived at 33 Cheapside in Codford St Mary; they had already lost their younger son Archie, killed in France. George was killed on 19th September 1918 at El Tirah in Palestine.

One of the reasons I knew that all the casualties of World War One were not recorded was because of a story told to me by Will Collins of Manor Farm. He was talking about Alice Sparey, the post-girl who had taken over the postal round from her brother when he went off to war. This was a temporary arrangement, the idea being that this would keep the job open for her brother on his return. The Spareys

A Rustic Lane, Codford.

The Spareys lived in the cottage nearest the camera

lived in one of the small farm cottages at the bottom of Frog Alley in Codford St Peter. The young soldier was killed somewhere in the Middle East so Alice continued as temporary post-girl till after the Second World War when she eventually retired. Will heard, but cannot confirm, that Alice could not obtain a pension from the Post Office because she had never been put on the permanent staff, and was still classed as 'temporary' after more than thirty years.

There were at least two other Sparey families in Codford, one living in the High Houses in the High Street, the other in Codford St Mary. They were still in the village during World War Two when siblings John and Mary Sparey ran the Milk Bar at the bottom of Chitterne Road. Two Spareys show in the records as having died in World War One. George was born in Codford St Mary, and died in France – wrong village, wrong battlefront. It is thanks to Joan Cole that the mystery was solved. While researching my book *Sterner Days: Codford During the Second World War* in 1994 she told me: 'Alice's father Henry Sparey was the village postman. She took on the round when her twin brother went off to fight in the First World War. He died of malaria in India in 1916.' Private Frederick Henry Sparey was born at Codford St Peter and died in India on 25th September 1916. He was with 'B' Company 2/4th Wiltshire Regiment, the twenty-eight year old son of Emma and Henry Sparey, married and living with his wife Beatrice at 42 Gorringe Road, Bemerton, Salisbury. Frederick Sparey is remembered on the memorial window in St Peter's Church, and on Face 7 of the Kirkee 1914-1918 Memorial. Kirkee or Khadki is a military cantonment adjoining the university town of Poona, on the plateau above Bombay. The Memorial commemorates more than 1,800 servicemen who died in India during the First World War, who are buried in civil and cantonment cemeteries in India and Pakistan where their graves can no longer be properly maintained.

Four more local men, fighting against the Turks on the Middle Eastern Front with 5th Battalion Wiltshire Regiment, were never to return home. It is very likely that Charles and Elizabeth Pretty of 31 Stockton lost two members of their family, possibly two sons. William Pretty, like George Pretty referred to earlier, was born in

Talbot's Stores with the Milk Bar cottages behind

Stockton, enlisted in Salisbury, and both are described as residing in Codford St Mary. George joined the Wiltshire Regiment on 1st September 1914, but there is no record of when William enlisted. He was only nineteen when he was killed in action at Gallipoli on Tuesday 10th August 1915.

The Regimental History takes up the story:

On 1st July 1915, the 5th Battalion sailed from Avonmouth in the *Franconia* and, a fortnight later, were anchored in Mudros Bay at the Island of Lemnos off the Dardanalles in the eastern Mediterranean. By the 17th July they were all ashore at Cape Helles, on the Gallipoli Peninsula, with the rest of their Brigade in the 13th Division. Two days later they were in the trenches facing the Turks. At the end of the month the Wiltshires returned to Mudros Bay in destroyers and minesweepers. Early in August they went back to Anzac Cove on the Peninsula. On 6th August the 5th Wiltshires and the 4th South Wales Borderers captured a ridge of hills in a night attack to help a British landing at Suvla Bay. Next the 5th were ordered to support the Lancashire Brigade at Sari Bair. On 10th August the Battalion and the 6th North Lancashires were holding the high ground there, having relieved some of the exhausted New Zealand, Nepalese and British Units, who had captured the ridge after tremendous efforts the day before.

William Pretty has no known grave. He is remembered between panels 156-158, one of the 21,000 names commemorated on the Helles Memorial. The Memorial takes the form of a tall obelisk standing on the tip of the Gallipoli Peninsula, visible to the ships passing through the Dardanelles in Turkey.

After fighting at Sari Bair and Suvla until their positions were evacuated in the middle of December the Wiltshires returned to the Peninsula in a blizzard.

In January 1916 Cape Helles was evacuated, the Wiltshires going on to Port Said, having received 750 reinforcements. In February the Battalion went to sea to Basra via Kuwait, at the top of the Persian Gulf. In March they continued up the River Tigris in barges to Amara. The 5th were to fight the Turks on this axis for two and a half years. From Amara their 13th Division went on up river to relieve the Lahore Division south of Kut.

Early in April the 13th Division attempted to break through the Turkish Division, which was besieging Kut, in an effort to relieve the British garrison there. After the 5th Wiltshires had rushed the enemy trenches at Hannah, they were held up in open country in front of Falahiyeh all day. At dusk they withdrew to bivouac by the river a mile in the rear, having suffered 194 casualties including 17 other ranks killed and 13 officers wounded. Falahiyeh was captured that night, and the Battalion took part in an attack on Sanna-I-Yat before dawn. Direction was lost through encountering a marsh on the line of advance. A few men of the 5th got into the Turkish trenches, but eventually the troops dug in under heavy fire 500 yards from the Turks and held on all day. The Commanding Officer, Second Lieutenant Binns and 21 other ranks were killed. In all the Wiltshires had 288 casualties and Captain Greany was wounded for the second time in the battle.

In one day the 13th Division had fought their way across six miles through the Turkish trench system in depth, and, in all, advanced seven miles. Further attempts were made to reach Kut. The 5th Battalion incurred a further sixty-five casualties in beating off a heavy counter-attack, on the opposite bank of the Tigris, with great losses to the Turks. Kut was not relieved, and the garrison was eventually forced to surrender.

The 5th Wiltshires were now only 413 strong, including 13 officers, under the command of Lieutenant Colonel R. H. Haseldine of the Kings Liverpool Regiment. May was spent in defensive positions, and then the 13th Division was relieved, going back to the Amara area.

Private Harry Cummins of Bapton died on 11th May 1916. He returned to Amara, a town on the left bank of the Tigris 520 kilometres from the sea, only to be buried in the War Cemetery there. Two more local men from 5th Battalion were buried in this cemetery in the next two years, twenty-year old Private Reginald Davis in 1917 and Lance Corporal Albert Frank Johnson in 1918.

Reginald Davis was born in Codford St Mary but residing elsewhere, possibly, given his age (twenty in January 1917) living with his parents in Lake, along the Woodford Valley outside Salisbury. He was killed in action on 25th January1917, the day the Wiltshires and the Royal Welch Fusiliers successfully assaulted the Turkish front line, one flank of which was on the Hai River.

The Wiltshires took 100 prisoners, and counted 234 Turkish dead. The enemy trenches were well sited in depth, and excellently constructed, much use being made of bricks. Their latrines were as clean as their rifles were dirty. The Battalion had 150 casualties; amongst the 35 killed were Captain Bosanquet and Second Lieutenant McInnes.

On 24th April 1918 the Wiltshires moved north to take part in operations on the Kifri front. Another British column had defeated the Turks farther north and occupied Kirkuk. On 29th April the 5th Battalion, acting as Advanced Guard to their column, drove the enemy from the hills near Tuzkurmati, which was captured with 1,800 Turks and much equipment. Lieutenant-Colonel Haseldine now commanded a force engaged in keeping the road open to Kirkuk, and occupied Tauq. Bad weather and floods prevented supplies getting through, and Kirkuk was evacuated before the end of May.

The Wiltshires remained as part of the garrison at Tuzkurmati till September. In the middle of October the Battalion, with supporting arms, moved north to prevent the enemy at Kirkuk from interfering with 1 British Corps advance on Mosul, further west. By the end of the month Baziyan and Kirkuk had been occupied, and the Wiltshires were at Altun-Kupri with the Turks in full retreat. On 1st November Turkey signed an armistice, and the Battalion went back to Kirkuk.

Lance-Corporal Albert Frank Johnson was the last casualty associated with Codford St Mary to die in Mesopotamia, sadly after the end of hostilities. He died on 16th November 1918 and was buried at Basra War Cemetery in Iraq. In 1935 the headstones from the graves were removed when it was discovered that salts in the soil were causing them to deteriorate. The graves of those affected are now recorded on a screen wall.

After demobilisation at Amara, the Regimental Cadre were sent as part of a composite Battalion to the North-West Frontier of India, and did not reach Devizes to be disbanded until September 1919.

[Sources: David Chilton, Curator, The Royal Gloucestershire, Berkshire and Wiltshire Regiment Museum, The Wardrobe, Salisbury; N C E Kenrick, *The History of the Wiltshire Regiment in World War I*; The Commonwealth War Graves Commission; *Soldiers Died in the Great War*; John Laffin, *Brassey's Battles*; Richard Holmes, *The Oxford Companion to Military History*.]

Chronicles of the N.Z.E.F. 1918

February 27th 1918
CODFORD NOTES Since I wrote last, we seem to have jumped into Spring weather, which has turned our attention to tennis and to gardening. Last year we had thirty acres under cultivation, and this year we hope to do considerably better. It is good to see the 'Diggers' once more happy on the land, even if it is only for a week or two before returning to the delights of trench digging.

In the District Football Championships our teams are doing well. The Depot Soccer people are still unbeaten, and Wellington Company is leading in the Rugger competition, with the other four company teams well up. The only game played recently by the Depot Rugger team was a return match against the South African Heavy Artillery a few days ago on a sticky ground. In spite of this, however, we saw some good play. In the first spell with the sun and breeze at their backs, our men pressed hard, play never going into their own twenty-five at all. Good opportunities were lost by over-anxiety and too hard kicking on the part of the forwards, with the result that the Africans forced down six times and only one score was made, a good try by Ogg at wing three-quarter, who dashed through three opponents and scored in the corner. The second spell was in favour of the Africans, who scored an unconverted try from a good passing rush, and so a keen game ended in a draw.

A foursome of M.O.s from the Hospital wandered over to Brockenhurst on Saturday, February 16th, and had a lively and enjoyable round of golf with the M.O.s there, ending in a draw. Col. Fenwick is very much missed by all the inhabitants on No. 3 General.

ONLOOKER

July 19th 1918
CODFORD COMMAND DEPOT NOTES We are finding out that England is not such a bad place after all – in summer. As a result of the good weather, interest in games is steadily increasing. The cricketers have a sound team and are leading in the District Competition. On the 6th they went to Bristol to meet a team captained by Lilley, of All England fame. Thanks to the good bowling of Torrance [8 for 27] and McFarlane, the home team were all out for 70 runs. Our men they reached 72 for the loss of two wickets, the runs being made by Torrance, Hadden and Gale. In the Inter-Company Competition, Otago carry too many guns for the rest, and have a strong lead.

Tennis is going strong with competitions of some sort at frequent intervals. The only outside match played so far was against Bristol, and was won by our men.

We are looking forward to a good Sports Meeting on the 12th, when we have several events open to Southern Command. At present we are well off for runners, and we have made a fair showing in outside meetings. Mason has won every half-mile he has started this year, and Lindsay, Mexted, and Brien, who have done well in sprints, make up, with Mason, a relay team that take some beating.

Our surprise packet at Australian Sports at Hurdcott, on the 6th, was a three miles team race, in which our team, almost untrained, came a very close second in a field of ten drawn from the Southern Command.

ONLOOKER

August 16th 1918
CODFORD NOTES In spite of such excitements as shifting camp and plunging into deep schemes of education, we have not a great deal to write about. Our chief interest lately has been our athletic team, which has had an almost unbroken success at sports meetings in a variety of places. At Aldershot Command Sports, on the 3rd,

Lindsay won the 220 yards open championship in 23 seconds, and Mason won the 880 yards in 2 min. $^{1}/_{5}$ secs. The relay team had hard luck to be disqualified, through a mistake in changing the flag, though they finished an easy first. The great event of the season was the Navy and Army meeting at Stamford Bridge on the 5th. In the chief item, an International championship, New Zealand was represented by three of our men, who had the honour of winning to the tune of 11 points over England's 7, Canada's 4, and Italy's 2. Lindsay, though very close off the mark in the 100 yards, finished with great dash, and won in $10^{2}/_{5}$ secs. Brien and Mason won the 440 yards and 880 yards respectively without much trouble in 54 secs. and 2mins $1^{2}/_{5}$ secs. The three-lap relay, run by the same men, who had competed in the individual events, went to England with our men second. In addition a relay race – four men to run 220 yards each – was won by our team, consisting of Capt. McPherson, Lindsay, Brien and Mexted. We are looking forward to our own sports.

November 8th 1918
CODFORD TODAY Poor old Codford, that queer collection of drab military architecture, slung on the cold slopes of a Salisbury Plain valley, is not such a bad home after all. 'Rotten hole' the Digger calls it, but then old Digger usually reckons that the last place he was in was much better than the present and, when first he looks upon its endless rows of huts, he is not in a frame of mind to view them through rose tinted spectacles. After a month or two of the free-and-easy cheery life in a tip-top New Zealand hospital, and a few weeks living like a lord on a grand tour of Scotland, coming to Codford Command Depot is not the happiest change of circumstance. Tea and toast in bed at 8.30 to reveille at six ac emma is too sudden an evolution to be accepted with philosophy. No, as a brusque N.C.O. bids him hasten to parade in a cold raw mist, the Digger, shivering, empty and fed up, does not approve.

But the camp improves on acquaintance, and some of those drab tin walls hide interiors less inhospitable than a forbidding exterior would lead one to expect. Codford is the habitation of an ever-changing multitude. Every day brings a miscellaneous little knot of men tumbling off the trains, and wandering despondently – and often a day or two overdue – along the camp road between untidy make-shift shacks, vending at high rates cheap articles to the troops. The men are divided now according to their classification as regards health and not according to unit; and so it is not exactly easy to find Jim Digger unless you happen to have made yourself fully acquainted not more than a day or two beforehand whether he is U14 or SWZ2 (I have long ago abandoned the more than human task of keeping pace with developments of military language, and no one having been enterprising enough to bring out a dictionary of military abbreviations, I have reverted to the ranks of the out of date.) Probably you don't find Jim just where his health said he ought to be, and so at last, having found him energetically exercising himself among those whose health has materially benefited

Catholic Women's League hut at Codford

through the excellence of everything which goes to make Codford what it is, you congratulate him on being A something in health, but no smile of appreciation lights Jim's features. No, being A something or other is far too strenuous for his liking, and besides Sling is in the offing.

The army has lost its dignity and becomes positively frolicsome in this, the fifth dark year of war. The cult of the 'hips firm-on hands down' has faded into the dim vistas of history, and now the bar numbers, the umpteenths and the old married birds all skip around together in childish frivolity at school games of the youngest generation. And the diggers enjoy them too, and put plenty of weight into the business, We are all no more than so many big kids, and it does you good to see them running round in a ring-a-ring-a-rosie circle, hot and laughing. The route march still maintains the dignity of old, headed by the band, though we must not hesitate to confess that there are those among us who consider it might be most happily varied by the band breaking from the dull old march into a one-step, then to the fox-trot, and from there to the turkey-trot. Tribal war dances, too, might replace the – but the time for this innovation is not, perhaps, yet.

The education infection has spread to Codford as elsewhere, and the diggers are becoming, if possible, a trifle more wily than before. Their knowledge grows as the day passeth and becometh night and is succeeded by another day – economics and electricity, cobbling and composition, agriculture and apoplexy, hygiene and what-not. But honestly, the education business is not a bad sort of affair at all, and, though some of us may not be much the wiser for all the economics, the classes pass pleasantly many a Codford hour. That is how depot days pass, games, education and route march – and now to the night, the dark, cold, dreary Codford night.

Inside the Ao-Tea-Roa Club, 1918

There is, of course, a wet canteen – much to the regret, we have heard, of people far away in comfortable homes in N.Z., whose hearts ache at this dreadful debauchery – but its adherents grow fewer as the beer grows colder. Then there is the Ao-Tea-Roa Club, the cheerful, china-rattling War Contingent home, where there is always warmth, something to eat, comfortable chairs, bridge, a library and nice, jolly sympathetic girls. Sometimes there is the camp orchestra playing sweetly, sometimes good concerts and occasionally drama of the vilest order. Yes, there are worse places to spend an evening than the old War Contingent Club. The Y.M., too, is good, but it is not so convenient. The round is completed at the establishment picture nightly, and many other things at all hours, of Digger. Padre Winton is Digger, and here he spends always a happy night with a hall full of Diggers, who sing popular songs to hymn airs – no, I'm wrong, it's the other way around. And they sing very nicely as they never do in church. The fact is that their singing in church is a disgrace. The hours from 6 til 9.30 can be passed pleasantly enough, Codford, with all its drawbacks, is not such a bad place after all.

Late in the evening the clouds which so often hang above the Plain have gone, and leave a starry vault above the quiet valley, and the old sweet call of the 'Last Post' sounds musically across the further side, and comes more faintly from other camps not so near. And the lights go out suddenly in the hutments, and soon a great stillness hangs over the camp, until in the early hour, reveille should wake it again to life, the cooks to their stoves, and half-clad men to the wash-places.

Two postcard views of the Aotearoa Club

Some Corner of a Foreign Field

Wiltshire contains 1,971 War Graves scattered over 196 cemeteries and churchyards. Of these graves, 1,114 are in six burial grounds (at Bulford, Durrington, Tidworth, Codford St Mary, Sutton Veny and Fovant) directly connected with the training grounds on or near Salisbury Plain. Most, though not all, of the rest are those of soldiers from Wiltshire who died at home.

Codford has the graves of eight British men from this period. Seven of the men are buried in St Mary's churchyard and one, Private F E Tullett of 8th Battalion East Surrey Regiment, in St Peter's. Privates Cooper (10th Bn. Cheshire Regt), McEwan, (4/5th Bn. Lancashire Fusiliers) and Short (17th Bn. Northumberland Fusiliers), Gunners Marsh (Royal Field Artillery) and Smith (32nd Div. Ammunition Col., Royal Field Artillery), Cpl. Fenn (7th Bn. Bedfordshire Regt.) and Sergeant Whitehead (3/8th Bn. Manchester Regt) lie to the east of the church and the south-east of the churchyard. Apart from dates of death the only soldier about whom there is additional information is Sergeant Whitehead. He died of pneumonia on 13th February 1916 aged 33. He was the son of Henry and Annie Whitehead, of 79 Cheadle Street, Higher Openshaw, Manchester and the husband of Annie Whithead (née Ellis).

In a quiet corner of the village across the lane from St Mary's Church is a small plot established by a deed of gift as a 'Military Burial Ground' with a small part reserved for future parish burials. Known as the ANZAC War Graves it contains 66 New Zealanders and 31 Australians from World War One with a single Welsh Guardsman from World War Two. The Cemetery, the second largest for ANZAC soldiers in the U.K., is in the care of the Commonwealth War Graves Commission; it has a War Cross erected between Irish Yews and other trees and is tended by local volunteers.

Since 1999 a special service has been held on 25th April, ANZAC Day, in the cemetery. Present and retired members of the British, Australian and New Zealand military, the British Legion, the Parish Council and villagers gather at 6.30am beside the graves to honour the men who never returned to their native shores.

Most of the men died in 1917 and 1918, 40 in the first year, 34 in the second, 9 died in 1916 and 12 in 1919. At least 73 of these men were in their 20s and 30s, 4 were 19, 8 in their 40s and one was aged 52. Of those where cause of death is listed 42 died of sickness, 14 of pneumonia, meningitis and bronchitis each claimed 3 victims, 1 soldier died of flu, 1 of nephritis (an inflammation of the kidney), 2 of phthisis (pulmonary consumption), one of wounds and another of accidental injuries. Of the 97 men buried in the cemetery we know the cause of death for 68 of them.

The oldest casualty was in the N.Z. Medical Corps. Fifty-two year old Corporal William Gilmore died of influenza on 7th April 1919, far from his home in New Plymouth. Of the four youngest, the first to die was born in County Cork, Ireland. Pte Lawrence Kinane of the 49th Battalion Australian Infantry died of pneumonia on 6th January 1917. The other three were Australians; Ptes Brookes, Cattermole and Patience are listed as having died of sickness.

The men of the Australian and New Zealand Expeditionary Forces travelled from the other side of the world, yet many originated closer to home. Pte Alexander Whitelaw was a Scot, Pte Harry Holder was born in Cornwall, Pte Thomas Chilton was a Yorkshireman, Ptes Cathcart and Magee, like Lawrence Kinane, were Irish, and Pte Oscar Cameron was a 37-year-old Canadian whose parents lived in Nova Scotia.

Among the entries is a soldier with an intriguing past: Pte 6809 J. Lessells of

ANZAC Service, April 2002 (photograph courtesy of Brian Marshall)

the 15th Bn. Australian Infantry died on 19th February 1917. It is noted he served as Morton but that Lassells was his true family name. We may never know his story but it raises interesting questions: Did he enlist under an assumed name because he was under age, on the run, needed to disappear or for family reasons? No cause of death, nationality or next of kin are listed so there are no clues as to where to begin to find the man buried beneath the chalk landscape of a Wiltshire village.

One of the last men to die was a member of the New Zealand Maori [Pioneer] Battalion. Private Hona Hape was 26, the son of Hope and Hera Inumia Tangiora, of Opoutama, Napier. He died of sickness on 11th April 1919, while waiting to return to the Land of the Long White Cloud, five months after the Armistice was signed.

Only one man is recorded as having died of wounds. Tasmanian Pte Albert Arthur Harris of the 4th Co. Australian Machine Gun Corps died on 27th July 1917.

The modern inhabitants of the village have not forgotten the sacrifice of the ANZAC and British soldiers. They are part of our heritage and in our keeping – in the words of Rupert Brooke, they lie with 'hearts at peace, under an English heaven.'

[Source: The War Dead of the Commonwealth.]

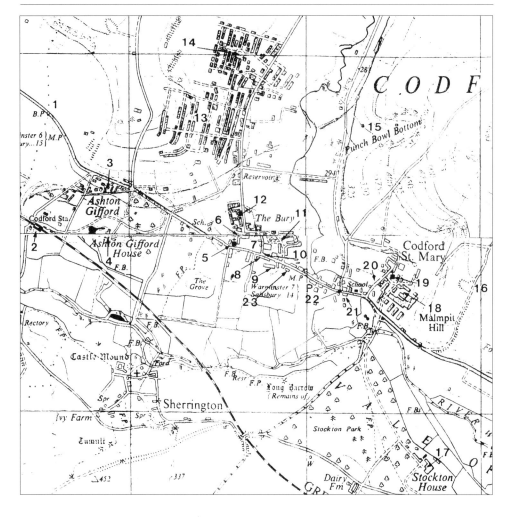

Codford 1939 – 1945

Key:
1   Hillside
2   Codford Station
3   Opposite Ivy Cottages
4   Ashton Gifford House/ Greenways
        Preparatory School
5   St Peter's Church
6   St Peter's Rectory
7   Bury Mead
8   The Woolstore
9   The Wool House
10 The George
11 Cherry Orchard Camp

12 The Bury and Green Lane
13 'A' Campsite
14 'B' Campsite
15 Punchbowl
16 The Dump on Malmpit Hill
17 Stockton House
18 Institute Camp: St Mary's
19 St Mary's Church
20 ANZAC Commonwealth War Grave
        Cemetery
21 17 High Street, Homer Bosworth's home
22 The Milk Bar
23 The Codford Club YMCA

WORLD WAR TWO

The Troops of the Second World War

In the Beginning

The 260th Field Company Royal Engineers [43rd Wessex Division] were the first troops to arrive in Codford since the First World War. Early in October 1939 a Territorial Company comprising about 250 local men, recruited from Chippenham, Melksham, Trowbridge and Bradford on Avon moved from Gillingham in Dorset to Codford. They were billeted in The Wool Stores and in the stables at Greenways [Ashton Gifford House today.] The Quartermaster's Stores were in the stables of Colonel Sneyd's Bradwell Grange, now the Wool House. The mess hall was in the Theatre Club, behind which was the cookhouse in a corrugated iron building. All the officers were billeted in Stockton House with the sick bay in the private chapel.

Early in the War the Pioneer Corps was in a camp opposite Ivy Cottages. It was known locally as 'non- combatant camp' as the men were either medically unfit for combat or were conscientious objectors. These were the camp builders – the huts were speedily assembled either alongside the World War One sites or on new sites. The principle camp was on the east side of the road from Codford St Peter to Manor Farm opposite Camps 13 and 14 of the previous war. There was also a camp between Codford St Mary Church and Little Wood near the site of Camp 5.[1]

Later the 'non combatant' camp was used for the Italian Prisoners of War, and finally for the Polish soldiers. Codford was the demobilisation Centre for the Polish units of General Anders after the war had ended.

The Guards

Prime Minister Winston Churchill was determined to create a British force to combat the formidable German Panzer Divisions, who in 1940 had rolled through Europe with terrifying speed and devastating effect. In the early part of 1941 a decision was taken to form a Guards Division, two Armoured Brigades and one Infantry Battalion commanded by General Oliver Leese. The 6th Guards Armoured Brigade, formed six months earlier, was selected to be one of the Armoured Brigades. It consisted of 4th Grenadier Guards, 4th Coldstream and 3rd Scots Guards, all commanded by Alan Adair who was destined to command the entire Division in North West Europe.

The Guards had never had any tank experience, so throughout the summer months of 1941 officers and senior sergeants were sent on technical courses for driving, maintenance, gunnery, wireless and tactics. On 22nd November 6th Guards moved into the Codford area and established its HQ at Stockton House. The 2nd Battalion Welsh Guards were at the Rectory Field Camp at the St Mary's end of the village, with part of their Battalion at the Wool Stores Camp, also known as Cherry Orchard Camp. There were two Battalions side by side in a corrugated Nissen hutted camp parallel to the Chitterne Road, in the New Road area – the 4th Battalion Grenadier Guards and the 3rd Battalion Scots Guards. The Coldstream Guards were situated on the Codford side of Heytesbury.

Whippet light tank in the ford, Codford 1938

The Tank workshops were in the Bury and Green Lane. At one time there may have been as many as 200 tanks in Codford, which were parked all along the Chitterne Road. Initially the tanks used for training were Covenanters, too lightly armed and armoured to be effective in battle. They also had a unique and confusing reverse steering system, a mixture of air pressure and epicyclic gear boxes. To turn left if accelerating, the left lever was used; if decelerating, the right. The result of this was that walls and hedgerows suffered as tank commanders going down hill pulled the left handle to turn left and found the tank veered to the right. Covenanter tanks and their crews, whose destination was the main road, so regularly found their way straight into the Milk Bar at the bottom of Chitterne Road that it became a standing joke in the Brigade HQ.

Among the Guards Armoured Division's distinguished visitors were Winston Churchill, King George VI, who came on 20th May 1942 and on 13th April 1943, the teenage Colonel of the Regiment, Princess Elizabeth [Queen Elizabeth II] on her first official engagement alone. She inspected the 4th Battalion Grenadier Guards at Codford, lunched at their mess and took tea at Stockton House.

In early 1943 the Guards Armoured Division was reduced to one Armoured Brigade, as the 6th Guards Independent Tank Brigade. In April re-equipped with Churchill tanks the Guards left Codford after eighteen months, exchanging the open spaces of Salisbury Plain for the wild Yorkshire Moors. Five weeks after D-Day the Guards Armoured Division landed in Normandy, followed a fortnight later by 6th Guards Brigade. This was the culmination of three years of intensive training, from the Wiltshire Plains and the Yorkshire Moors on to the European battlefields.

The Welsh Guards

A mong the Welsh Guardsmen posted to Codford during World War Two were men who had either made their mark or would go on to great things after the conflict. A future Director of the Bank of England, Hugh Kindersley, Lord Chamberlain and Chief Scout, Chips MacLean, and George Mann who was to captain England at cricket, were just some of the Guards officers at Codford. In early 1941 the Regiment boasted that it included two world-famous artists, three Oxford professors, a brilliant Welsh author, a well known film actor and a prominent racehorse trainer. One of the artists was certainly Rex Whistler, the actor possibly Anthony Bushell and the racehorse trainer Peter Cazalet. The author was probably Richard Llewellyn, a captain in the Welsh Guards whose most famous novel, written in 1939, was *How Green Was My Valley*.[2]

The Conservative statesman William Whitelaw, made a Viscount in 1983, was in 'S' Squadron 3rd Armoured Battalion Scots Guards. He joined the Guards Armoured Division in tanks and despite admitting to having limited mechanical ability, was appointed Technical Adjutant. His early tank training was in Codford Camp, during the winter of 1942/43.

Robert Runcie, later to become Archbishop of Canterbury, passed out of Sandhurst at the age of 21 as a Second Lieutenant and was posted to 3rd Battalion Scots Guards in November 1942. The Battalion was organised into four Squadrons; each Squadron had six troops, each troop three tanks with a crew of five. The three tanks in the troop were individually commanded by the troop corporal, the troop sergeant and the troop commander; Robert Runcie was the troop commander. In a private conversation many years later he remembered his time in Codford, recalling his tank hitting one of the village walls – a very common occurrence, especially in the Covenanter Cruiser tanks.

1st Northamptonshire Yeomanry

The 1st Northamptonshire Yeomanry arrived in the village in May 1943 to join the 42nd Armoured Brigade. The emphasis during the summer-long troop and squadron training and divisional exercises on Salisbury Plain was the importance of close artillery support. The parade ground was right next to St Mary's School, and the children would peer over the wall during playtime to watch the soldiers drilling.

The Yeomanry's time in Codford was very brief. In September after the 42nd Armoured Division was disbanded the Regiment moved to Gloucester to be re-equipped with Sherman tanks as part of the preparations for the invasion of Europe with the 33rd Armoured Brigade.

The American 3rd Armored Division

September 1943 saw the arrival of the American 3rd Armored Brigade, a heavy tank division with 16,000 men and more tanks than a regular outfit. The 3rd Armored were stationed within an area of less than 100 square miles, about 1,000 in the immediate Codford vicinity.

The Codford Camps were around Manor Farm, St Mary's Church and close to Codford Station. The GIs were mostly in Quonset huts, half-round corrugated iron structures approx 50-60 feet long, 8-10 feet high and between 16-20 feet wide with doors at each end. The huts had vents at the top and a few windows cut into the walls for ventilation, with oil- or wood-burning stoves for warmth. Twenty to twenty-four men at any one time bunked on cots 30 inches wide and 6 feet long. The officers were billeted in local homes or in smaller Nissen huts made of wood and covered with tarpaper. The officers' quarters were about 30-40 feet long, 8-10 feet wide and 8 feet high, they consisted of three small rooms and a bathroom, and were built close to the wall of St Peter's Church.

The Maintenance and Supply Battalions, the Battalion HQ and the gun park were behind St Peter's Church. The workshops of the tank and repair depot were where Bury Mead is today and the 32nd Armored Regiment was at Hillside. Stockton House was 3rd Armored Division Combat Command 'A'. The 45th Medical Battalion and Trains HQ Officers and men were quartered in the House, the enlisted men in the servant's quarters, and the medics, Train HQ's and non-enlisted men in Quonset huts in the grounds.

The ford, looking towards St Mary's church, World War Two

The Woolstore was a billet and mess hall, the USO Club canteen and recreation area, and the base of the American Red Cross. Malmpit Hill was one of several areas where unwanted supplies were dumped by the Yanks and liberated by the villagers.

The 3rd Armored Division left Codford between 16th and 19th June 1944 for Normandy, landing at Omaha Beach. Their first battle was at Villiers-Fossad on 29th June, their last fight was at Dessau on the Elbe River, 21st-23rd April 1945. They took part in many battles including the Battle of the Bulge in the Ardennes, 19th December 1944 – 16th January 1945. By the end of World War Two the 3rd Armored Division had 10,371 battle casualties with 2,214 killed in action. They had captured 76,720 prisoners, won five battle stars and made the greatest one-day advance in the history of mobile warfare – 101 miles, a record not broken until the Gulf War.

[Sources: [1] Plain Soldering by N.D.G. James (Hobnob Press) [2] Regimental Archivist, Welsh Guards; other material from Romy Wyeth, *Sterner Days: Codford during the Second World War,* and regimental histories]

Refugees From Les Îles Anglo-Normandes

Edith Chivers's father was an Alderney stoneworker; she was the eldest of fifteen children, having seven brothers and seven sisters. At the age of fourteen she went to live and work on her grandparents' farm after her grandmother suffered a stroke. In 1940 Edith was twenty, working a farm that was large by island standards, with eight cows; many farmers had only three or four. The family, including her widowed, invalid grandmother and Edith's fiancé Frank Le Cocq, a young farmer three years her senior, were among the 1,400 residents of the most northerly Channel Island of Alderney who left their native shores to an uncertain future on 23rd June 1940. Their tranquil island home, with its wildflowers and birds, three and a half miles long by one mile wide, came into the possession of the English monarchy in their capacity as Duke of Normandy almost a thousand years before. It was now under threat as the forces of the Third Reich swept through France towards the English Channel. Paris fell on June 14th, all too soon the German Panzers would be at the ports, with only seven miles of water between them and the first of Les Iles Anglo-Normandes: the French name for the Channel Islands.

The population of Alderney in 1940 was 1,432, living in 514 houses; there were 79 shops, 9 licensed premises and a fleapit of a cinema. The total livestock numbered 511 cattle, 362 pigs, 175 sheep, 41 horses and just 7 goats. Most of the cattle, just over half the horses and some pigs were relocated in Guernsey when the Island was evacuated, and the rest were either slaughtered or turned loose.

The Judge and the Procureur were Crown appointees, at the head of an independent court and legislature. Judge French posted the following notice eight days before the German occupation of the Islands:

I HAVE APPEALED TO THE ADMIRALTY FOR A SHIP TO EVACUATE US.
IF THE SHIP DOES NOT COME IT MEANS WE ARE CONSIDERED SAFE, IF THE SHIP COMES TIME WILL BE LIMITED.
YOU ARE ADVISED TO PACK ONE SUITCASE FOR EACH PERSON SO AS TO BE READY.
IF YOU HAVE INVALIDS IN YOUR HOUSE MAKE ARRANGEMENTS IN CONSULTATION WITH YOUR DOCTOR. ALL POSSIBLE NOTICE WILL BE GIVEN.
22nd JUNE 1940.
Judge French

The independence of the Channel Islands meant that young men were not eligible for conscription. Edith doesn't recall anyone volunteering for the services while living on Alderney, as most people were facing an uncertain future and closely watching events in Europe. There were a few troops training on the island but on 9th June 1940 they were removed out of harm's way to the mainland. Those islanders remaining would stand on their cliffs to watch the huge pall of dark smoke from the German advance bombing in the skies above Normandy. Before the embarkation the Luftwaffe had bombed the coastal lighthouses. The warning beacons that had safeguarded the ships for generations were now blinded and impotent, echoing the sense of foreboding, of awareness that time was running out, felt by those who could only await their fate and pray for deliverance.

On the peaceful Sunday morning of 23rd June the church bells pealed their grim defiance and their poignant farewell. Edith remembers that activities on the Sabbath were usually restricted to Sunday school, church and perhaps a gentle stroll. This Sunday would mark the mass exodus of the inhabitants aboard six 1,000-ton vessels.

One or two farmers refused to leave their animals. Much of the livestock had already been removed to Guernsey, and the farmers were to follow them. For the rest of the population the heartbreaking task of destroying their pets was now inevitable, many shot their dogs, while some turned their cats, caged birds, fowls and cattle loose hoping they might survive. Edith still remembers the horror of that last morning, with dead animals in the fields and in the outbuildings. The Chivers's farm had two strong young bulls, Brigadier and Rupert; unable to set potentially fierce animals at large, the bulls were shot in the stable. The Islanders gathered all the money they had, carrying their portable valuables with them, burying the rest in the hope they would be able to recover them after the war.

Edith arrived in Weymouth, where she remained for a few days, sleeping on straw bales and being fed by the WRVS. Edith's mother kept her three youngest children with her. The others, of school age, had been evacuated with their classmates to the home of Gracie Fields in Lancashire. Edith recalls that Mrs Chivers was less than anxious to have her children returned to her, and insisted they remain in the north of England either until they were old enough to seek employment or the war ended. The family were not to be reunited until the last week in 1945 – an estrangement that had lasted for almost six years.

Edith's group was taken by train to Glasgow. For many islanders this was their first train journey, as the only trains needed on such a small island as Alderney were used in the stone quarries. Frank, who had arrived in Weymouth on a different steamer, followed her on his arrival in Weymouth. He immediately set out for Scotland, where the couple were married as soon as the required three-week residency was established. Edith smilingly told a newspaper reporter that 'We may not be getting married at home but at least we have our own organist, from St Anne's Church, Alderney.' They were the first Alderney couple to marry after the evacuation. Frank's brother Nicholas acted as best man and his sister Harriet was the only bridesmaid. One sad note: Edith's grandmother died in Glasgow Infirmary on her wedding day.

While in Scotland the young couple were allocated to work for Farmer Lush of Codford. Harriet Le Cocq was working for another farmer, John Stratton of East Farm, as a domestic. It was a job she was happy in; however she confided that the most horrible thing she experienced while about her duties was finding old Johnnie's eye under the bed!

Edith's in-laws were living in Chitterne, and when she and Frank arrived in Codford they set out on foot to visit. They decided that they wanted to live close by and asked Mr Lush for permission to live in Chitterne, staying until 1941 and the birth of their first daughter Jean. Frank, Edith and their baby moved to 39 Cheapside into one of Mr Lush's farm cottages and this was where their second daughter Sheila was born, in 1943.

Edith found the Codford of 1941 very quiet, apart from the tanks. There were plenty of shops within the village. At the bottom of Church Lane was a shack with a thatched roof that leaked like a sieve, where the owner sold fresh vegetables. The Milk Bar at the bottom of Chitterne Road was a café, there was a paper-shop next to Vine cottage, run by the Stacey family, and Mr Chick sold provisions a little further on where the present Codford Stores is situated. There was a Post Office, a hairdresser, Doughty's shoe shop, Mr Pike the butcher, the Norris Bakery, Dewey's Hardware Store, Goodsall's clothes shop and Paul Cole's petrol station in the middle of the village along the High Street. At the St Peter's end of Codford at the top of the hill just beyond the Church on the opposite side of the road was where Mr Bee sold provisions, while on the site of the present New Road service station Mr Phelps had a sweet shop.

Social life for Edith consisted of a weekly outing to the whist drives, where there would be 12-14 tables in the YMCA hut, known locally as 'The Club' and run by Mr Dunbar. Sometimes the local soldiers organised good nights' entertainments there in the form of dances, which were very well attended. The local pub, *The George*, was a village focal point and popular with the troops. Edith was not averse to the odd gin and orange while catching up on the news and meeting her friends.

When the 3rd Armored Division arrived one of the American soldiers turned up one evening with a sack full of laundry to ask one of Edith's neighbours if she would do his washing. Soon Mrs Bray at 37, Mrs Ploughman at 38 and Edith at 39 Cheapside were all washing for the GIs. The soldiers would deliver tunics, shirts and socks, the women would wash the clothes, hang them around the fire over night and iron them the next day ready for collection. They seldom saw their customers, but the soldiers would leave money, tins of fruit and cigarettes as payment.

In 1945 the Le Cocqs reluctantly left Codford to return to Alderney, where their third daughter and only son were born. They worked on the family farm for sixteen years, returning to Codford in 1964. Frank and Edith worked for the Collins family at Manor Farm, living first in Ivy Cottages, then in the early 1970s moving into the newly built Anzac cottages in Green Road where they remained until 1984.

Edith Le Cocq, now a widow living in Cherry Orchard on the site of one of the World War Two camps, has recently celebrated her eightieth birthday.

[Sources: Edith Le Cocq; *The Alderney Story 1939-1949* compiled by Michael St. J. Packe and Maurice Dreyfus]

The First Casualty of War
Homer Bosworth

At 51 Charles Homer Bosworth was the first and the oldest local man to die in the Second World War. At the time he was living at 17 High Street with his wife Edith, who taught at Stockton School, and their three daughters, Doreen, Marion and Vera. Homer was born in 1888, serving in the Army during World War One, spending time in Russia when Britain went in to help the Czars during the Revolution. After World War One, when the Royal Flying Corps, the forerunner of the Royal Air Force, was formed he joined up, serving as a regular until his death in 1939.

During his service with the RAF the Bosworths, like many other service families, moved around regularly. In 1926 they accompanied Homer when he was posted to Aboukir in Egypt for three years. On their return to England the Bosworths settled briefly in Netheravon before moving to Codford. Homer was stationed at Old Sarum in 1929/30 transferring to *HMS Courageous* in either 1938 or 1939.

Homer Bosworth (third from left) in 1937 (Mr Chick – see page 126 – is on the left)

At the onset of World War Two Homer Bosworth had all but completed his twenty years of service and was about to retire. In his last letter to his daughter, Doreen Rafdal, dated 31st August 1939, Homer was hoping desperately that war would be averted. At this time he was a Flight Sergeant, not flying but in charge of the maintenance crew. According to the Ministry of Defence Air Historical Branch it appears that Flt.Sgt. Bosworth was among those RAF personnel seconded to the Royal Navy Fleet Air Arm to provide technical and other expertise in aircraft handling [ground duties]. There was a shortage of these skills in the Fleet Air Arm at the beginning of the war. Homer Bosworth was part of *HMS Courageous* ship's complement.

The *Courageous* was one of a class of only two ships (the other being the *Glorious*), and was originally built as a cruiser at the Armstrong Yard, Walker on Tyne. She was completed and commissioned on 4th November 1916. She was first a flagship of the Rear Admiral commanding 3rd Light Cruiser Squadron, then the Vice-Admiral commanding the light Cruiser Force. In her first months of service she completed her sea trials and on 17th November 1917 was engaged in the first naval battle of the Great War, the Heligoland Bight Operations, the object of which was to intercept enemy minesweepers. Her first salvo, just after 7.30 am, hit a minesweeper and set it on fire. Despite coming under heavy fire from German cruisers neither the Courageous or her sister ship the Glorious were hit. The British suffered just 33 casualties and no ships lost, the Germans lost approximately 1,000 sailors, three light cruisers and a destroyer plus three other cruisers crippled.

At the end of World War One the Courageous was allocated for service in Portsmouth Dockyard, remaining as Turret Drill and accommodation ship for boy seamen. In June 1924 the Courageous was taken in hand for conversion at Devonport Dockyard. Most of her original superstructure was removed and a flight deck 480 x 100 feet was fitted. In May she emerged as an aircraft carrier designed to carry 50 aircraft. In 1928 she sailed to service in the Mediterranean, and in 1929 transported officers and men of the 2nd Battalion South Staffordshire Regiment to Jaffa in Palestine where they were to restore order in an outbreak of inter-racial riots. After disembarking the military personnel and stores, the Courageous put out to sea where some of her aircraft were flown to be temporarily land-based at Gaza. She remained in the area until 5th September 1929. In October she sailed to the Dardanelles, proceeding on to Constantinople to take part in the first Royal Navy visit since 1923, when the last ship of the British Occupation, HMS Ceres, sailed for home. On 18-19th October the Courageous aircraft gave the first flying display ever seen by the people of Constantinople, who were greatly impressed.

The Courageous returned home in 1930 for further structural additions and alterations. She was in Lisbon in 1932, then cruised home waters until returning to the Mediterranean for aircrew training and the development of air equipment. She then served with the home Fleet, her service taking her to Copenhagen and Oslo in the years preceding the beginning of the global conflict. At the end of 1938 the Courageous was paid off and taken in hand for repairs and refit. She was recommissioned for further service on 31st July 1939, and joined the Channel Force at Portland.

At the outbreak of World War Two HMS Courageous formed part of the Naval Forces, which protected the route of the British Expeditionary Force to France. On Saturday 16th September 1939, she sailed from Plymouth for the Atlantic, escorted by four destroyers, to carry out offensive air operations against enemy submarines off the south-west coast of Ireland. In the late afternoon of 17th a message was intercepted indicating that an enemy submarine was attacking a merchant ship. Two of the escorting destroyers were despatched to assist aircraft flown off from Courageous.

At about 6pm unknown to those in Courageous, the German submarine U.29 was in the vicinity. Her commander had no previous warning of the close proximity of the carrier and it was with some surprise that he sighted her through his periscope. The Courageous with her two destroyers, proceeding on the standard zigzag course for protection against such risks, left U.29 no alternative but to follow patiently and await his opportunity. This was not to be until dusk. At about 7.45 pm the *Courageous* suddenly altered to a steady course into the wind to fly-on her returning aircraft. This action, and the absence of half her destroyer screen, placed this valuable ship in a vulnerable position, which Lieutenant Schuhart of U.29 exploited to the full.

At 7.50pm he fired three torpedoes at a range of less than 3000 yards, and two of them hit the *Courageous* on her port side, just abaft the bridge. She sank in fifteen minutes with the loss of her commanding officer, Captain W.T. Makeig-Jones RN, and 518 of her complement of 1,260 officers and men. The destroyers picked up the survivors and U.29 was vigorously hunted until midnight. The hunt was taken up by other destroyers and continued for two days after, but the U Boat escaped and returned safely to her base.

Just seventeen days after writing his last letter to his daughter, two weeks after War was declared, Flight Sergeant 237295 Homer Bosworth died in the Atlantic with his captain and 517 of his crewmates aboard the first aircraft carrier lost in the war. He is remembered with pride by his daughters, and on Panel 1, Runnymede Memorial, Egham, Surrey.

[Sources: The RAF Air Historical Branch, Ministry of Defence; Doreen Rafdal (née Bosworth); The Admiralty: Summary of Service H.M.S. Courageous.]

A Scots Guardsman's Memories of Codford, 1942

Lt. Col. Thomas Hyslop

The 3rd Battalion Scots Guards arrived at Tilshead on Salisbury Plain from London to form part of the new Guards Armoured Division for re-enforcement in North Africa in 1941. The Battalion settled into what became known as Airborne Camp, where it was visited by the then Queen Mary and her entourage.

After a few months, when vehicles and equipment were more plentiful, together with the 4th Grenadiers and the 1st Welsh Guards we moved to Codford 'B' Camp. The Grenadiers were in 'A' Camp, the Welsh Guards in the village. All tanks were parked along one side of the Codford–Chitterne Road, where maintenance bays and petrol points had been installed. After training the tanks were washed in the river ford before reaching the tank park. From our tanks to our accommodation we used the footpath across the meadow to 'B' camp, over the footbridge.

No. 4 Troop, Right Flank, 3rd (Armoured) Batallion, Scots Guards, 1942. Back row, from left: Guardsmen Clark, Watt, Billingham, Sgt. Tayne, Lt. J Elliot, L.Sgt. Hyslop, Guardsmen Gilchrist, Tait and Coulson. Front row, from left: Guardsmen Munn, Miller, Dobson, Small, L.Cpl. Garnet, Guardsmen Harris and Lees

A favourite destination on foot was the café by the pub in Chitterne for a fresh fried egg sandwich followed by cider if funds allowed. Weekend recreation transport ran from the camp to Bath, Salisbury and Devizes, where we enjoyed the company of the local talent.

Having now reached the rank of sergeant I was able to enjoy the Warrant Officers and Sergeants Hogmanay Ball in the gymnasium in 1942. Importing female partners from the ATS at Devizes, WRENS from Bath, nurses from local hospitals and WRAF helped a great occasion. All went well, with the CO and all officers joining in about 11pm, followed by Pipe Major and Master Cook as escort to the rum punch near midnight.

One of my duties was to return our ATS friends back to Devizes at 0200 hours. Counting the hats in the blacked-out coach appeared to tally with the required numbers. Only when I reached Devizes Road did I find five fellow sergeants in place of some ATS left behind – Happy Days!

During our stay at Codford the Grenadiers were visited by their then Colonel H.R.H. Princess Elizabeth [now Queen Elizabeth II]. Great preparation was made in the true Guards fashion – though some incidents blamed on the Scots Guards may best be forgotten! Even the red, white and blue ladder to climb on to the tank was a picture.

The Milk Bar in the village was many times damaged by tanks. No sooner had the engineers repaired it than another learner driver had a go! The proprietor used to stand across the road waiting for the inevitable.

We left Codford to make way for the Americans, changing tanks and our role.

Preparing for D Day we joined together with the 15th Scottish Division in the Yorkshire Dales.

Wounded and discharged in late 1944 I returned to Potterne to marry and settle down to normal post-war years. I retain a great affection for Codford and Wiltshire.

Codford Home Guard 1941

Front Row:

Percy Gurd, farm worker

Bill [Ginger] Chapman, railway worker

George Butt, gardener

Arthur Spiller, worked for butcher Larry Pike

Walt Conduit, farm worker

Maurice Furber, shepherd

Frank Phelps, farm worker

Middle Row:

Ted Snelgrove, worked for Norris the Baker

Bert Simper, owned the bike shop

Capt. Guy Woods, lived in Chitterne Road where Oxbarn is today

Sgt. David Blatch, barber

Capt Henry Wightwick, farm manager/ surveyor: lived in The Cottage

Edgar Snelgrove, bootmaker

Fred Cox, carter for Collins, Manor Farm

Albert Sheppard, odd job man/ gravedigger – father of Ben

Albert Doughty, builder/undertaker

Back Row:

Bert Ford, gardener for Colonel Sneyd

George Smith, worked for Dyer the coalman

Bill Gadsby, dairyman for Spareys of Milk Bar

Henry Veal, drove Wilts and Dorset bus

Stafford Veal, worked for butcher Larry Pike

Ben Sheppard, apprentice blacksmith at SuttonVeny. Died March 1944

Ron Sutton, worked for Sparey's

William Target, smallholder at Hillside, lived at Cleeve House

Michael Armstead, schoolmaster at Greenways School

Codford - a Wartime Memory
John Waite

L ike many of my generation who were young children at the outbreak of the
second world war, memories of our early years are often ones of great change
and upheaval, as fathers left home to join the services, and, as in our case, our
mothers moved around the country, sometimes to be near their husbands and
sometimes to find a refuge for the family from the growing threat of German bombers.

Although my brother Robert and I had been born in Exeter in the latter half
of the thirties, my mother had left the city after our father had joined the Army.
Initially we had moved to Plymouth to live with our grandparents in their large
terraced house a couple of miles from the town centre. It was not long before the
city, with it's dockyard, became a prime target for the Luftwaffe, and some of my
earliest memories are of nightly visits to the cramped, and somewhat damp, Anderson
shelter that my grandfather had constructed in the back yard of the house, and
which we also shared with the tenants of the flat on the ground floor. The nightly
routine of the trek to the shelter after the warning siren had sounded, the straining of
ears to hear the first drone of the approaching enemy bombers, and then hearing
the crack of the anti-aircraft guns throwing flak at the enemy planes as they reached
their target area, acquired, for me at four years of age, a strange but terrifying
'normality'.

In 1942, after some particularly ferocious raids on the city, our mother felt
that we would be safer moving to Codford, where my father's mother, our Gran
Waite, was working as a cook/housekeeper for Mrs Roney-Dougal, at The Rectory.
This stood, and indeed still stands, at the Codford St Mary's end of the village on
the corner facing the bridge over the Wylye.

Initially we lived at Middle Farm, owned in those days by a Mr and Mrs Lush,
and standing, as its name implies, beside the street in the centre of the St. Mary's
end of the village. If my memory serves me right we were in a ground floor flat,
possibly Mr and Mrs Lush lived upstairs in the same house.

I think one of my earliest memories of life in Codford was a personal
demonstration of milking a cow by hand, given to me by a friendly land-army girl
called Mary, who worked for Mr Lush. The milking parlour stood, if I remember, in
the field on the other side of the road opposite the farmhouse. It was whilst we were
at Middle Farm that I started my schooling at the Codford St Peter primary school.
The school, now long since closed and converted into a private house, stood on the
Warminster road leading out of the village, just before Ashton Gifford House. I
recall being a reluctant and tearful pupil during my first few days at the primary
school, and remember mother warning me not to let Sgt. Thomas, Codford's resident

policeman, hear me crying as we passed his house at the top end of the village. My mother told me in later years that this threat had the desired effect, and that I was silenced – at least in the vicinity of Sgt Thomas's residence!

Our mother worked for a while in the village post office, which was run at that time by a Mr and Mrs Parker. The military presence in Codford was growing rapidly by the time we arrived in the village, and this meant that the post office was a hive of activity. My mother told me that she well remembered serving the artist Rex Whistler, who was then a Guards officer stationed at Codford, and sending telegrams for him on several occasions. Sadly Rex Whistler was not to survive the war, losing his life during the early days of the Normandy invasion. My mother told me that she was invited, with Mr and Mrs Parker, to a function at the officers mess, and remembered that during the course of the evening, Rex Whistler was called upon to use his artistic skills to provide a sketch of the winning couple as a prize in the 'spot waltz' competition.

The presence of so many soldiers and so much military equipment in the village held an understandable fascination for two young brothers of our age, and this fascination was to prove somewhat painful for me during the early days of our stay. Our new-found friend, Gordon Norris, who was a few years older than my brother Robert and me, was the son of the village baker. On one of our first visits to the bakery we played with a canister of tear gas which Gordon had, somehow or other, acquired, and which I had managed to open, with dire consequences. Its contents got into my eyes and I was led home in anguish to have the noxious powder flushed from my eyes. Gordon, whom I recently spoke to for the first time since those days, reminded me of this incident which, strangely, I had almost forgotten, and told me that he has included some of the exploits that we got up to, when he recently wrote of his reminiscences of his Codford childhood. The painful incident with the tear gas did not, however, put me off revisiting Gordon at the bakery, for not only did he allow us to play with his rather splendid collection of toys, but I found the mouth-watering aroma of the newly baked bread from Mr Norris's ovens a great attraction. To this day I am instantly transported back in time to the wartime Codford bakery, whenever I smell freshly baked bread. It is strange how potent the power of the sense of smell is to return us, in memory, to the scenes of our childhood's first experiences.

I do remember, very shortly after we arrived in the village, exploring the river [the Chitterne Brook] that ran behind the Norris Bakery with Gordon and some of his friends. The wire I was standing on collapsed, pitching me into the water – and getting myself into, shallow water, but deep trouble with my mother when I arrived home soaking wet and covered in mud.

As I was only some six years of age my memories of life in the village of Codford in those wartime days are somewhat fragmentary, as childhood memories often are, but I can recall the 'mile of pennies' we helped to complete along the kerb of the village pavement during one of the village's efforts to raise money for a war-time good cause. I also remember a 'Meet the Army' day, when some of us children were given the immense treat of a ride up the village street from the Rectory in a tank. Peering through a periscope beside the driver as we rattled up the village street was a thrill I vividly recollect to this day.

On visits to my grandmother at the Old Rectory, my brother and I were sometimes allowed, as a special treat by Mrs Roney-Dougal, to play with the toys that had belonged to her two sons, by then both grown up and serving in the army. As our own collection of toys was a meagre one, to be able to assemble, and play with, a huge Hornby 'O' gauge train set in the attic of the old house, was, for me at least, an excitement beyond words. I remember once finding a set of skis at the rectory that had once belonged to the late Colonel Roney-Dougal, and wondering what on earth they could possibly be. Such exotic items were well outside the range of my experience, at that time.

Sometime in mid-1943 my mother took up a position as housekeeper for the Reverend Dr. Tupholm, and we left Codford to live in the 'Old Rectory' at Steeple Langford further down the Wylye Valley. Early the following year our mother's health broke down and she was hospitalised, leaving my brother and me to return to our grandmother's care in Codford. It was then that a place was found for me as a boarder at Greenways preparatory school, which then occupied Ashton Gifford House. My brother lived with our grandmother and, I believe, attended the Codford St Mary School at the lower end of the village.

At less than seven years of age when I first joined the school, I must have been one of the youngest pupils at Greenways at that time, and although I was only at the school for six months or so, I can clearly remember being somewhat in awe of the formidable school matron, who was inclined to apply the back of a hairbrush to the bottom of such pupils who did not toe her required line. I believe I suffered from her attentions at least once, for what misdemeanour I cannot now remember. I remember playing cricket for the first time on, what seemed to me then, the huge lawn in front of the school surrounded by massive trees.

I can also recall, on more than one occasion, clinging to the back of a delivery lorry with other pupils, as it sped up the school drive towards the Lodge, where we deftly dropped off, hoping that no member of the school staff had seen us. Boys would be boys, even, or especially, in wartime.

Looking back, my memories of Greenways are, on the whole, happy ones. My first experience of cricket played on the lawns between the great trees at the front of the schoolhouse, is something I still recall with pleasure. School walks, when parties of us boys marched, singing, down across the meadows and alongside the River Wylye, introduced me to the joys of country walking that remain with me to this day.

Other memories of wartime village life: . . . Eating, in 1942, a final ice-cream from Mr Fry's shop, at the Codford St Mary end of the village, before this luxury was withdrawn for the 'duration'. (It was to be three long years before I tasted another one.). . . . Having a milk shake, presumably *sans* ice cream, at the 'Milk Bar', in the main street on the corner of the Chitterne road. . . .The great searchlights up on the downs above the village sweeping the skies as the bombers passed over on their way to Bristol and beyond. Once, during break time in the playground at the Steeple Langford school, we saw a German fighter plane crash into fields up the valley near to Codford, and I remember being warned not to go looking for souvenirs in case the ammunition exploded. For once I believe we took notice and did not go searching for the wreckage.

Our association with Codford came to an end when our father, who had recently landed in Normandy on D-Day on the 6 June 1944, was allowed home from the front, shortly after the invasion, on a brief compassionate leave, to sort out more suitable living arrangements for the family whilst our mother was hospitalised. As a result of this, our grandmother left her employment with Mrs Roney-Dougal, and took us boys to a cottage in a remote Devon hamlet near Newton Abbot, to await the return of our mother and, as it turned out, the ending of the war in Europe a year later.

My memories of wartime Codford were certainly happy, and the rare occasions that I have revisited the village have been pleasant ones. But for my mother, the time we spent in the valley of the Wylye was one of stress and unhappiness. It was while we were there that the sad news of the death of her youngest brother reached us. Uncle Joe had been serving with the 1st SAS regiment in North Africa and was one of the first to land on Sicily in the initial invasion of Europe. His death at the age of twenty-three, at Termoli in southern Italy in the last SAS battle of the Italian campaign, was a blow which had contributed to the temporary breakdown of her health.

When I was last in the village, in the autumn of 1996, I was surprised to see Romy Wyeth's book on wartime days in the village on sale in the post office, and even more surprised to see that my brother Robert and I were briefly mentioned in the reminiscence of our old friend Gordon Norris, the baker's son. This was even more gratifying to me, for on my previous visit to Codford, some fifteen years earlier, I had not been able to find anyone with memories of the village during the war, and I admit that I had felt, on that occasion, rather like Rip van Winkle.

Although I spent only a relatively short period of my early life in Codford, it was a time when great events were taking place. The village of Codford, like so many in Southern England at that time, was full of soldiers, many of whom would shortly take part in the invasion of France that would eventually bring the war to its long awaited close. I will not forget my association with the village at such a momentous time in its long history.

6th Armoured

When the 6th Armoured left Codford in April 1943 the villagers were sad to see them go. The Guards had been extremely popular– according to Harry Cole they were the most popular troops to come to Codford in World War II. The Reverend

Meyrick who had billeted some of the officers at St Peter's Rectory obviously thought very highly of them. His letter to the various regiments has not survived, however the responses lend a footnote to the history of Codford and the Guards.

From: Brigadier G.L. Verney, M.V.O.
  Headquarters,
6th Guards Tank Brigade,
  Home Forces
Friday 16th April 1943

    Dear Mr Meyrick,
On behalf of all Ranks of the 6th Guards Tank Brigade, I write to thank you for the extremely kind letter which you have addressed to me as their Commander.

    We are indeed grateful for all the kindness which has been shown to us during the last 18 months. We could not have been in a more pleasant locality, and it is with real sorrow that we shall march out in a few days time.

    We hope that before long we may be engaged with the enemy. We shall always carry with us the memory of these happy days, and the hope that peace and prosperity may come to all our friends here.

    I would be grateful if you would kindly convey our thanks to the people of Codford and the neighbourhood, and our very best wishes for their future happiness.
Yours sincerely,
  G.Verney
Brigadier Comdg. 6:Gds. Tank Bde

3RD BATTN. SCOTS GUARDS
'B' Camp, Codford,
16th April 1943

    Dear Mr Meyrick,
Your very gracious letter of April 14th has brought considerable pleasure to all ranks of the Battalion under my command.

    Our stay in Codford has been a happy one for all of us and we shall leave here with the most friendly feeling towards Codford St Mary itself and all its inhabitants who have done so much to make our life here a pleasant one.

    On behalf of all ranks I thank you for everything you have done for us and your good wishes for the future.
Yours sincerely,
H K M Kindersley
Lieut.Colonel, Commanding, 3rd Tank Battalion Scots Guards.

4th Tank Bn. Grenadier Guards, Codford 'A' Camp
17th April 1943

Dear Sirs,
On behalf of myself and my Battalion I thank you very much indeed for your kind letter
and the nice things you have said in it. Our stay here has been made all the more pleasant
by the friendliness of the people of Codford. Troops are not always welcome and a letter
such as yours is all the more appreciated for that reason.

We are all very sorry indeed to leave this delightful part of England and do so with
many regrets and pleasant memories. Movements are inevitable in the Army but we
consider ourselves extremely lucky to have been stationed here for such a long time.

We thank you for your good wishes and on our part we wish Codford all good fortune
in the years to come.

I, for my part, hope that one day I shall again be able to visit Codford in the Wylye
Valley to which I have become very attached.
Yours sincerely,
H R Davies
Lieut-Colonel, Commanding, 4th (Tank) Bn, Grenadier Guards.

22 April 43
2nd Armoured Bn. Welsh Guards, Thetford, Norfolk.

Dear Mr Meyrick,
An extract from your letter to Brigadier Verney had already reached me so that your
personal one was a very real pleasure to receive.

We very much enjoyed our time at Codford which was made all the pleasanter by the
way in which you all accepted the overwhelming descent of a newly formed Guards
Armoured Brigade in your village and land!

Your kind messages, which I have been delighted to pass on to all ranks, are most
touching and we in our turn will not forget our stay in the Wylye Valley and all our friends
in Codford.

As, I suppose, a Commanding Officer should, I am intensely proud of my Battalion,
which I know to be militarily as good as I can make it; it is therefore all the more gratifying
to know that these soldiers are none the worse citizens through the training they have
had to receive.

May I assure you that Codford and its residents are often in our conversation and
constantly in our hearts.

May War quickly end so that we can all join together again in peaceful pursuits as
God intended us to do.
Yours sincerely,
 Douglas Greenacre
[Lieutenant-Colonel]

From Dunkirk to Chungkai
Percy Conduit

Percy F. Conduit was born on 8th May 1920, the oldest in a family of three boys and a girl. He worked for Mr Norris the Codford baker and was a member of the T.A. before the war began. He was always fascinated by radios and telephones, an interest which gravitated him towards the Signals Corps. He was part of the British Expeditionary Force who, in May/ June 1940 faced the might of the German Army with their backs to the sea at Dunkirk. Between 29th May and 2nd June he was one of the 224,585 British soldiers, together with 112,546 French and Belgian soldiers, who were evacuated over five nights in a flotilla of miscellaneous vessels.[1]

After a period of leave Signalman Percy Conduit 5569479 was posted to the Far East. When Singapore fell in February 1942 he was one of the 16,000 British soldiers [2] captured by the Japanese. Percy was sent to work up-country on the Thai–Burma Railway, and in early July 1943 he was evacuated to Chungkai Base Hospital suffering from a general debility resulting in chronic diarrhoea and dysentery. In a letter written on 21st October 1945 by a Lieutenant in the RSC to the Reverend Meyrick [3]

> This hospital consisted of 9,000 such officers and men, and supplies and staff were wholly insufficient to cope with them.

Percy Conduit

Percy was under observation for several weeks and the expected signs of avitaminosis [vitamin deficiency] appeared. He was admitted to a ward devoted to malnutrition patients, where he died in the early morning of 11th September 1943. The cause of death on the certificate, forwarded to the Royal Signals Records, Reading, from Rangoon, was given as Pellagra-Malnutrition.' [Pellagra is the result of a diet lacking vitamin C; symptoms of the disease are scaling of the skin, diarrhoea and mental disorder].

During his entire period in hospital he had been on what special diet they could supply and in addition extras from the R. Signals Sick Fund and anything else that I, or two or three men of my section could obtain. The medical officer stated that this could not be assimilated due to the terrible sloughing [loss of the lining] the digestive tract had undergone from dysentery.

I was with him daily throughout the entire period and he was thoroughly cheerful, though not I am afraid optimistic. It was difficult to be so under the conditions, for there were over 1,000 cases of malnutrition in the hospital and 530 of these died. His last three days were spent in partial coma and though I was present at the last night he was not conscious. His closest friend during captivity had unfortunately also died in mid-year 1944, but I feel I could add nothing further to the above. Personal belongings such as pay book, documents etc. were handed in to the Japanese Head Office and I doubt whether many will be distributed.

Throughout his service with me in the Malayan Campaign, Signalman Conduit was a cheerful and willing soldier fitting in with the small line-laying team [of which he was a part] to perfection. Though he was with me when we moved to Thailand as POWs we were split again and I did not see him 'til we both reached Chungkai, in the sad state described.

Please reiterate to his parents my profound sympathy at their bereavement, and accept my thanks for your helpful intermediation.

Percy Conduit's war had lasted almost four years, and his captivity nineteen months, when he died in Siam [present day Thailand] at the age of twenty-three. The manner of his death is perhaps the most poignant of the men who are remembered on the war memorial tablet in St Peter's Church. Three of the others died in the heat of battle, two in the comfort of Allied hospitals, and one in an accident. Far from the grey skies and green fields of his Salisbury Plain village, one of Codford's sons endured barbaric and inhumane treatment with courage and humour. Percy Conduit is buried in War Grave no.3, Row B, plot 4 of Chungkai Military Cemetery, North-West Bangkok, Burma Railway, Siam. Both his younger brothers are still living in Codford at the time of writing.

Sources:
[1] *Brassey's Battles* by John Laffin, 1995(London: Brassey's)
[2] Ibid.
[3] Personal family papers, Walt Conduit
Other details from Romy Wyeth, *Sterner Days: Codford during the Second World War*

Guarding the Railway Line
Percy Bundy

With the Home Guard we used to go on guard every two hours. We walked from Albany Bridge, down to the signal box at Codford Station, and back up again, that was our job. One night we was walking down one side of the railway line together, my argument was that while we were together anyone could drop in the back of us, both sides should be guarded.

This special night we was down beside our signal box when we heard someone coming. It got closer and I shouted 'Halt who goes there' and I never got no reply. I shouted three times! Then I said 'I've got one up the spout'– that's how we used to talk in them days, 'I've got one up the spout, I'm gonna drive 'em into you.' And this was Perc Harvey from over there, he said 'It's me, Perc' and when he got close to us, he was a sergeant in the Home Guard. I said 'My God Perc, you're lucky, I could'a shot you, that's what we're here for.' He was lucky, I would have shot one into him, we had rifles and ammunition!

A Country Girl's War
Doreen Cole's Story

The family patriarch, Harry Cole [born 1888] was a tall man, just under six feet tall, while his wife, Lillian, was a diminutive four foot ten and a half inches – their six children Paul [b. 1914], Doreen [b. 1916], Gwen [b. 1918], Godfrey [b. 1920], Christopher [b. 1921] and Maurice [b. 1927] were all relatively short. Harry and Lillian were both Londoners. Harry first came to Wiltshire as a civilian attached to the Army in World War One – working for London waterworks engineers the Candy Filter Company, building pumping stations for the military camps, one of which was opposite Codford Railway Station.

Harry moved from Stapleford to Codford in 1919 and began to breed Wessex Saddlebacks. His gilt, Codford Mayflower, won the Royal Bath and West Show at Romsey in 1922. He sold her for a staggering amount, 365 guineas – a record for gilt that was not beaten for thirty years. He bought the land he was renting in Codford with the proceeds and renamed it Mayflower Farm.

After World War One Harry ran a canteen for the troops. In the 1920s he organised a concert party in the Red Triangle Club, which was on the main roadside of the present New Road Service Station. Harry would go out singing and when Doreen was old enough she would accompany him on the piano. He would run fêtes regularly and eclectically, regardless of religion or politics.

This was a time when people in the general way were not as well educated as today, when the owners of the big houses run by servants seldom mixed with the *hoi polloi*, except at cricket. The wealthy householders even told villagers how to vote, and such was their power that no one dared do other than they were bid.

In 1927 the Coles bought their first wireless, a huge cumbersome set, bringing immediate news and popular music to the masses for the first time. From 1925, for more than half a century, Harry was writing Salisbury market reports for the Ministry of Agriculture and Fisheries. The reports were published nationally and in the local paper, and soon Harry was covering local news as well. He was also actively involved in local politics and amateur theatricals, ran the local football team, was the conductor for the Choral Society and a member of the exclusive reading circle, made up of all sections of rural society who were avid readers.

In the autumn of 1939 life changed dramatically. The Coles's safe, predictable world disappeared and an unknown future loomed on the horizon for all the young people. Paul, immediately returned from London where he had been working for MacFisheries, to help run the farm. Nineteen-year-old Godfrey and eighteen-year old Chris were both farming at home in Codford, Maurice the youngest was still at school. Godfrey joined the RAF Voluntary Reserve immediately, followed a year

Godfrey Cole

later by Chris; both men were aircraft engineers who served on Bomber and Fighter Command stations in England throughout the war.

Gwen was also in London, working for the Admiralty in the Civil Engineering Department. At the outbreak of war she was moved to the Battleship Department drawing office, her job was to trace the engineer's drawings so that the plans could be printed. In 1939 the Admiralty were evacuated to Bath, and this enabled Gwen to return to Codford at weekends to see her family. It was during a visit home that Gwen met her future husband Geoffrey Twist, who was a member of 260th Field Company Royal Engineers [43rd Wessex Division]. Geoffrey was one of the soldiers welcomed at Mayflower Farm who came to play billiards and snooker. Geoffrey was invalided out of the Army in 1940 after a motorcycle accident, when he was acting as a Despatch Rider on a new Norton belonging to the M.T. Sergeant. Riding along Green Lane towards the Chitterne Road, Geoffrey hit a succession of deep potholes, the result of constant use by tanks that tore up the surface of the lane, and came off the bike. He woke up the next day in Bath Royal United Hospital – his military career ended. He was working as an engineer at Corsham when he and Gwen married in 1942. They were living in Bath during the heavy bombing over two nights of the Bath blitz. At night Gwen would retreat to a dark cellar in use as an air-raid shelter. Her enduring memory of the Blitz is of the view from Widcombe Hill; Bath was in flames, with a thick pall of smoke across the sky. As she left for work in the morning at the neighbouring farm Mr Silcox the farmer was getting his cows in to milk, a peaceful rural picture against a backdrop of the devastated Georgian City below. She thought

how even in the midst of death and destruction normal life had to go on, and as a farmer's daughter she understood that the agricultural routine of tending the stock took no account of human suffering nor acts of war.

Doreen Cole was twenty-three and a teacher at Codford St Peter infants school when war broke out in 1939. Teachers were a reserved occupation and not subject to call up, but Doreen volunteered to help on the Home Front, as a helper at the YMCA and an air raid warden. The YMCA was initially in a dark wooden weatherboarded barn-like building, on the banks of the Chitterne Brook just before it joined the River Wylye. A rota of people prepared to help was drawn up, and volunteers served tea and coffee, and cooked bacon and eggs each evening.

Doreen Cole in her Air Raid Warden's uniform

YMCA, in about 1944

The first manager of the YMCA was an Australian caught in England and unable to return home because of the war. He courted and eventually married Eileen Lewis, the doctor's daughter. The next manager was Mr Daly, a mad Irishman with a flaming temper. One of the very well brought-up ladies, the product of an aristocratic upbringing and a finishing school, particularly irritated him. Doreen recalls that she would roll her sleeves up and muck in with the physical work, but was less well adapted to the practical everyday experience of giving change! Mr Daly would rail each time he saw one particular volunteer: 'Every time she's here she costs me so much money!'

Doreen worked throughout the war at the YMCA. The original weatherboard building was pulled down and a tin one erected where the Broadleaze houses are today. After the war it became the village hall and was commonly known as the Codford Club. The YMCA always had a large chalk and pastel picture of Montgomery, painted by one of the soldiers, hanging on the wall. Fairly early on in the war the shutters were painted with regimental badges.

The third manager of the YMCA was Mr Dunbar, a Scot with a hunchback who lodged with Mrs Fred Doughty at St Mary's end of the village. He was a small but feisty man who always stood up for the girls – woe betides any soldier who stepped out of line! He fell in love with Doreen, a fact she was unaware of until, alone one evening clearing up, he asked if she would consider marrying him. For once the young schoolteacher was almost lost for words, however she gently explained she couldn't marry without being in love, and she wasn't in love with him! Later Mrs Doughty told Doreen she knew he was going to propose.

The first troops into Codford early in October 1939 were the 260th Field Company Royal Engineers [43rd Wessex Division]. Their billets were in the Woolstore and the Stables at Greenways [Ashton Gifford House]. They slept on bare floorboards, and used the Woolstore as a mess hall, trestle tables and benches each seating eight men. The cookhouse was in a corrugated iron building behind the Woolstore with field kitchens nearby. The soldiers were local men recruited from Melksham, Chippenham, Trowbridge and Bradford-on-Avon. Some of them had been in Codford in 1937 working in the area of Codford Station. Geoffrey Twist was one of several men who married local girls.

In the early months of the conflict the Pioneer or Non-Combatant Corps were in a camp near Ivy cottages. Doreen and her family got to know one of the men well. Len Buckley was a staff photographer working for a Press Agency, Fox Photos, who was a gardener at Greenways school. In September 1942, Len's wife Beatty and their baby son Keith were in the village too. It was thanks to this friendship that there are photographs recording intimate family moments; during the war years film was not readily available.

Lillian Cole, Beatty Buckley and baby Keith. The Camp in the background is on the site of the present day Bury Mead. September 1942.

The first winter, 1939/40, was terribly bad. One ice storm coated the branches of trees an inch thick until they broke under the pressure, leaving the roads covered with three or four inches of broken ice. The weight of ice on telegraph wires brought down a pole, which fell on the bus bringing Doreen back from Salisbury from her music lesson. There was a panic among the passengers, but Doreen quickly took charge of the situation. Her main concern was for the bus driver, who was fortunately unscathed despite the pole having fallen on the front of the vehicle.

The Guards arrived in Codford in the autumn of 1941 when the weather was very wet. The High Street and Chitterne Road were covered in liquid mud, churned up by the tanks and other military vehicles, which splashed unfortunate pedestrians as they passed.

On her first official engagement, Princess Elizabeth, the present Queen, inspected the 4th Battalion at Codford. The Grenadier Guards were camped behind the Cole home, Mayflower Farm. This was a period when the Labour movement was on the rise, and certain ingrained attitudes were changing. Doreen remembers that the night before the visit the tank that the Princess was to see was cleaned and polished, the next morning it was discovered that someone had emptied a bucket full of excreta from the latrines and written, 'And this isn't bullshit either' on the tank. The tank was hastily cleaned again and the visit passed smoothly with few people any the wiser.

Major Houston, who lived in the Manor House, owned fields neighbouring the Cole family's Greenhill Farm [the old piggery]. Each landowner kept a bull in adjacent fields, and on one occasion the Cole bull got into Houston's field and the two animals fought, head to head, push and jostle, to the delight of the Guards who lined the fence to watch the action. Paul, Doreen's eldest brother, small of stature but game to the last, took a stout stick and went into the arena to separate the bulls, to the sound of indignant cries of 'Spoil sport' from the Guards.

Doreen volunteered as an Air Raid Warden, regularly going on parade with the Home Guard, taking part in their training exercises and learning to shoot a 2.2 rifle. Some Sunday mornings they would have a casualty exercise, with mock wounded laid out all over the village to be found and assessed. Parish Councillor Mr Bee, who owned the grocer's shop, was instrumental in organising training for the wardens. They would meet in the back room of the *George* and he would religiously read through the *War Conduct For Wardens*. Doreen always felt she would have preferred to have read the information herself rather than listening to the interminable long passages.

Small units of the Free French and the Belgians came to Codford intermittently, but the soldiers who made the biggest impact were the Americans. In September 1943 Doreen remembers her mother calling her, 'Come and look at these men!' They stood together on the veranda of the farm house facing New Road, and watched the GIs marching from the railway station, in a seemingly endless stream of humanity which came past the house for at least three hours. Like the Guards before them the American camps were all around Mayflower Farm. The American soldiers were much more hands on than the British troops had been, but they were still very well behaved despite the lack of streetlights. Doreen was only slightly bothered twice, even though there were thousands of soldiers inhabiting the very small settlement of Codford. There were black GIs in separate units but they were stationed elsewhere, at Teffont and Fovant.

Mayflower Farm, Christmas 1942

Inevitably, the Cole family came to know the group of soldiers in the hut just beyond the farm boundary. They would come into Mayflower Farm to socialise, but would always refuse refreshment with a polite, 'I wouldn't care for any ma-am.' Before arriving in England the GIs had been issued with a little red book that told them how to behave. As Britain was in the grip of rationing the etiquette book instructed the men not to eat anything in their host's house as it might be all the family had in the way of food. Doreen always told the men it was OK to accept, as living on a farm there was always something to be had – eggs or meat were easier to come by.

From 1939-45 Mayflower Farm was a small livestock farm producing food. There was no refrigeration; poultry and eggs in wooden boxes packed with straw were placed on the first steam train from Codford Station to Waterloo for the London markets. As well as poultry the farm contained 20 to 30 cows and 200 pigs. The cows needed to be milked twice a day; it took an hour on average to milk eight cows. When he began farming after World War One, in the 1920s, Harry Cole had collected swill from the Army Camps as far afield as Durrington. In the 1920s and '30s during the Depression he ran a feed mill on a siding at Codford Station. At the beginning of the World War Two Harry was managing the farm while his sons worked it. With Paul and Maurice the only boys at home until hostilities ceased, Harry continued to collect from the camps in the vicinity to feed his pigs.

Just before D-Day the Americans already in the village were moved into pup tents and their replacements were billeted in the recently vacated huts. They also had all their radios taken away so they would come into the farm to hear the 9 o'clock news every night. After D-Day when they were being shipped out without warning very early in the morning, some of the GIs came to say goodbye. Doreen was still in bed but her mother allowed the soldiers to go to her bedroom to bid her farewell.

After D-Day there was a feeling of anti-climax. There were still Italian prisoners of war around, and the Coles had two German POWs, Heinrich and Erik, working on the farm about six months before victory in Europe. At the end of the house was a room that had been used as a young men's club room for whist, billiards and darts in the 1930s. It was no longer in use so it was partitioned in one corner and made into a billet with beds, a table and chairs. The prisoners were not guarded; there was nowhere for them to escape to and they were not fluent in English. The POWs seldom met their fellow countrymen and Doreen felt sorry for their isolation. They had nothing to do when their work was finished. The world she lived in made its own entertainment, in which listening to the wireless, reading and doing jigsaw puzzles were regular evening activities. There were even puzzle libraries, the complicated many-pieced jigsaws were passed around to new devotees. Doreen collected some jigsaws together and offered them to one of the men. He looked at her with scorn, and coldly told her ' they were just for children!' After that she made no more attempts to communicate with either man. Maurice recalls that Erik was very aloof and arrogant but that Heinrich was a rather nice man.

Social events in the village were likely to be concerts, theatricals, whist drives and dances. During the war years the local girls would be picked up in army trucks with curtains to screen those on board, and taken to dances in various locations, including Wilton and Salisbury. After VE day there were parties of men clearing the camps so dances were a welcome distraction from the daily grind.

Among the units who at the end of hostilities had crossed Europe under Monty, and later forming an Army of Occupation in Germany, were the Poles. They returned to England in 1947/48 and were camped along Green Lane. The Polish Resettlement Corps needed someone to teach the troops English and asked Doreen to help. The pay was good. Doreen was a teacher earning perhaps between £7 and £8 a week, however 10/- in every £1 was taken in income tax, some of which was put in post-war credits.

It was now that she met Captain Wojciech Szeliga, a decorated and gallant Polish officer, who began to walk her home after class using the excuse that he wanted extra English practice. He eventually asked her to go to the pictures, and this was the beginning of a courtship that was to last about a year.

Wojciech Szeliga was born in the Tatra Mountains and trained as a regular Army Officer. He was the commander of the mortar platoon of the Artillery Support Company of 9 Rifles Battalion, which formed part of the 3rd Rifles Brigade which in turn formed part of the 1st Armoured Division. He served with the Polish Army in France in 1940 taking part in the French Campaign. Following the fall of France and the dispersal of the Division orders were given to make for the UK and rejoin the

Polish Army being formed there. Wojiech escaped to Czechoslovakia, into northern Italy, crossing southern (Vichy) France during Partition. As the Germans pushed southwards Wojciech, together with other Polish soldiers, crossed the Pyrenees on foot into Spain, where he was interned, possibly at Mirande del Ebro Camp, for about eighteen months. Having obtained false papers he was transferred to and then evacuated from Gibraltar and taken to Scotland where he joined a Polish unit.

After D-Day he was with the 9th Flanders Battalion of the Polish Armoured Division, fighting across northern France and into Holland, where the Battalion liberated Breda. He was awarded the French Croix de Guerre and the Polish Virtuiti Militari [the equivalent of the Polish VC.] His VM was won for action at Soignolles in August 1944 when he led a platoon under fire and despite heavy losses silenced the heavy artillery. The citation, roughly translated by Andrzej Suchcitz, the Keeper of the Archives at the Polish Institute and Sikorski Museum, reads:

> Wojciech Szeliga commander of a mortar platoon under fire from German artillery, mortar and machine-gun fire led effective fire by which he was instrumental in a critical moment to steady the situation. Through his outstanding example and greatest courage which was seen by the largest part of the Battalion he was responsible for giving heart to men and ultimate victory. One of the most beautiful heroic silhouettes of that battle. Despite large losses in his platoon he was always cheerful, he increased the effective fire and neutralised the enemy on hill 111 at a time when he had no supported fire.

At the end of the war the Polish soldiers were given various options. They could return home (an offer taken up mostly by married men), remain in Britain, or emigrate to Canada or Australia. Wojciech was a man of the mountains, he thought that the Canadian scenery and weather would be more familiar than the Australian environment. He didn't make the Canadian quota, but was accepted in the Australian quota early in 1950. He asked Doreen to marry him, and this time the proposal was from someone she loved, so she accepted and they were married in Australia.

Their two children Sylvia and David were born in Australia, returning to England with their mother in the early 1970s after Wojciech's death. Doreen settled in Durrington as a temporary measure, and thirty years on she is still in the village just across the Plain from her childhood home. At the time of writing her widowed sister Gwen has been a resident of Chippenham for almost sixty years, while her two surviving brothers, Godfrey and Maurice, still live in Codford.

[Sources: The Polish Institute and Sikorski Museum; Doreen Szeliga; Gwen Twist; Maurice Cole]

With the 'Dukes' at Anzio
Ben Sheppard

Albert Ben Sheppard was only twenty, the youngest of the local men who lost their lives in the Second World War. An apprentice blacksmith in Sutton Veny and a member of the Home Guard in 1942 he became private 14260269 in the 1st Battalion Duke of Wellington's Regiment (West Riding).

The Regimental Secretary Lieutenant Colonel T. J. Isles believes that: 'Given his age, and the fact that he was a member of the 1st Battalion, it is probable that he sailed from Africa to the Battalion in Italy in December 1943 and was launched onto the Anzio beachhead in January 1944. It was a period of fearsome fighting, and the Battalion suffered many casualties.'

The Regimental History takes up the story. 'By December the Allies had occupied Southern Italy and the battle front stretched from coast to coast, roughly in an east and west line north of Naples. The next objective was Rome, and the preparations were made to resume the offensive in January. This was to take the form of an amphibious scoop designed to land a large force south of Rome, at Anzio – combined with an advance on the main battle front. The Dukes were destined to play a great and glorious part in the operations of the Anzio beachhead. On 17th January the Dukes moved to Castellamare, where they embarked on the 19th in Land Craft Infantries (L.C.I.s) and Land Ship Tanks (L.S.T.s) for the operations at Anzio. Moving out in line ahead with barrage balloons as far as the eye could see, Capri fell astern at noon on 21st; the Fifth Army front was passed during the night of 21st/22nd, intermittent flashes telling of the watchfulness of friend/and foe.'

Eyewitness descriptions tell of a lovely morning and a vast Armada of assorted craft; 36,000 men and 3,000 vehicles were landed from 253 ships. The following day three battalions of the Brigade marched into the environs of Anzio, past handsome villas, bright little farms and plentiful trees.

On 28th January the 3rd Brigade was briefed for an attack on Campoleone station. In the order of battle the 1st and 2nd Battalions Duke of Wellington's Regiment were positioned left for the attack, which was launched on the night of 29th/30th. The fighting was fierce and prolonged, heavy shelling and mortar attacks on the battalion positions continued, and by the 4th February the main Anzio–Albano road was controlled by an enemy armoured division. The Dukes were in close proximity to Panther and Tiger tanks, fighting every step of the way. It was not until the night of 15th February that the Battalion was relieved and was able to retire to reorganise, refit and rest, but the respite was short lived. By 6.30 am the following morning the second German offensive was launched with great ferocity. During the last five days of the month in appalling conditions and constant rain, the Dukes were grimly holding on to positions in the wadis.

The Allied breakout began on 23rd May and Rome was eventually entered on 4th June. After four months of fighting the Allied casualties were 21,000, while unreliable German casualty figures were estimated at around 11,000.

At some stage during the hell that was Anzio, while pulling a dead friend from a machine gun, Ben was wounded in the shoulder. He was sent back to England aboard ship, but during the voyage his wound turned gangrenous and he died on 11th March 1944 in Cambridge Military Hospital, Aldershot. He was buried in St Mary's Churchyard, Codford, with full military honours.

[Sources: Regimental Secretary Lieutenant Colonel T. J. Isles; *The History of the Duke of Wellington's Regiment.*]

Ben Sheppard

'Ben'

In Wiltshire, ancient hamlet, lived many friendly men
One whom I will remember a blacksmith, known as Ben
He struck the anvil all day long, with efficiency and skill
The clang of iron on iron re-echoed o'er the hill.

The sweat ran down his youthful brow, his cheek and down his chin
But still he worked midst dust and heat and never did give in
He struck the shoes and links of chain his pattern and design
The lengths of iron and bits of steel, stacked away in line.

He worked all day never to pause, vibration in his bone
And though he toiled and hammer clanged, his heart was still at home
A future lay before him, he had visions of a bride
The hammering ceased and Ben stood still, the anvil at his side.

A premonition on swift wing was racing in his brain
Had his years as smithy been wasted all in vain?

He heard the sound of hurrying men, the third day of September
His smile was gone, his jaw was set I know he will remember.
   The Drums of War were beating, he braced his wide set shoulders
He knew the darkening days had come, a smithy, No, a soldier,
But time went by, the War went on, and Ben continued working
He had a duty still to do, a Home Guard and no shirking.
   Conscription speeded in our land, the rate of men had soared
And Ben received his papers, he had a medical board
He stood before the Doctor, examining had began
And before his senses came to him he was classified A1
   His heart was beating faster now he's waiting for his call
When he would leave his loved ones, a breaking, what a fall
He bade farewell to Mum and Dad and paused outside the gate
His brain was muffled, Home was his all, but now it was too late.
   Incidents had happened, a bus ride then a train
But thinking what his duty was, he knew 'twas not in vain
To Colchester he travelled and met men on the way
The Barracks known as Goojerat, that's where he had to stay.
   The 20th August, and the year was '42
Ben was now a Soldier, he learned now what to do
But two days later, being browned off, a lovely girl he'd seen
And Ben could not forget her, he called her My Moreen.
   Well days had passed and in due course, he met this lovely girl
But Ben was slightly bashful, his head was in a whirl
They met on different days and dates, and friendship grew more close
Her heart was opened up to him, like petals on a rose.
   At last the day had dawned, when he really had to go
To Burnham-on-Crouch for why, well no one's yet to know
A short stay in that place and once more he flees
To a town in North England called Stockton-on-Tees.
   It's true it was a short way out of this lovely town
But being from his Lady, made poor Ben fret and frown
Letters he wrote, when he had a chance
Writing of past times, pictures, walks and a dance.
   A blow came in August, it hit him oh, so hard
To play ones hand freely, to be trumped by one card
The card of calling him overseas
No one can rebuke, he's down on his knees.
   Like flashes of lighting, the days swiftly sped by
Time marches on, you can hear the war-cry
The train to the docks, the ship at the berth
Ben's heart sank more deeply, 'twas like nothing on earth.
   One foot on dear England, one foot on the plank

To drag it from the homeland, his heart ne'er sank
He faced it as the ship tugged at the ropes
He faced it with courage, new life and great hopes.
          Though distance divides you Moreen and Ben
You still live with each other by thoughts and by pen
The things that you think of, the letters you write
The future before you, 'tis already in sight.
          Now I must close as night closes the day
One word about Ben that's all I will say
A friend and a comrade through thick and through thin
He's not like the 'Ities' he never give in.
          Moreen you've a man you can look on with pride
He'll depend and protect you, always at your side
To Ben's Mum and Dad, you deserve what is due
Your Son is a Pal, straight, honest and true.
          Last words that are spoken as true as can be
I write as I know him you can take it from me
Here's to Ben's people can you hear my call
Good-bye and Good-luck, God Bless you all.

George Lanning

          This poem, written by a pal of Ben's, was given to me by one of Ben's best friends, Ron Sutton. Together with Walt Conduit and Arthur Spiller the four Codford youths were inseparable before the War split them up. When Ben died Ron and Arthur were two of his pallbearers, and the poem was printed on a card and given to each man. It was at his funeral that Arthur Spiller met Ben's sweetheart, Moreen. When Arthur was conscripted he was also sent to Colchester, and while stationed there he courted and eventually married Moreen. At the time of writing both Ron and Walt are still living in Codford.

The Sheppards of Chitterne Road

Ben Sheppard's life in Codford is recalled by Derek Williams, a year his junior, whose memories of the village date from the time he was eight years old, when his mother's eldest sister Ellen became Albert Sheppard's second wife. The couple married in 1932 and from this time, during the summer holidays throughout the thirties, Derek with one or other of his siblings, cycled from Salisbury to spend several weeks at a time at no 45 Chitterne Road. The day war was declared Ben and Derek were together at no 45, and they switched on the wireless to listen to the sombre announcement – Ben was fifteen years old.

Ben's home was converted from an 1850s racing stable with a hayloft to two cottages in the 1860s. Albert bought the two houses, one of which he rented out, for £100 in the 1920s and when Ellen moved about 1959/60 it was sold for £500. It was the semi-detached stone cottage with a thatched roof closest to the Chitterne Road, consisting of a kitchen, living room and three bedrooms. There was no electricity, and light was provided by oil lamps and candles. Water came from a pump in the kitchen and cooking was done on a primus stove or the living room fire. There were a tin bath and copper in the tin shed outside. In order to bathe, water from the pump in the kitchen was carried through the living room to the copper, then the fire would be lit beneath it. The outbuilding doubled as the only toilet, a home made wooden seat over a bucket, which was emptied once a week on the allotment that adjoined the house.

There was always a 12-bore shotgun in the corner of the living room, which no-one but Albert ever touched, and in the woodshed at the bottom of the garden were two vicious ferrets. Albert would go on to the Punchbowl and shoot rabbits, keeping some for the pot and selling the rest for 6d each. Financially things were very tight in the thirties, the family living off rabbit stew, rabbit pie and home grown vegetables. As boys Ben and Derek would go to the orchard (the site of Apple Orchard today), beside the Chitterne Brook at the bottom of Chitterne Road to scrump apples. They also played football with Walt Conduit, Ron Sutton and Arthur Spiller, two of whom are still living in Codford in 2002.

It was a daily ritual for the boys to go to the shops to buy bits and pieces. Farmer Sparey had a milk round and the International Stores called on Tuesdays and delivered on Thursdays. Derek remembers that the delivery man for the International Stores had a penchant for young boys and was always asking them to come out with him.

Ben loved the cinema. He would go to Warminster cinema on a Sunday night and catch the 10.30 pm bus home. He would also cycle into Salisbury and go to all three cinemas in a day, having seen at least six films. Derek recalls that on one of their outings Ben got chatting to a girl, who lived at Wilton, and took her home, only to turn up at Derek's house in Salisbury at 1 am to ask for company cycling back to Codford.

Albert Sheppard's octogenarian father was knocked down and killed in a traffic accident towards the end of the war, and his eldest son, a policeman in Plymouth, was killed in an air raid.

Albert was a staunch supporter of St Mary's church. For many years a bell ringer and a sidesman, he also tended the War Graves Cemetery. His association with the church came to an abrupt end when a member of the War Graves Commission saw him tending the graveyard and commented on the splendid job he was doing and asked if they were paying him enough. A figure was quoted and Albert realised that he was only getting a small proportion of the funds allocated;

the church was retaining the rest. From that time on he ceased his religious activities and refused to be buried in St Mary's churchyard – when he died in the late 1950s he was buried in the War Graves cemetery he had tended with such loving care.

Two Little Girls, the Nit Nurse and a Pink Hairbrush

C athy Fry was born in 1937 while her family were living at French Horn cottages. The Frys moved when she was two years old to number 5 Council Houses in New Road. Her memories begin at about five, a small girl living in the midst of a Wiltshire village turned into an enormous military encampment during wartime. For family outings Mr Fry had a motorcycle and sidecar, his wife rode pillion and the four children of his second family were all fitted into the sidecar. Her father worked as a coach driver for Mr Couchman the local carrier, and later for the REEME. Her mother utilised the family copper and flat iron to supplement the family income by taking in American Officers' washing.

Cathy Fry (sitting on father's lap)

Cathy remembers being taken with her brother in an old pushchair by their mother behind St Peter's Church, where Gracie Fields was entertaining the troops. They could hear her singing but only see Miss Fields's bright blonde hair in the distance. She also remembers going to the Woolstore, watching films starring Joe E. Brown.

For a young child with an imagination the black-outs were a very worrying occurrence, especially when the Air Raid Warden came to check there was no chink of light to guide the Luftwaffe to the camps. She was even more afraid when she heard the bombers going over, undoubtedly sensing her parents' silent apprehension.

On one occasion the children at St Peter's School were the recipients of Red Cross Parcels, a great excitement. Cathy says,

> My parcel had flannels and soap inside, but my friend had a doll with hair, I was very disappointed with what I had. When I went to play with my friend at Anzac Farm I combed her doll's hair and it all came off! We all used to go to Star Brigade at the Old Chapel, boys and girls together, we played games and things!

The Fry family home had four bedrooms, so it was inevitable that they would take in evacuees. The children had separate bedrooms, the two boys sharing a bed in one room, Cathy and her sister Stella sleeping together in another. When their half-sister Joan came home on leave from the ATS she slept at the bottom of the girls' bed. Cathy thinks her parents may have given up their room to evacuees, but if so, she can't remember where they slept. One lady was from Scotland. She lived in the small bedroom with her tiny baby. Another woman, Mrs Wright, came from up North and had a large family. The house was crammed full of people, and sometimes the crowded conditions, either at home or at school, led to that dreaded infestation. . . NITS! The nits took a liking to young Cathy's head, and she has memories of being taken out of class to see the 'nit nurse'. On one occasion she was marched off by her mother to have her hair cut very short. She still shudders as she recalls that the hairdresser may have used his clippers! Mr Fry, like many people of the time, was shamed by 'nits', believing them to stigmatise the family as 'dirty.' His wife was afraid to tell him about Cathy's nits, so she waited until they were on a train journey to Bristol Zoo to break the news.

Just over the brow of the hill from the Council houses opposite the old pig farm to the north of New Road there was a huge lorry park. Cathy remembers seeing Montgomery standing on the top of a Bren Gun Carrier chatting to the troops.

A Royal visit stands out from Cathy's wartime childhood days. She says that while at St Peter's School the children were taken to the Green Lane/Green Road junction with the New Road. They made daisy chains as they awaited the open-topped vehicle to travel along New Road taking Queen Elizabeth on her way to lunch at Stockton House. She has a vivid recollection of the Queen Consort dressed in a powder-blue outfit which matched her eyes.

It was really the American troops who made a lasting impression on Cathy, as their camps were behind the council houses on the hillside. The children would see them stripped to the waist, shaving and washing, and sometimes they heard them swearing as well. The GIs were so smart and so exotic, they used Nivea Cream [perhaps for shaving – Cathy recalls seeing the tins around!] and they made a fuss of the children, often taking her two brothers, aged 5 and 8, with them into the mess for meals. One day they took Cathy too, her enduring memory is of the delicious chocolate pudding in tins she tasted that day. At one end of the Woolstore the Americans had a NAAFI where they cooked doughnuts with holes in the middle – unlike anything Cathy had tasted before. She wasn't that keen on the doughnuts but was fascinated by the holes!

One of the soldiers gave Mr Fry a comic book with Sad Sack as the hero. Cathy was intrigued by the ladies with huge breasts adorning the pages, she had never seen their like in English comics!

There were tanks everywhere, parked in front of the council houses, all along the local roads. The children would watch the Americans taking their tanks through the water-proofing pool, and on one very special day Cathy and some of her friends were given a ride inside the belly of a monster tank. They were taken up the Chitterne Road for about a mile and then back. Cathy found it exciting and frightening in equal measure.

In June 1944 the Americans left Codford, and Cathy was very sad to see them go. The GIs had been in pup tents, so close to the ground and so small that it was difficult to see how they could accommodate the soldiers. With the Normandy Invasion in the offing and then a reality men were limited as to what they could take with them into battle. They discarded equipment and food on to the dump at Malmpit Hill and handed out personal possessions to the local people. One GI left with one of the Fry boys a beautiful blue butterfly in a glass case, which he had bought as a gift for either his mother or girlfriend.

Two of Cathy's half-brothers were in the midst of the fighting. John was with the Desert Rats, while Jack was a Paratrooper who had parachuted into Arnhem and been captured. He spent the remainder of the War in a German Prison Camp having originally been reported 'missing believed killed'. Jack had received a shrapnel wound in the neck that was tended and sutured by a German doctor. Cathy can still visualise her beloved elder brother walking down the road after the war.

Another little girl was living with her mother Rhona and her maternal grandmother, Martha Salter, three miles away in Chitterne, at 75 Shrewton Road. Sue Wilson's father Jack was away during the war serving in the Royal Artillery, spending some of the time stationed close by at Larkhill. He would hide his motorbike in the barn on his surreptitious forays home after dark!

Sue's earliest memories are from about the age of four. She remembers that it was just getting dark when she went to visit her auntie down the road, leaving the door open and the lamp lit [there was no electricity!]. She heard the enemy planes drone above her in the darkened sky and the sirens shrilling their urgent warning as the searchlights arced and circled overhead. She also recalls receiving a smack on the backside for not observing the blackout regulations.

Sue Wilson aged three, with her parents Jack and Rhona, and her paternal grandmother May Wilson

At the edge of the village on the road to Codford was a crater-filled field known as 'bomb field.' The Luftwaffe would offload their bombs after their sorties to the ports and the industries of south-west England, Bristol being a regular target.

Sue travelled to Codford on Mr Couchman's bus en route to Salisbury, past the Punchbowl with its complement of tanks and soldiers. Chitterne was also full of soldiers, and when the Americans came Sue says that they were camped in the Chitterne Lodge/ Townsend area on the Tilshead Road, and the local children would stop and salute as they marched by. Sue's grandmother used to threaten her that a 'black man would get her' when she was naughty. The first time she saw a coloured GI on duty she was terrified that the moment of reckoning had come!

The American troops were known to give nylons to the girls they dated, and the children received bananas, cakes, sweets and chewing gum, unheard of and exotic luxuries! Some GIs would throw packets of condoms out of their trucks to the children, who were universally delighted with their 'balloons' and would put them in their mouths and blow them up. Their female relations were less impressed. Sue's grandmother snatched her treasure away when she saw what it was.

Rural children roamed far and wide, but the barns were not just used for childish or agricultural pursuits – illicit romantic dalliance thrived in the hay-filled isolated buildings. Sue recalls seeing one of the ladies from down the road enjoying a sexual encounter with a GI. As the soldier got up a young Sue saw an erect penis for the first time, a sight, which she says, she can still see now! When she heard that one of the local women was 'up the pole' she was unaware that the term referred to pregnancy. Thinking it must be an interesting condition, women climbing telegraph poles, she repeated the phase publicly. The result was a close encounter with a pink hairbrush – something else that she never forgot.

The Italian prisoners of war had tents at the edge of the village on the road to Tilshead while they were working and sandbagging the water-cut. They were cheerful and friendly, especially with the children, and would make rings from three-penny pieces for the girls. Sue was forbidden to have anything to do with them; her uncle had been killed in Italy.

At the end of the war Sue's father returned home. Her earliest recollection of him is of a strange man picking her up and of her tears of fright! Her father left the Army to work for the railways, and the family moved into a house by the crossing in Station Road, Codford.

[Sources: Cathy Lock and Sue Poolman.]

Spearhead

In 1974 Robert M. Stevens, the editor of the United States Army's 3rd Armored Division newspaper, *Spearhead*, was planning to write a series of articles to commemorate the thirtieth anniversary of the division's entry into the combat in World War Two. He wrote to. 'The Honorable Mayor, Codford, Wiltshire, England' asking if there was anyone still living in the village who had any personal reminiscences of the period between autumn 1943 and June 1944 when the 32nd Armored Regiment, an element of the 3rd Armored Division, was stationed in

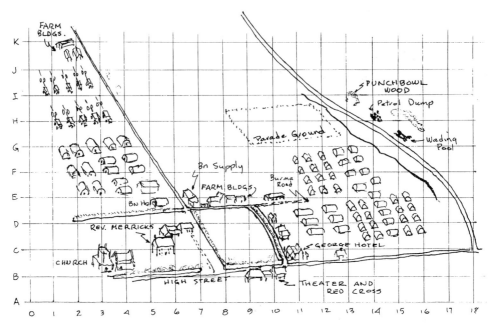

Sketch of 3rd Armored Division sites

Codford. The letter was passed to eighty-six year old Harry Cole who had lived in Codford for sixty years and had a clear recollection of those turbulent times. This was his reply.

I might say in passing that they were not the first American troops to have been stationed here. This village has twice during two world wars been completely occupied by military forces, and at the end of 1914-18 conflict there were small detachments of American troops passing through here, as Codford was a transit camp.

However the American Armored Division was the first to arrive in 1943 during the 1939-45 war. They followed the 6th Armored Brigade and the 11th Armored Division, and it is quite safe to say that everyone was most impressed by the number and size of mechanised vehicles. The enormous transport vehicles with their teams of drivers and the mechanisation of everything appertaining to war, which could be mechanised, was an education in modern warfare.

The men too seemed built on the same scale. Those that came here seemed to have come from the country towns and the quiet places, homesteads and farms. Softly spoken, happy, kindly natured men who missed their homes and loved to sit in the houses and homes of the village people and smoke their endless cigarettes and cigars, and just talk of their Pops and Moms. Delightful companions they were, just as we had met them in books and it brought home to us that not all Americans did come from New York or were Chicago gangsters. They made many friends and we were impressed by the fact that they were very proud of their British ancestry – where they had any.

It must be made clear that the village had nothing to do with the training or anything else appertaining to these men, although we extended our hospitality and were pleased to welcome them in our homes.

A large American Club was set up for their use in the Wool Store – a large building formerly used for a wool sorting business in the 19th century, in which they had social gatherings of all sorts. They gave the schoolchildren a wonderful Christmas Party, as they, at any rate, had no rationing problems.

It was during their stay that a visiting E.N.S.A. party gave a performance in the large repair hangar, which was situated in the Manor House paddock, and the programme included Gracie Fields.

I had the pleasure of playing contract bridge with a group of officers billeted in the Manor House and they were very good players. Mrs Moneypenny, who was the wife of one of them, became a good friend of our family. We wrote to some of the friends and relations of these Americans and kept in touch with them for some time after the war was ended.

The Division left in 1944 and was succeeded by a different type of man entirely. They were not from any Armored Brigade and came from a different background. This was illustrated by a comment I frequently heard from them. I had a full-sized billiard table, which they used to play on. They did not understand billiards too well, being pool players, and I occasionally heard the phase 'too much English,' following a shot. I was puzzled by this, and then it dawned on me: 'too much side'.

During their stay here many of the Americans slept in pup tents and it was an odd sight to see a field covered by these small tents. Their Headquarters were at Stockton House, a fine Elizabethan Manor in Stockton Park, built by John Topp in the early 17th century. Stockton Park adjoins Codford.

Several local girls married GIs and went to live in America, their children having since visited their relations here, so there is a tangible link with the U.S.A. forged out of war. Neither the men of that time or their cartons of cigarettes will be forgotten here for many years.

A Tattered Dollar Bill

It was Christmas Day in Codford and the year was 1943. Ten young American soldiers, boyhood pals from Wisconsin, gathered together, perhaps for the last time. They came from Port Washington, a city about 20 miles north of Milwaukee on the Lake Michigan shoreline (population in 2002 – 10,467). The soldiers were assigned to various units of the 3rd Armored Division, one of the élite Corps of the U.S. Army, stationed in England to prepare for the invasion of Europe. The 32nd Armored Regiment, the Maintenance Battalion and the Supplies Battalion were based in Codford; Combat 'A' Command, the 45th Medical Battalion and Trains Headquarters were close by, at Stockton House.

The 3rd Armored Division had arrived in the village in September 1943. as noted earlier, the 32nd Armored Division were at Hillside, while the Battalion HQ, Maintenance and Supply Battalions, and the gun park were behind St Peter's Church and Rectory, with the tank and repair depot sited where Bury Mead is today. The Maintenance and Supply Battalions used Cherry Orchard Camp [also known as Woolstore Camp,] other campsites were on Manor Farm, with a firing range at the Punchbowl. There were billets in the Woolstore, which also housed the Mess Hall, the USO Club and the American Red Cross.

One of the GIs, Ralph Ansay, pulled out a dollar bill. He wrote 'Codford, England, Dec. 25, 1943,' and the note was passed round and all the soldiers signed it. Ralph Ansay put the dollar bill back in his wallet and carried it throughout the war. The 3rd Armored Division left Codford between 16th and 19th June 1944. They were to Spearhead the US 1st Army from Omaha Beach to the Elbe River, winning five battle stars, and at the end of the war they had 10,371 battle casualties.

Jim Stingl of the *Milwaukee Journal Sentinel* takes up the story in December 2001, almost six decades after that last Christmas before the Normandy Invasion.

> The dollar bill is carried by Ralph Ansay for the rest of the war. He brings it home to Wisconsin and eventually puts it in a frame and hangs it on the panelled wall of his

Ten GIs from Wisconsin, Christmas Day 1943

basement room. During a rummage sale at his house, an unscrupulous shopper walks away with the war memento. 'Someone took that dollar bill, stole it from me at least 30 or 40 years ago,' Ansay says. He felt pretty sure he would never see it again.

Four or five years ago, a Pewaukee woman named Mary Miles is at the Bradley Center to see a Bucks game. She steps up to the concession stand to get a hot dog and a beer and then returns to her seat with the refreshments and her change. She notices that one of the bills looks tired and tattered around the edges. There are 14 glue marks on the back, suggesting the bill had been in a frame or a photo album.

The tattered dollar bill, about 2001

It's a 1935 silver certificate, serial number B51237373C, on of those old dollars you almost never see in circulation any more. And its signed by ten soldiers. Many of the names are hard to read. The clearest is Charles W. Wolf, just to the right of George Washington's face. You can make out Smiley Sceper and Sgt. Richard F. Husting. And one name looks like Sgt. Tony Dickman. Printed neatly at the top of the bill in the same black ink is this: Codford, England Dec. 25, 1943.

Mary, who is 41 and works in marketing for an insurance company immediately starts to wonder about these men. She's not sure whether to picture them in a bar over there or a bunker. She can feel their loneliness so far from home on a holiday, but she can also sense the camaraderie of being together and a part of history.

The mystery gets hold of her. How did the bill get back in circulation? Did an old soldier die and have his belongings scattered and, in this case, spent? How could she find at least one of these 10 guys?

She calls the Department of Veterans Affairs and asks around at an American Legion post. She surfs the military sites on the Internet. Many of the names are hard to read exactly. For all she knows they're dead by now or living many miles away. Nobody seems to be able to help her. 'We have no way of determining from the records in our custody the names of military personnel assigned to a particular locale or even military installation. Regret we cannot assist you in this matter,' says one typical e- mail.

Last week she brings the bill to me, hoping that an article would lead to some answers. The Christmas season had her thinking about these soldiers again. 'I really have no interest in this except to find its rightful owner and get it back in the hands of someone who really cares about it,' she says.

Charles Wolf (83), Mary Miles and Ralph Ansay (82), Christmas 2001

Using an Internet search service called AutoTrackXP, I find a listing for a Richard F. Husting and for a Charles W. Wolf. They both list Port Washington. When I call I get Husting's grandson. He says his grandfather is deceased. He's not sure if he was in World War Two.

When I dial Charles W. Wolf, he answers yes three times when I ask him if he served in the war, if he was in England in December of 1943 and more specifically if he was in Codford, a little village south-west of London. I tell him that a dollar bill he signed back then has been found. 'I could tell you most of the guys who signed it,' he tells me. Then he starts to recite the names on the bill. 'Most of them are dead already,' he says, but all of them survived the war and came home to raise families and take jobs. He says somewhere he has a copy of a photo of the 10 men the same day the bill was signed.

Charles, 83, thinks that Ralph Ansay is still alive and calls him. 'This is unbelievable!' Ralph tells his old friend when he hears about the bill. He tells him about the day he and his wife had the rummage sale at their home near 84th and Center streets in Milwaukee and made the mistake of allowing people to enter the basement to look at items for sale.

The bill, which was absolutely not for sale, had been hanging on the wall for only weeks or at most a couple of months when it was stolen. Ralph still lives in that house and even now he thinks about the bill whenever he looks at the spot on the wall where it hung.

Ralph, now 82, has a clear memory of pulling out the dollar on that Christmas Day 58 years ago and passing it to his buddies. I said 'Why don't we all sign it and I'll keep it as a souvenir.'

On Friday, Ralph comes to visit Charles at his home in Port Washington. They have not seen each other since the day they signed the bill. Mary Miles, whose honesty and curiosity made this day possible, stops by, too. She hands the dollar to the two men. Other family members snap pictures and preserve the moment on videotape.

No one can believe it's been found, and everyone wonders where it was for all the lost years until it landed in Mary's hand. Ralph says he plans to reframe the bill, but no more rummage sales.

Everyone looks at the picture of the 10 young men in their dress uniforms. Every name is recited: Wolf and Ansay, Sceper and Husting and Dickman. Clarence Bartelt, Gerald Ziehr, Arnold Bach, John Kranz and William Karasch.

Then Ralph takes out a crisp dollar bill. He signs it then Charles signs it. They hand it to Mary. For them, this will be a Christmas, much like the one in 1943, that will never be forgotten.

It is amazing how circumstances and connections coincide and things seem to happen at exactly the right time. In January 2002, while I was writing this book, I received a phone call from Bimp Simpkins of Chippenham. He had been corresponding with an American lady from Wisconsin, helping her with her genealogy. She had seen the story of the Codford Dollar bill that went AWOL for decades in the *Milwaukee Journal Sentinel*, and realising that the story originated in Wiltshire she sent a photocopy to Bimp. Bimp Simpkins belongs to the

Chippenham History Society, and by coincidence he read in his society's magazine that I was speaking to the Warminster History Society in February, my subject 'Codford During Two World Wars.' Like all good historians he wanted to share the story, so he contacted the secretary for my phone number and asked if I was interested.

I contacted the newspaper reporter Jim Stingl, who willingly gave permission for me to use his story and gave me the phone numbers for Ralph Ansay and Charles Wolf, I phoned them both. Ralph, recovering from recent surgery, was sitting at the kitchen table, looking through his photos when I called. This is what he told me:

> We left the United States early in September 1943 and docked at Liverpool for transfer to Codford. We were part of a VERY LARGE convoy.
>
> My girlfriend, Jane, [now my wife] saved every letter I wrote during the war. Hoping those from Codford would reveal many stories, I have now read them all. But to no avail – they were censored. Therefore, those letters were 'love letters' at most. We couldn't even mention we were stationed in Codford. I did mention cities I visited on pass or official duty: London, Bournemouth, Salisbury, Bristol, Exeter, Edinburgh and Loch Lomond.
>
> I usually stayed at the American Red Cross facilities while on pass. I met Cissie Porter, a W.A.A.F., aged 19, of London in Bournemouth. I don't recall how or where we met, there being a blackout. We met again on a second visit. We saw a movie and walked about town chatting until she had to return to her quarters. She told me of her experiences during the London bombings.
>
> Codford must be a very small community. I recently acquired an AAA map and Codford isn't on it. Stonehenge is shown so I have a fair idea of where we were stationed. While in the Codford area, the 32nd Armored Regiment, 3rd Armored Division, lived in Quonset huts. Each hut housed 17 soldiers. We had wooden bunks with metal strips and a straw mattress and pillow. We used four blankets and jackets to keep warm.
>
> I was Personnel Sgt. Major of the 32nd Armored Regiment. Our office was in a building. We maintained the Service Records of all the soldiers in the 32nd Armored. Each company had a company clerk – must have been well over twenty clerks in all including a mail clerk. We also had two commissioned officers in charge of the Personnel Office.
>
> In April/May 1944 we were moved out of the Quonset huts into 'Pup Tents' for two. We had straw on the ground and two blankets. The army was growing. New arrivals now occupied the Quonset huts. The Personnel Office eventually moved into two-and-a-half-ton trucks. Then came June 6, D-Day. Our Division moved to Bournemouth and eventually Omaha Beach.
>
> I entered military service on June 16, 1941, and was assigned to Co. F, 32nd Armored Regiment, 3rd Armored Division, as Company clerk. Some time later I was transferred to HQ Company and designated to be the Personnel Sgt. Major. After VE Day, the time arrived that I had enough points to be returned to the United States. I was discharged on September 17, 1945, and married Jane on October 24, 1945.

One GI
and Two Little Kids

The American was McNamara. The children were Joey and Kenny Brian. Their friendship grew in the midst of war during the months of May and June 1944 in Codford. McNamara had landed with the American Forces in Scotland in January 1944, and the troops were taken to Frome in Somerset by train and billeted at Marston Bigot. In May they shipped to Codford for about a month. McNamara writing home tells the story:

> There are two little kids who live across the street from the camp. We're great pals. They're Joey and Kenny Brian. Joey is seven and Kenny is six. Gee, are they cute! Joey reminds me an awful lot of Billy. Same colour hair, and curly just like Billy's. We have a great time. They love me to twist them around and give them piggybacks. They come in the camp and the fellows give them money, gum and candy. They're swell kids.
>
> The other day Kenny made me take him for a walk down through the fields, across the brook, down the road, and, through town to the camp again. Now he's always after me to go walking with him. He's always wearing black rubber boots just like Billy. Every time he sees me coming, he runs to me and I take him up in my arms. I love to play with them. They're a lot of fun.
>
> Well, I'll have to close now, and get to bed, as I have K.P. in the morning. That means rolling out at 5am. I'll feel just like it too.

Sometime in June McNamara moved to Tidworth, then across the Channel from Southampton, landing at Omaha Beach on June 17th. He marched inland, joining up the next day with 747th Tank Battalion and being assigned as an assistant driver. The Allied advance from the Normandy beachheads had been halted between Caen and Lessay. The U.S. First and Third Armies were involved in the Saint Lo breakout, code named Operation Cobra, which took place between 25th July and 8th August 1944.

McNamara was with the 747th Tank Battalion from the battle of St Lo until he was wounded when his tank was knocked out on 21st November in Germany while trying to reach the Ruhr River. He was eventually sent back to England, remaining there until he shipped back to America in December 1945.

More than fifty-five years later, writing from Millville, Massachusetts, McNamara recalled, ' Having spent so much time in England, I developed a deep love for that beautiful country and a great respect for the English people. I was always treated with such courtesy everywhere I went.'

First Ashore on D-Day
Guy Westley

From Argentina to Codford and on to the D-Day beachhead, Guy Napier Westley was born at Hayward's Heath in Sussex on 5th October 1919. His father William was a Buenos Aires businessman, an Englishman who had moved to the Argentine with his wife Lillian. The couple had four sons, Barry, Guy, David and Ivor, all born in England and schooled at Gresham's School, Holt in Norfolk. Guy entered Gresham's in 1933 and a year later became friends with Arthur Meyrick, the son of the Rector of St Peter's Church in Codford. Arthur remembers:

> I first met the Westleys in 1934. The eldest brother Barry, was 17 and having left Gresham's was about to start his career in Buenos Aires, where he became a businessman of considerable importance. Guy, about 15 [I think] was at Gresham's and David, 13 was about to start there. The youngest, Ivor, about nine, was returning to Buenos Aires with his mother and eldest brother. Guy and David spent their holidays with us in Codford.

Guy was a popular and attractive young man, full of enthusiasm for life, described by Arthur Meyrick as, 'the sort of straightforward Englishman who was totally honest and would never let anyone down.' He spent his holidays in the Meyrick's home at St Peter's Rectory, where he enjoyed playing tennis, socialising and the rural lifestyle. Guy left Gresham's in 1936 and returned to Buenos Aires to begin life as a dairy farmer. When war broke out he returned home, enlisted in the Black Watch embodied in the Territorial Army on 20th August 1940, and was posted to Infantry Training Centre. Shortly after his 21st birthday, on 12th January 1941 Guy was posted to 163rd officer Cadet Training Unit. He was discharged on 28th March, and the next day appointed an Emergency Commission as 2nd. Lt. P/180302 the York and Lancaster regiment and posted to Infantry Training Centre. Four months later, on 24th August 1941 he was posted to Infantry Base Depot, a month later he received a posting to 1 Palestine Company, The Buffs. Their strength between February and December was 6 Officers and 164 other ranks, and they came under HQ Lydda Area and were based at Sarafand in an internal security role. When Guy arrived in September of 1941 they were in Tel Aviv before moving on to Haifa in November. In February 1942 the 1st Palestine Company, The Buffs moved to Athlit, and then to Khiryiat in August still in a security role.

On 1st March 1942 Guy was attached to the Middle East Mechanics School for 27 days. He was promoted to Lieutenant on 29th October 1942 and on 23rd December the 1st Palestine Company was redesignated 'A' Company, 16th Battalion Palestine Regiment, on the formation of this new regiment. Guy appears to have been posted to no.3 Company of the Buffs, designated 'C' Company of the new regiment at this time. This company was at Haifa in January, moving to El Mansura for training purposes in April 1943. He joined the 1st Batt. Hampshire Regiment on 3rd June 1943, and was posted to the Transit Camp on 23rd July that same year.

His overseas service was in the Middle East Force from 24th August 1941– 29th July 1943, Sicily from 30th July 1943 – 8th October 1943, North Africa from 9th October 1943 – 20th November 1943 and North West Europe from 31st May 1944, to his death on the morning of 6th June 1944.

The 1st Battalion of the Royal Hampshire Regiment to which Guy was assigned on 3rd June 1943 successfully completed two D-Day assault landings that year, Sicily in July and Italy in September. Guy's record shows that he arrived in Sicily on 30th July, too late to take part in the Sicily landing. His battalion was part of the 8th Army landing on the west coast of Italy at Porto San Venere near Pizzo. When the 1st

Guy Westley

Battalion returned to Britain on 18th October 1943 after a twenty-three year absence Guy was not with them; nine days earlier he is listed as being in North Africa. The Royal Hampshire Regimental Archivist, Lieutenant Colonel John Darroch is of the opinion that Guy was a medical evacuee, either sick or wounded, and was sent to the nearest medical facilities to the Front. Casualties from Italy were invariably hospitalised in North Africa.

Guy Westley spent from 20th November 1943 until the end of May 1944 in Britain. The 1st Battalion were at Long Melford near Sudbury, then Southwold in Suffolk. In February 1944 they were stationed at Cadlands Camp near Fawley in Hampshire, at Inverary for training and rehearsal for the Second Front, returning to the West Country for a brief period in the New Forest (Lyndhurst/ Beaulieu) before returning to Cadlands Camp prior to the Invasion. On 24th May the camps were sealed, the men embarked for the Normandy beachheads from Southampton on 31st May 1944 and anchored off the Isle of Wight.

On 3rd June 1944 Guy wrote to Mr and Mrs Meyrick from aboard ship:

In exactly 12 hours from now we shall be rushing for our objectives on the coast of France, and while I write our ship is rounding the Needles off the Isle of Wight and as I want to get on deck and watch Old England fade away in the distance this letter must needs be brief. Today we have been very busy and this afternoon we received messages from Generals Eisenhower, Montgomery, and our Divisional Commander General Graham, then later the ship's captain gave us a farewell good wish: and I mustn't forget the Brigadier who came on board this morning and asked us as he has often mentioned before to go in with Dash and Determination, the convoy commander who was with him bade us God speed also, so we have had a good share of farewells and although none of us is particularly enthusiastic about going into another battle, we look forward to getting a move on so that the war will be finished the sooner. I hope this finds all at Codford well and in good spirits, and Emily too. I found 10 clothing coupons which I once promised to give to Mr Meyrick if I had no use for them so here they are. The fact is however that were we on dry land I shall immediately push off and buy a pair of drawers as my Batman packed my valise and sent it off leaving me a thick pair of winter drawers to wear which can hardly be worn in this weather. You might let me know where it was Ken and Arthur stayed when they went to France we may pass that way someday.

Love and best wishes to you all – Guy

At 6.30 pm on June 5th the convoy sailed down the Solent and out to sea past the Needles. Guy Westley and the Royal Hampshire Regiment were about to take part in the greatest amphibious operation the world had ever known. They were part of the 231st Brigade and were to spearhead the assault force on Gold Beach between Le Hamel and Arromanches. The assault convoy anchored in a choppy sea, seven miles off the Normandy beachhead at 5.30 am on 6th June. The men were soaking wet and many were seasick by the time they landed. The Hampshires were the first regiment on Gold Beach that morning, A Company leading the attack.

On D-Day Guy Westley was the Battalion Assistant Unit Landing Officer, whose tasks with his Pioneers was to land with the Assault Rifle Companies on Jig Green Beach (Gold Beach West) to the east of Le Hamel. Its many tasks included the direction of Reserve Companies and other troops coming ashore to 'cleared' exits taped by the Royal Engineers. Another responsibility was collecting and dumping vital weapons, ammunition and stores at beach exits, for the Asnelles area. Most troops landing that Wednesday morning were concentrating on getting off the beach. For Guy the job was to ensure a swift, safe passage for incoming waves of men, while he remained on the beach under heavy fire. There were 182 members of the Royal Hampshire Regiment killed on D-Day, and of these five were officers. Sometime during the morning of 6th June 1944, in the first hours of 'The Longest Day,' 25-year-old Lieutenant Guy Westley died on Jig Green Beach.

After Guy's death, Mrs Meyrick received the following letter, dated 26th July 1944, from Captain Thomas of the Hampshire Regiment.

I am glad that you wrote me as Guy is one of the very few people I can give any information about, and even that is second hand.

As you probably know Guy was the Battalion Pioneer Officer. We were an assault battalion in the landing, and his job was to help supervise the clearing up of the beaches as soon as we landed. The assault troops had to carry ashore mortar bombs and gas capes and dump them on the beach. Guy was in my assault landing craft, which was the first to reach the shore with several others. He, with a small party of pioneers, followed us out as soon as the boat reached the shore.

The Germans went to ground when the preliminary bombardment was on, and their defences were so deep that the bombardment had little effect. As soon as we started to land the bombardment stopped and the Germans started to appear again. I, as first out of the boat, was lucky to be able to get to the top of the beach before the Germans started their defensive fire. Those following behind, however, came under very heavy mortar and machine gun fire. From the time I left the boat I never saw Guy again and was told later he had been killed. I cannot say whether he was killed coming ashore or later, but as his job entailed staying on the beach he would have been under fire for several hours until the German positions were cleaned up.

I would like to say how very sorry I am not to be able to give you better news. Guy was a great chap and one of the most hard-working officers in the Battalion. There was an enormous amount for him to do before D-Day and he did it with efficiency and zeal which I do not think many people appreciated fully, as he was the last person to complain or say a word in his own favour. His troops would do anything for him and he had made his specialist platoon as good at their job as any in the Army.

If there is anything else I can do for Guy do let me know and I will certainly do anything I can.

Guy was awarded the 1939-45 Africa Star, Italy Star, France and Germany Star, Defence Medal and the War Medal 1939-45. He is buried at Ryes War Grave Cemetery, Bazenville, France in plot 4, Row E, grave 2.

In 1995 when I was researching the World War Two casualties listed in St Peter's Church for my book *Sterner Days – Codford During the Second World War*, I wrote to the York and Lancaster Regiment for information about Guy. Mr D.W. Scott, Keeper [Militaria] at Rotherham Department of Libraries, Museum and Arts responded. He had been at the 50th Anniversary of D-Day landings in Normandy in 1994, and by coincidence had been in Ryes War Grave Cemetery, and come upon Guy's grave. He wrote:

> The photograph of this officer's grave at Ryes, was all that was held in the archives to say he existed. There is no mention of him in the official history, so your donation will become the archive record of this man. I am pleased that he 'turned up again' so to speak, as he was a bit of a mystery last year when we 'discovered' the grave at Ryes. The mystery of course was the date of death, as no York and Lancaster units arrived in Normandy until D-Day + 4. So this officer had to have been operating with some other unit. Your information solved the puzzle and added more besides. You have, in effect, brought him home.

[Sources: Arthur Meyrick; David Westley; Commonwealth War Graves Commission; Ministry of Defence; Archivist for the Royal Hampshire Regiment Lieut.Col.[Retd.] C.D. Darroch DL; Gresham's School Register; Field Return of Officers, No 1 Coy Palestine Buffs, September 1941]

A Sapper on Sword Beach

Bert Doughty was born in 1916 while his parents were living at 7 Riverside in Codford. The family lived next door to George and Eliza Simper, who had lost a son serving in the 12th Battalion King's Royal Rifle Corps in the Great War. Bert's father told him that when the young rifleman left home he went out to bid him farewell. The soldier shook his hand and said, 'I won't be coming back!' He was to die somewhere in Belgian Flanders on 13th February 1916. A.F. Simper is one of ten local men remembered in St Mary's Church and one of 65,000 soldiers commemorated on the Menin Gate, whose bodies were never recovered from the battlefields of the Ypres Salient.

From the age of fourteen Bert worked with his father who was the local builder and undertaker. He joined the Royal Engineers in Salisbury the day after war was declared, going to France in early October 1939, with the 18th Field Park Company R.E., as one of the sappers whose main tasks were building bridges and clearing mines. Remarkably unaffected by the task of dealing with mines, Bert told me that he was trained to de-fuse them, the worse thing he remembers about the task was the fear that the mines would be booby trapped!

When, on 10th May 1940, the Germans invaded Belgium, Luxembourg and northern France, Bert was at home on leave. Hurriedly recalled to France, at the time of the Dunkirk evacuation with the British Expeditionary Force cut off with their backs to the sea, Bert was in Le Mans. In June 1940, after Dunkirk, his unit travelled by rail in cattle trucks to Cherbourg before setting sail across the English Channel.

Bert Doughty

On returning to the U.K. the unit spent three days in Cheshire, then entrained to Codford, where Bert re-mustered as a Sapper and was transferred to 17th Field Company. He was billeted almost on the doorstep of the Doughty Riverside home, so was able to visit his parents most days, but happily slept out, as the weather was particularly fine. The Company were at Stockton House for a week, then under canvas in a field by St Mary's Church. After three weeks the 17th Field Company was sent to the South Coast near Folkestone as part of the First Line Defence for the expected invasion. The Company remained in the area and around the South Coast locations from Dover to Weymouth for most of 1940-1. Bert takes up his story:

In 1942 we went to Scotland to train for the landings. We trained with the Navy at Invergordon, at Inverary and at the Battle school at Moffat. Most of the exercises were using live ammunition. In 1943 we were to embark for North Africa for the landing on Sicily, I remember coming home on embarkation leave and being taken ill. On Sunday morning my father went to the Guards H.Q. at Stockton House and the Medical Officer came to see me. I was taken to Bapton House where I stayed for the whole of my leave. On my return we were told that the Canadian Division was to take our place.

We continued training in Scotland until May 1944 when we returned south to a location outside Waterlooville to await the Second Front. After travelling down from Scotland we were in a sealed camp, with troops with fixed bayonets to keep us in. The three weeks we were there we had two lectures a day telling us in code where we were landing and studying a mock-up of the area showing the beach, the surrounding hills and countryside.

I went to Normandy on D-Day with my unit landing on Sword Beach as part of the 185 Brigade, 3rd British Division. Although a sapper I was also a relief driver. Three weeks before on our way from Scotland to the embarkation point, one of the drivers broke his leg in a motorcycle accident so I had to take his truck.

On 5th June 1944, the night before D-Day, we boarded a transport landing craft at Gosport, landing about 10.30 am the next morning. The lorry was loaded with 4 ton of explosives, the platoon's greatcoats plus one blanket for each man, and a Despatch Rider with his motorcycle. As we were the only ones from our Company on this L.C.T. [Landing Craft Tank] I was given a sealed envelope not to be opened until we had sailed with instructions where to go and what to do on landing. Just before dark the Captain held a short service with prayers, which everyone on board attended. After we sailed I laid down in the back of the lorry on the blankets and went to sleep.

When I awoke the next morning I could clearly see the French Coast with H.M.S. Ramelies close to us, firing broadsides into the shore defences. This must have been what woke me from a very deep sleep! We had had a good crossing but nearing the coast things hotted up with our naval guns firing inland and artillery fire from the shore. As we came in towards the beach our L.C.T. was one of three in line abreast. We were all keyed up to get ashore, but the shelling from shore batteries and 88 Artillery guns became very heavy with shells dropping in the sea on either side of us. We were fairly close to shore when all three craft turned about and went back out to sea. In a very short time we turned to try again; although the shells were still coming over it was not as intense as before.

As we came in we hit the beach with quite a thud, the ramp went down, first off was the M.P.s jeep and trailer. They stalled on the ramp so we turned it over the side of the ramp into the water. We all had our engines running by this time, I believe I was about the fifth vehicle off – as I descended the ramp I went into four feet of water which came right up into the cab and over my feet. I was in four-wheel drive and low gear so it was quite easy to travel up the beach on to dry sand. There was so much equipment on the shore that vehicles were queuing to get off the beach. I was very relieved to get away after about half an hour of stopping and starting before we were able to get on the road.

I had read my instructions and turned left along the coast road. Having travelled a short distance the shelling became intense again. We took shelter by the side of a tank which had been knocked out earlier. We soon got going again, and at the next crossroads we turned left and proceeded to our destination – the bridge at Benouville. I had a large notice on the front of the lorry which read 'Bridging / Priority' so had right of way over most other lorries. Having reached about halfway we were stopped by our old Sergeant Major who had been transferred to one of the other Companies in the Division. He said we couldn't go on, as there was a pillbox which hadn't been cleared about 100 yards from the road on the right. Also wanting to get to Benouville was an Officer and half a dozen paratroopers who had been dropped miles from their target. They were desperate to get to Benouville and said if I were willing they would ride with me and give what protection they could with their small arms. The Officer got into the cab with me and mounted a Bren gun in the notch for that purpose on the top of the cab. The Sergeant-Major gave us permission to travel at our own risk so I got up as much speed as possible, I don't think we were fired on at all although with the noise of the engine I probably wouldn't have heard it anyway! We arrived in Benouville by nightfall and I met up with 17th Company RE who were awaiting instructions before starting the bridge building. Our orders were if the enemy had blown up the bridge we were to build another. In the event the bridge was only partially damaged, but our tanks were not allowed to use it. In two days we had built our own bridge across the Caen canal.

Our M.T. Sgt. came and told me our billet area was in an orchard close to where I had parked. As I was the first vehicle he said I had better back in, in case there were hidden mines. I'm sure with my load of explosives it wouldn't have mattered which way I went in! At about 9 o'clock a glider pilot came in the orchard and asked if I had a shovel. I gave him a small one, he just took the turf off where his hip would be and laid down to sleep having said he would be back in England in the morning. He also told me he had landed in Sicily, so, thinking he must know what he was doing, I copied him and lay down for the night, as we couldn't break out of the bridgehead.

We were there for sometime and each day we were subjected to intense shelling, after a few days I had a trench about 3 feet 6 inches deep to shelter in. The next few weeks we spent east of the Orne River supporting the 6th Airbourne around Benouville and laying mines at the perimeter of the bridgehead as protection against counter-attacks.

The bridges at Benouville and Ranville were the first Allied objective on D-Day. They were about 400 metres apart, crossing the waterways which ran from Caen to the sea at Ouistreham, and were the key to troop and supply movements from the landing areas. They needed to be captured intact before the German Army had time to detonate the explosives, which were known to be in place to facilitate speedy detonation. At Benouville the bridge crossed the Caen Canal, and it was captured by the paratroops, whose shoulder flash is the mythological winged horse, Pegasus. The bridge was renamed Pegasus Bridge as a tribute to the red berets who secured and held both bridges; the second one at Ranville was the Orne River crossing.

The first troops into Normandy as part of Operation Overlord came by air. Towed by RAF Halifax bombers six fragile Horsa gliders were released over Cabourg, landing just after midnight on the 6th June. They carried D Company, 2nd Battalion, the Oxfordshire and Buckinghamshire Light Infantry. The enemy were taken totally by surprise and within ten minutes the bridges were safe in British hands, with an Allied loss of two dead and fourteen wounded. The Germans counter-attacked through Benouville, but D Company held fast until the 7th Parachute Battalion who had been part of a huge parachute drop at 12.10 am reinforced them. Within two hours the 7th Paras were in Benouville, holding their positions despite fierce opposition until the evening, by which time the troops from the beaches had fought their way inland to join them.

The 17th Company R.E. fought across Normandy and the men were in action continuously until they reached Bremerhaven at the end of the war. They sustained very heavy casualties, and only 40 or 50 of the original 260 men who landed on Sword Beach on 6th June 1944 survived unscathed. The rest were either killed, wounded or taken prisoner.

Bert Doughty returned home three days before Christmas 1945 and picked up the threads of his life. He carried on his father's building and undertaking business

Bert Doughty (left), and Pegasus Bridge (right)

with his brother Fred, continued as the local undertaker after his retirement, finally giving up at the age of 84 after seventy years.

He is a member of the British Normandy Veterans Association and of the Royal British Legion, and has returned on many anniversaries to Normandy and to Pegasus Bridge. Four years from his ninetieth birthday, Bert now lives with his wife Hilda just across the Codford Parish boundary in Upton Lovell.

[Sources: Bert Doughty; *Red Berets into Normandy*, by Sir Huw Weldon (Jarrold, 1982)]

An Artist For All Seasons
Rex Whistler

O ne of the most brilliant artists of his generation, described by his Commanding Officer as 'one of the most delightful men the Welsh Guards has ever carried on its roll,' Rex Whistler was 35 when he applied for an emergency commission in September 1939 at the outbreak of war. Rex was a prolific painter, book illustrator, theatrical, ballet and graphic designer. Prior to World War Two he had tried to get into a Territorial Army Regiment, and when war was declared he initially applied to the Grenadier Guards but they were up to strength. A new order was in force that prohibited the granting of any commissions except through the ranks, the exception being the Brigade of Guards.

On 17th March 1940 Rex was granted an emergency commission and noted for the Welsh Guards. According to the *Army List* Rex had been a 2nd Lieutenant from the beginning of October 1939 in the Oxfordshire and Buckinghamshire Light Infantry, though he never served with the Regiment. He took his commission with the Welsh Guards in the spring of 1940, joined his unit on 2nd June and was posted to a Training Battalion at Colchester. In July he was officially attached to the 2nd Battalion Welsh Guards, and in August he attended a commander training course in London.

Rex probably moved to Codford St Mary on 17th September 1941 with the majority of the 2nd Battalion (Armoured) Welsh Guards. From sketches and communication with former officers it is obvious that the Officer's Mess left a great deal to be desired when Rex arrived on the scene. Squalor, glaring lights, narrow table, lack of leg-room and erratic service were the order of the day. He transformed it in late September, painting the inside of the hut as a Bedouin tent with plaques featuring the heads of his fellow officers, depicted in the style of Roman commanders. Unfortunately all trace of these exquisite paintings has been lost. It is very likely that when the camps were pulled down after the war the paintings were destroyed, burned on the bonfires of Boylands, the West Country based firm dismantling the

Rex Whistler

buildings.

Later the sitting room was decorated with Rex's version of framed Old Masters on a green wall. The painting of Colonel Blimp in the dress uniform of the Welsh Regiment of Foot Guards is now in the safe keeping of the Welsh Guards HQ in Birdcage Walk, London.

Life in Rex Whistler's Codford during World War Two has been captured in numerous sketches, drawings, paintings and anecdotes. The Covenanter Tank featured together with the regimental badge, arms and battle honours in the 1941 Welsh Guards Christmas card. A drawing of the Queensbury-Cripps Mobile Cinema indicates that it first visited Codford in December 1941, when 400 Welsh Guardsmen attended the show. The venue, according to the illustration, was the Wool Stores.

Rex's parents had moved into the Walton Canonry in Salisbury Cathedral Close in 1937, and he had many friends living in Wiltshire. London was an easy train journey away, so his off-duty periods were sociable and relaxing.

As a small boy Alexander Thynne, the present Lord Bath, met Rex on many occasions.

> I remember Rex Whistler very well. He often would come over for weekends when my mother was entertaining at Sturford Mead in Corsley. This was during the months which he awaited the start of the invasion of Normandy, where of course he was killed in action.
>
> As children, we much admired his upside-down [reversible] drawings: also his scribble drawings. He would ask one of us to make a scribble: then incorporate those lines within a life-like action sketch – of a drunken Father Christmas or whatever. I also remember how he enjoyed participating in our snowball fights.
>
> He was painting a portrait of me which was never fully completed by the date of the invasion. It was an uncharacteristic pose for me of holding a shotgun. But he wasn't to know that I would grow up as someone anti-blood sports! I suppose this portrait which I do have here at Longleat might be the very last picture that he painted.

The Battalion left England for Normandy on 29th July 1944, landing near Arromanches on Gold Beach. The rain was continuous and the weather deplorable, but Rex caught tantalising glimpses of an ethereal beauty in the failing light and the ancient landscape. He had a metal box specially made and welded onto his tank for his canvases and paints. He had been appointed the Battalion Burial Officer, and as such carried the white crosses used to mark battlefield casualties. Ironically and tragically, he was to be the first in his battalion killed in action.

The preparation and the waiting to go into action was over, and the battle for Caen was about to begin. On 18th July the Guards Armoured Division was advancing through marked minefields along the eastern bank of the Orne River. As the Squadron turned towards Caen on a hot summer day, the tank crews endured stifling, suffocating conditions as they crossed open tracts of French countryside, supporting the Canadian infantry.

In the afternoon the advance was halted, Rex's tank tracks became entangled in cut telegraph wires and the tank was unable to negotiate the railway cutting which other troop tanks had successfully crossed. It was against military procedure to evacuate the whole crew from a tank, only two of the five crew members were needed to cut the wire, but in what was to be a fatal decision, Rex ordered his men out. Without any warning the tank crew came under small arms fire and were unable to return to their vehicle to radio for help. Rex made a gallant gauntlet run of approximately 60 yards to his sergeant's tank to appraise him of the situation, but was killed by a mortar blast as he dismounted from the tank to return to his own vehicle and crew. Rex Whistler had just tasted his first action, he died of a broken neck but his body was unscathed. Rex was thirty-nine years old when he was killed. He is buried at Banneville-la-Campagne.

[Sources: *Rex Whistler's War 1939–July 1944: Artist into Tank Commander*, by Jenny Spencer-Smith (National Army Museum); *The Laughter and the Urn: the Life of Rex Whistler*, by Laurence Whistler (Weidenfield and Nicholson); Lord Bath, personal communication; anecdotes from locals and Guards Officers, Guards HQ, Wellington Barracks, Birdcage Walk, London; Commonwealth War Graves Commission]

The Poet Warrior
Anthony Strangman Hancock

The second youngest local casualty, Anthony Hancock, was an organ scholar at Wadham College, Oxford – a poet, composer, and musician who played the flute, viola, piano and organ. His father, Captain Dugald Strangman Hancock, had been a signaller in the Buffs during World War One, and his widowed mother, Vivien, had moved her prep school, Greenways, from Bognor Regis to Ashton Gifford

House in Codford in August 1940. After the Dunkirk evacuation, Operation Dynamo, over five nights in late May and early June, Britain stood alone against the might of Hitler's Nazi Germany.[1] The south coast of England was declared an emergency zone in anticipation of an invasion by German Forces. All civilians whose presence in the south of England was non-essential were encouraged to leave the area and move inland.

Anthony was born on 9th September 1923, in Hanworth, Middlesex. As the eldest son, one of three boys and a girl, he was very conscious of his position and determined to carry on the school in a way his father never did. He was just sixteen when war broke out, and he enlisted while an Oxford undergraduate into the Queen's Royal Regiment embodied Territorial Army on 5th March 1942.On 17th July that year he joined for duty and was posted to 164 Officer Cadet Training Unit, was appointed an emergency commission in the Buffs and posted to the 9th Battalion as 2nd Lieutenant [P/249763] on 31st October 1942. He was promoted to Lieutenant on 1st May 1943, and six weeks later posted to 44 Holding Unit, before being posted to 2nd Battalion Lincolnshire Regiment for a brief period between 30th June and 9th July 1944.

On 11th July Anthony was admitted to 81 General Hospital. He was discharged to a Holding Unit on 16th August, and posted to another Holding Unit a week later, before his final posting to 2nd Battalion Royal Ulster Rifles on 25th August 1944. Anthony served in north-west Europe from the time he joined the Royal Ulster Rifles to early July when he was wounded. He returned to this theatre of war on 21st August 1944, serving until his death on 26th April 1945.

The actor Roy Purcell, MC, served with the RUR and remembers:

Tony joined us in September '44 at a small village near the river Seine -- we were taking in reinforcements after the battle for Normandy. We were with the 2nd Battalion of the Royal Ulster Rifles, part of the 3rd British Infantry Division. Tony was appointed Platoon Commander in a Rifle Company, and I can assume from personal experience that these chaps are always at the sharp end when it comes to doing battle. They fought with the battalion through Belgium, Holland and Germany. He was a modest fellow, but proved cool and courageous in battle. He soon captured the trust and affection of his men.

Excerpts from Anthony's letters, regimental history and field diaries and relevant passages from Norman Scarfe's *Assault Division* chronicle his experiences. He was with the 3rd Division from Caen to Bremen.

Caen

... late in the evening of July 7th. . . 450 heavy bombers swarmed like black dragons over the sky, unloaded their bombs on the old Norman city, and, as they returned, the Division was for a time in total darkness beneath a great vaulty cloud of ashes . . .'

I saw a wonderful sight last night – a really colossal raid on Caen by heavy bombers. . . I have never seen so many planes in the sky at one time, flying through flak as if it just wasn't there!...When they had finished there was such a dense pall of smoke over Caen that one could hardly see, and there was a red glow over the town all through the night. [ASH]

His sister Patricia remembers that two days later he was in hospital in Oxford having received a severe head wound.

Wanssum

Anthony was wounded again on 30th November 1944. An excerpt from *History of the 2nd Battalion R.U.R. in N.W. Europe 1944-45*, in the chapter 'Twilight Towards the Meuse', reads:

At 0415 'D' Company, commanded by Major Bird [awarded the MC], moved out from Blitterswijk, along the Wanssum road, leaving their defensive responsibilities to 'A' Company. At 0500 the Pioneers under Corporal Genovese began a breaching operation to clear the wire. They had expected that the obstacle would be mined, however the Germans had attached explosive charges to the wire, ensuring that the Pioneers could not reach the explosives to neutralise them, leaving them no alternative but to cut the wire, and pull it to detonate the explosives.

The Company came under heavy machine gun fire, but took the first three objectives, two windmills and a thick wood, by rushing in and throwing grenades. The Regimental Diary records: 'The leading platoon under Lieutenant Hancock experienced similar opposition. These men came under heavy fire from a wood between themselves and the objective, but getting into the wood they worked forward employing the tactics of throwing a grenade at a position and then taking it. This was done with great initiative and dash by Lt. Hancock in spite of two slight wounds, and his leading section commander Cpl. Harrigan. The denseness of the wood made progress slower, and when the Boche positions were reached, again the bird had flown, though in great haste judging by the amount of equipment left behind.'

Anthony wrote to his mother:

You may be getting informed that I have been wounded recently – don't worry, as it was nothing serious, and I was not evacuated. We have only just come out of a very hotspot. I got back from Brussels to find myself in the middle of preparations for it, and we started that night. It was the toughest fighting I've met yet. I had two very narrow escapes. A bullet grazed my throat, hardly drew blood! And a bit of shrapnel went through my cheek. Not enough force to go through both cheeks, so I spat the bit out! The CO seems to be very pleased with my work, for some unknown reason. We are having a rest now. I have had four hours sleep in the last three days and nights
Lots of love   from Anthony

In another extract from *The History of the 2nd Batt. RUR*, Major General Whistler's summing up of Anthony's performance is given as follows: ' I congratulate you on your excellent leadership and courage in leading your platoon against the enemy in the Wenssum area.'

The Maas

An extract from the Regimental Diary:

In the last fortnight of our Watch on the Meuse, active patrols across the river were initiated along our entire Corps front. After the restoration of the situation in the Ardennes, the allies had taken up the offensive again when the Second Army attacked north and east of Geilenkirchen to close up to the line of the River Rohr. On the Eastern front the Russians were making striding advances across Poland into Germany, and it was soon obvious that great events were impending on our own front. It became of vital importance that the enemy's layout should be effectively pinpointed and identifications should be secured, and in fact that the slightest change in enemy dispositions was at once made known to the Higher Command.

With this background the first patrol was planned. It was to be led by Lt. Hancock of 'D' Company assisted by Lt. Hogan of 'A' Company and composed of the Battalion's Battle Patrol, which had been reborn at the beginning of the year. Under Captain Baudains, MM, it had journeyed to Grave on the lower Meuse for training in the science of boating, and there had mastered the technique on a far broader and more stormy stretch of the river than opposite Lottum. They came from Grave proficient at probably the trickiest part of their task.

The patrol's objective was a group of houses called Hocken, which lay between the hostile village of Lomm and the east bank of the river, that lay opposite our own right hand Company in the village of Lottum. The intention was to discover whether Lockum was held by night and if so in what strength. If possible the patrol was to take a prisoner.

On the night before the patrol was to cross, the boat was carried down to the small creek a few hundred yards up the stream from Hocken. At last at 2000 hrs 31st January, the boat was slipped down into mainstream, and at the very moment of the crash of the opening salvo of the anti-sound programme, the paddles of the patrol hit the water. In five minutes the whole party, Lt. Hancock, Lt. Hogan, and the seven men were on the other bank. Here they had the misfortune to land on a mudbank, and sink in almost to their waist in mud, extracting themselves only with the utmost difficulty. This was a wretched start, but the patrol soon recovered itself, cut the wire, and when Lt. Hogan and three Bren guns had been left to cover the boat on the bank, Lt. Hancock and four men started forward.

Hocken consists of five houses in a line of some two hundred and fifty yards back from the river. What used to be the gardens of these houses stretch 75 yards down towards the river and are hedged off parallel to the river line forming an enclosure about 100 yards long. South of this enclosure is a scraggy orchard, so thinly peopled with trees as hardly to deserve such a name. Between the orchard and the enclosure is a track leading up to the southernmost house in Hocken.

The patrol had almost reached this track when the excitements began. Sounds of footsteps were heard coming from the southern end of the orchard and, throwing themselves flat, they saw three of four men pass within a few feet of them. Simultaneously they heard coughing in the direction of the point from which this party seemed to have come. This was subsequently confirmed by the boating party and the first enemy position was established. Moving northwards after this tense moment, the patrol lay up within view of the southernmost house at Hocken in which much activity was observed; light flared out as the door was opened and closed, sounds of occupation could be heard, and tracks in the snow could be observed heading away from the house in the direction of the position which had already been located. Clearly it was the platoon billet and headquarters. Now the party continued north to halfway up the enclosure and then forced their way through the thick hedge and fence that bounded it. Scarcely had they done this when two more sentries walked past not two yards away from the patrol; who, baulked by the hedge, were badly placed to seize them quietly. When they had passed, the patrol moved back out of the enclosure hoping that they would return, but in this they were disappointed. Another piece of ill fortune came later when Lt. Hancock having laid up close to the northern houses of Hocken and heard nothing, returned to the track between enclosure and orchard just in time to see two more men walking from the HQ across the orchard to the located position. Once more the patrol was unfortunately placed for snatching a prisoner.

After moving about and lying up for four and a half hours, the patrol now returned to the bank, since Lt. Hancock considered his men too cold profitably to continue. Recognition signals with the boating party were successfully made and the whole party re-embarked without further incident. Having left at 2000 hrs they were back again by 0030hrs. No prisoner had been brought back, because of being unfortunately placed on the two most promising occasions, the patrol found no opportunity in which silent success was certain to be the outcome; and Lt. Hancock felt that with only four men at his disposal, any sound of struggle would place the whole enterprise in jeopardy. As it was the patrol was able to return with exact information about the enemy dispositions and habits in Hocken without the enemy even realising that anyone had been there. It was the perfect reconnaissance patrol.

Anthony's letter home was typically modest: 'I have a lot to tell you when I see you.'

Four nights later another patrol was able to take advantage of the detailed information received and as a result captured two prisoners, one of whom turned out to be a Company runner who was able to identify his own and neighbouring positions, as well as delineate the inter-divisional boundary. The Regimental Diary records this final patrol as a fitting swansong for the Battalion's Watch on the Meuse. After a limited offensive over the River Rohr the Cologne Plain lay open; as the operation was completed 3 Division were drawn out of the line for a brief respite in a peaceful area North of Louvain.

Weeze, February 1945

Once again Anthony is praised by Major General Whistler: 'I congratulate you on the courage and daring you displayed in leading your platoon in the face of heavy fire near Weeze.'

Bremen, April 1945

The day after the Battalion moved to a concentration area to the north of Barrien, Anthony wrote his last letter home. It was dated April 18th, just eight days before his death:

I'm sorry I haven't written for so long, but we have been moving fast and far – the newspapers madden me more and more daily; the atmosphere of the war being virtually over is very much absent here, where we have seen monthly stiff opposition. After having done attack after attack on a stubbornly held position it is very hard to read of columns rolling on into Germany with no opposition. The war is definitely not over, and I can't hazard any guesses as to when it will be over – some time yet. If some war correspondent would come and see for themselves they would get a very different picture.

Anthony Hancock

The following day at 0700 hrs the Battalion successfully attacked Moordyke, 'D' Company's objective being the main crossroads. Within six hours, 94 prisoners together with considerable quantities of arms were captured.

On 21st Anthony and the 2nd RUR were about to go into what was to be the final amphibious battle of World War Two – the battle of Bremen. They had specialised in assault river crossings and had battle experience of all but one type of amphibious craft. For the first time they were to attack in Buffalos, tracked amphibian troop carriers. Bremen, south of the Weser was strongly defended, and was protected from attack by the line of the Ochtum canal. Artificial flooding of its banks had submerged about 2,000 yards of land on either side. The depth of the water was erratic, from 4 inches to the Canal depth, with uneven and boggy ground which would prove a challenge for the Buffalos. They also had to cross a waterlogged dummy airfield covered with immense bomb craters, and negotiate flooded fields and wire cattle fences. The brigade was to attack the main road crossing the canal; their objective to take Kattenturm and secure the bridge. They would be traversing flooded embankments, moving in blind using educated guesswork as there was no solid intelligence of either enemy numbers or positions.

The last entry in Anthony's diary was on April 23rd: 'We learnt last night about Bremen. I recce the ground for the attack in the morning.' On the night of 24-5th April a squadron of 47 Buffalos, all that were available, absorbed the whole of the fighting strength of the battalion. During the afternoon each company practised loading its own men and equipment on to their designated, numbered craft. At 2100 hrs the companies boarded their Buffalos, moving to a forward assembly area. Morale was high, the men cheerful with an air of suppressed excitement. Everyone was aware that this would be the longest advance the Buffalos had attempted.

The barrage that was to mask the attack began. The silhouettes of the lumbering Buffalos were visible within 700 yards in the bright moonlight of the spring evening, as they crossed the start line at midnight. Anthony and 'D' Company crossed twenty minutes later. 'C' Company were leading the column, and they came under bazooka and small arms fire while still 50 yards from the place on the embankment that they intended to make a bridgehead. The Germans resisted fiercely, 'A' Company meeting the most determined opposition, as the enemy were dug into the bund and entrenched in a house defended with panzerfausts and spandaus.

'D' Company had advanced simultaneously with 'A' Company. Their opposition was not dug in, consisting mainly of snipers which were dealt with speedily. The attack had taken the Germans completely by surprise, so that a total of 133 prisoners, 5 of them officers, were taken and a 88mm and five other flak guns were captured. The Bremen garrison commander had been so certain that the attack would come along the line of the road that the 88mm gun had been taken off its wheels and given an arc of traverse which was limited to a particularly vulnerable part of the main road. He thought that the turning manoeuvre which the Battalion carried out was the finest thing tactically that he had seen in the whole campaign, and with the rest of the prisoners he gazed goggle-eyed at the 'Schwim-Panzer', which had traversed what was considered impassable country.

One disaster clouded the completeness of triumph in Bremen. When 'D' Company had reached their objective, Major Bird, Lieutenant Hancock and a section set off in the company carrier to contact the 51st (Highland) Division in Huchting. Not far from the company headquarters there was a fearful explosion and it soon became apparent that the carrier had activated one of the most diabolical of all

German mines, the magnetic mine. There were no survivors. Major Bird, a gallant leader, who had brought his company triumphantly through many actions; Lieutenant Hancock, whose unassuming bravery and steadfastness in action had won acute admiration; and Lance-Corporal McCoy, Rifleman McGlennon, MM, Rifleman Stevens, and others constituted the very core of 'D' Company. The loss of these men in this cruelly wasteful manner stunned and shocked the whole Battalion.[2]

In Anthony's obituary his Commanding Officer noted:

Tony Hancock joined my company in September 1944 and was immediately posted as platoon commander. His quiet manner and scholarly appearance demanded respect, and before long his was the best platoon in the company. The men in that platoon, and in the company loved him, both for the excellence of his leadership and for his profound understanding regarding all personal matters.

In action he was outstanding, a fearless leader always cool and unafraid no matter how trying the circumstances or how fierce the battle. Typical of him was a remark he passed when a bullet narrowly missed its mark in the course of the action at Blitterswijk. He appeared at Company Headquarters bleeding from the throat saying he'd got a slight scratch. On examination I discovered that the enemy bullet had passed underneath his chin and dented his 'Adam's Apple'!

Although wounded twice in battle he always refused to be evacuated and remained with his platoon until the end of the day. His untimely death right at the end of the campaign was a cruel blow. But we shall long remember his quiet unassuming personality, and in recalling his worth as a friend we can offer our deepest sympathies to his bereaved relatives.

Captain George Johnson wrote to Mrs Hancock on 13th August 1945:

My dear Mrs Hancock,

I am so terribly sorry. I find it very hard to believe that I shall never laugh with Tony again. He was such a grand lad – I valued his friendship very much. We were together in the Buffs from the time he joined us in October '42 until he left from Antrim station one afternoon last June. We had much in common. Tony and I used to row together in Belfast.[3] He had a grand sense of humour and was always so cheerful, even on the most depressing exercise. He was very popular in the Battalion and I know that Colonel Coates had a very high opinion of his work as Signals Officer. I thought it was a dreadful thing that he wasn't allowed to do Signals work in France – the job at which he trained so hard and which he carried out so competently. He spent a weekend with me in Enniskillen after he returned to the RUR Depot. I thought he looked wonderfully fit after his head wound – and he certainly had not lost anything of his boyish gaiety.

I heard from him several times after that – I knew that he had been wounded again and I hoped that he would have been given a rest.

He often spoke to us about the school[4] – he was so happy about his future. I can just begin to understand what his loss must mean to you. I hope some day to be able to visit you with my wife when this insane business is over.

In the eleven months from the invasion of Normandy to the German surrender 1,570 members of the 3rd Division were killed in action. Anthony Hancock was among the very last of the RUR casualties. He was twenty-two years old when he died on 26th April 1945. He is buried in grave 4, row G, plot 8 in Becklingen War Cemetery, Soltau, Germany.

In his book about the 4th Somerset Light Infantry, *18 Platoon*, Sydney Jary wrote:

> There is a mathematical formula: aggression increases the farther one goes behind the lines. Opposing infantry, with a few exceptions like the SS, are joined by a bond of mutual compassion which few but the aristocracy of the battlefield can understand. The public, influenced no doubt by writers with little or no experience of battle, have strange and sometimes silly ideas about what makes a good soldier. Ill informed television programmes have added to this misunderstanding. Few professions have been so misleadingly caricatured. Had I been asked at any time before August 1944 to list the personal characteristics which go to make a good infantry soldier, my reply would indeed have been wide of the mark.
>
> Like most I would no doubt have suggested only masculine ones like aggression, physical stamina, a hunting instinct and a competitive nature. How wrong I would have been. I would now suggest the following. Firstly sufferance, without which one could not survive. Secondly, a quiet mind which enables a soldier to live in harmony with his fellows through all sorts of difficulties and sometimes under dreadful conditions. As in a closed monastic existence, there is simply no room for the assertive or the acrimonious. Thirdly, and no less important, a sense of the ridiculous, which helps a soldier surmount the unacceptable. Add to these a reasonable standard of physical fitness and a dedicated professional competence, and you have a soldier for all seasons. None of the NCOs or soldiers who made 18 Platoon what it was resembled the characters portrayed in most books and films about war. All were quiet, sensible and unassuming men and some, by any standard, were heroes. If I now had to select a team for a dangerous mission and my choice was restricted to stars of the sportsfield or poets, I would unhesitatingly recruit from the latter.

Anthony Hancock was such a man, a poet, a dreamer, a leader and a warrior. 'His life was gentle, and the elements so mix'd in him that Nature might stand up, and say to all the world, "This was a man".'[5]

Notes:
[1] Roger Hedley, *Sterner Days: Codford During the Second World War*, by Romy Wyeth.
[2] *History of the Royal Ulster Rifles*, volume 3
[3] Anthony's father Dugald rowed for his college, Corpus Christi.
[4] Greenways in Codford
[5] from Julius Caesar by William Shakespeare

[Sources: Patricia Windsor [née Hancock]; General Sir Roger Wheeler KCB, CBE; Colonel W.R.H. Charley OBE, JP, DL; *History of the Royal Ulster Rifles*, volume 3; The Royal Ulster Rifles Regimental

Association Secretary, Major M.B. Murphy; Roy Purcell MC; Brigadier David Shaw; Ministry of Defence; Norman Scarfe, *Assault Division*, p.177; *History of the 2nd Batallion, Royal Ulster Rifles, in North-West Europe, 1944-5*]

Under Fire
Tom Stacey

Thomas Robert Stacey was born in Hackney, London on 14th February 1903, the fifth son of a Metropolitan police officer. Later the family was to increase by two girls. Shortly after his birth, his parents Charles and Eliza Stacey moved from London to a farm in Chitterne, eventually settling at 58 High Street, Codford. Pete Stacey, the son of one of Tom's older brothers, remembers his grandparents' general store and newsagents at number 58. As a child he noticed an old potato chipper at one end of the village store, from things he recalls his grandmother saying he believes that the Staceys may have had a fish and chip shop in the First World War.

Pete remembers his Uncle Tom as a quiet, gentle man, fair haired, fresh complexioned with grey eyes, and like all the Stacey boys a keen footballer. Tom

The postman with his tricycle is outside Stacey's Newsagents (Wellin Cottage today), opposite Couchman's Yard, where coaches and buses were kept

was a newsagent in civilian life, working in the family store. He would get up at 5.30 every morning, rain or shine, take the daily newspaper delivery, sort and mark the papers up, then go on his round, which included Codford St Peter, St Mary and surrounding villages including Stockton and Sherrington. Afterwards he would take his young nephew Pete mushrooming on 'The Pimple' (Lamb Down where the World War One Badge is carved) or to the river to tickle trout.

Tom volunteered to join the R.A.F. on 19th September 1941. He trained as a gunner, and at some point in his service he served as an aircraft gunner. He took part in the North African Campaign, then went through Italy, returning to Egypt for a few months at the end 1943 or the beginning of 1944 before returning to England. He was stationed close to home, at Old Sarum just outside Salisbury, before being posted to Eshott.

Leslie (left) and Thomas (right) Stacey, about 1923

On 7th March 1945 Tom was mustered to a fire-fighting unit. Official records from the Air Historical Branch [RAF] of the Ministry of Defence state: '1468187 Leading Aircraftman Thomas Stacey was under training as a fire fighter with 54 Operational Training Unit [OTU] at RAF Charter Hall, 15 miles WSW of Berwick on Tweed. On 30th May 1945 he was tragically killed when his fire tender overturned on the perimeter track.'

Pete Stacey says that with the war in Europe over Tom was waiting to be demobbed and intending to return to the family business in Codford. On the night he died he had swapped shifts with a friend who wanted to go out for the evening. He was on Fire Tender duty when the crew were called out to an emergency. Tom was forty-two years old when he died on active service; he is buried close to Ben Sheppard in St Mary's churchyard.

[Sources: Pete Stacey; Ministry of Defence Air Historical Branch [RAF]; Commonwealth War Graves Commission]

A Farmer in South Africa
Alan Roney-Dougal

Alan Richard Roney-Dougal was born in Paignton, Devon on 23rd September 1917, the younger of the two sons of Alaistair and Edith Roney-Dougal. Ian and Alan were the children of a service family. Between the wars they lived almost continuously around Salisbury Plain, in Amesbury, Durrington and Bulford. Their father was a Brevet Lt. Col. in the Royal Artillery, who was awarded the D.S.O. and bar in World War One. After his death at Bulford Camp in 1933, their mother moved first to Heytesbury and then to the Old Rectory in Codford St Mary.

Alan was educated privately and at Bradfield College, Berks (1932-35). During 1936-37 he had a private tutor, and it was during this period, on 26th August 1936, that he was appointed to a Supplementary Reserve Commission as a 2nd Lieutenant [P68748] in the Somerset Light Infantry. Alan's health had always been poor. He suffered from sinusitis and bronchial trouble, conditions aggravated by the damp cold climate of the Wiltshire winters. In 1937, after resigning his commission on 29th May, he emigrated from his widowed mother's house in Codford, to Tarke Training Farm, Cradock, South Africa, intending to make a career in farming.

Alan Roney-Dougal

At the age of twenty-four, on 20th December 1941, he enlisted as a private in the South African Medical Corps for full-time voluntary service at Port Elizabeth. His description on the Oath of Attestation is fair complexioned with blue eyes and light brown hair, his deflated chest measurement 34ins and his only distinctive mark was an operation scar. Alan's health was still precarious, and medical records show that he was hospitalised between 5-8th January and again between June 14th and July 2nd with frontal sinusitis. On 3rd May 1944 he was again admitted to hospital for a seven-month stay until 13th January 1945, this time suffering from pulmonary tuberculosis. In January of 1945 the nature of Alan's disability, 80% pulmonary tuberculosis, led to him being declared medically unfit by the Medical Board [medical

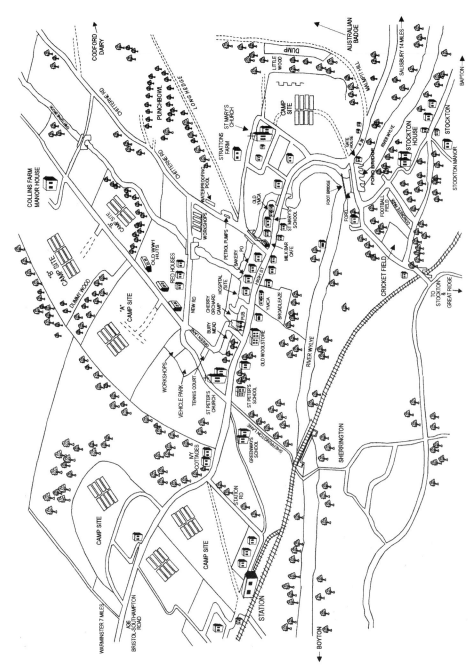

Codford 1939-45: computer-drawn map by Brian Marshall based on an original drawing by Martyn Lock

category C on attestation]. He was discharged from service, medical category E, with benefits, on 31st of the month.

Alan Roney-Dougal was just twenty-eight when he died after a brief illness in Queen's Central Hospital, Cradock, on the 13th August 1945. The causes of death are listed as acute intestinal obstruction and congestive heart failure. He is buried in Grave 577, Row P, St Peter's [Anglican] Allotment, Cradock Cemetery, Cape Province South Africa.

[Sources: Ian Roney-Dougal; South African National Defence Force; Ministry of Defence]

The Wartime Adventures of Gordon Norris and His Pals

Gordon Norris was born in Codford in 1931, where his father, David, was the local baker. When war broke out Gordon was eight years old, and for the next six years he and his friends experienced a childhood filled with adventure and excitement. The size of the group of children changed day by day, sometimes large, sometimes small, always inquiring. Gordon moved from Codford in 1955. He worked in Trowbridge in the aircraft factory making Spitfire wings, did his National Service in the Air Force at RAF Lyneham, and became a draftsman and illustrator.

The Bakery, with Mr Spiller on the steps to the flour loft, and delivery vans in the garage

Gordon's wartime adventures are recounted in my book, *Sterner Days: Codford During the Second World War*. He has a remarkable ability to recapture the youthful enthusiasm of a country childhood during an extraordinary time and to bring it alive. He made a map of his adventures, scrupulously plotting the locations, allowing us see the 1940s through the eyes of the village children.

1 Rubbish Tip:

This was where Gordon and his friends found enamel chamber pots. By using ingenuity, paint and sand they turned them into first-rate copies of paratrooper helmets. The children knocked off the handles, made holes to attach the chinstraps and used rubber and felt for the inner padding.

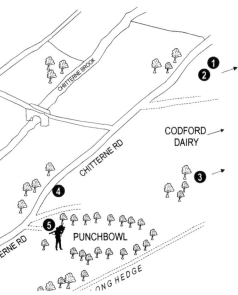

2 Owl Rescue

The scouts would go off for evening manoeuvres in this area. They once attempted to rescue an owl caught by the leg in a tree, but unfortunately it was already dead.

3 An American Tank Lost in Fog:

This happened above the Australian Badge. The scouts came to the rescue and showed the way.

4 Road Widened For Tanks:

The Codford to Chitterne Road was widened prior to D-Day, but allowed to revert to its original width afterwards.

Hill For Trolleys

'Chitterne Road was a favourite place to try out home made trolleys. Some of the trolleys had cast iron wheels from the farm, very popular because they skidded and made a lot of noise, others made from old pram wheels were much faster and quieter.'

5 The Punchbowl Range:

This was used for bazookas, etc. The bazooka shells had concrete instead of explosives in their heads. The children collected them for swaps. Gordon once swapped one for a German bayonet. All manner of things, many lethal, would be collected and hidden in the barn at the back of the bakery, unknown to unsuspecting parents.

Gordon remembers that when his father moved from Codford in about 1955 a bazooka shell was discovered, and the local police and the bomb disposal team were summoned to dispatch it. It was at the Punchbowl that Gordon and his friends had found a pristine hand grenade.

D-Day Model:

' A panoramic view of houses, rivers and roads along the French Coast was laid out at the far end of the Punchbowl. It was very well guarded and we were asked to leave when we came upon it. It was protected by an existing wire fence with armed guards patrolling in the trees.'

Old Tank:

At the Punchbowl this was used for target practice. It was situated centrally on the roadside of a large bank, which had been constructed for use as sentry security for the aforementioned panorama. The owner of Punchbowl Farm, Greg Puddy, has heard that a tank was buried somewhere in the area, but has yet to discover its whereabouts.

6 World War One Hand Grenade:

'We found hand grenade fragments in a red brick building in the area of the water pump beneath the hillside to the north.' This was along the small private road that leads from the Chitterne Road by the entrance to Long Hedge to East Farm.

7 Trenches and Mine:

Constructed by the soldiers of the British Expeditionary Force who had returned from France. Dating from 1939 the men dug trenches similar to those used on the Somme in World War One. It made an excellent play area for several years but is now filled in.

8 American Shot at Ghost:

'An American soldier was on guard one night in a sentry box located adjacent to the cemetery of St Mary's Church. He thought he saw a ghost and took two shots at it.'

9 Decorated Polish Church:

This was in a Nissen hut with elaborate paintings on the walls near St Mary's Church.

10 Marquee Slide:

'Before the camp was built we were chased off by a soldier for sliding

Vickers medium/heavy tank opposite the Bakery in the High Street, 1938

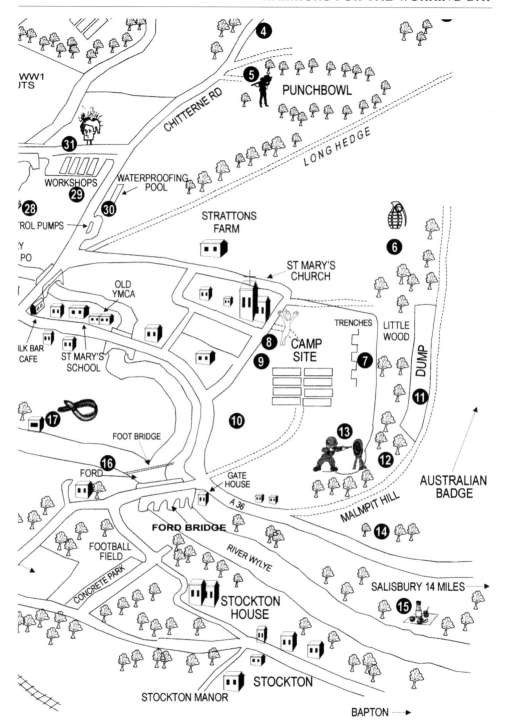

WW1
JTS

CHITTERNE RD

4

5

PUNCHBOWL

LONG HEDGE

31

WORKSHOPS **29**

WATERPROOFING
POOL

30

28

ROL PUMPS

Y
PO

STRATTONS
FARM

6

OLD
YMCA

ST MARY'S
CHURCH

ILK BAR
CAFE

ST MARY'S
SCHOOL

TRENCHES

LITTLE
WOOD

DUMP

8

CAMP
SITE

9

7

11

17

FOOT BRIDGE

10

13

12

16

FORD

GATE
HOUSE

A 36

14

MALMPIT HILL

AUSTRALIAN
BADGE

FORD BRIDGE

RIVER WYLYE

FOOTBALL
FIELD

CONCRETE PARK

SALISBURY 14 MILES

15

STOCKTON
HOUSE

STOCKTON

STOCKTON MANOR

BAPTON

down from the ridge of a marquee. The sagging top of the tent broke our fall to the ground.'

11 The Dump:
'This was on Malmpit Hill. During World War Two everything was in short supply, and food and clothing were rationed. However on the Dump American uniforms, badges, underwear, boots and full kits, haversacks, shovels, bayonets, tents, sheets, blankets, towels, radio spares, mess kits, knives, forks and spoons were among the luxuries that could be found. There were often boxes, larger than coffins, made of straight grain deal with no knots, plus sweets, cookies, American comics, pens, pencils, shoes, books, cigarettes, pipes, and prophylactics. America was the land of plenty, Britain was not!'

12 Littlewood:
'We had a sledging area here in the winter, snow was rare and we were very keen. I made some skis, which I tried out at night, but they went too fast and the next day the snow had gone. We had home made toboggans, which we used on snow, frost and then mud after everything had melted. People strolling on Sunday afternoons would find violets in Littlewood. It was also the place where we saw fox cubs playing. Another thing we found was a rusty hand grenade or Mills bomb from World War One.'

Foot and Mouth Disease:
'Cows and sheep were cremated on Stratton's Farm near Littlewood.'

13 Rifle Range:
The American soldiers used pop-up targets activated by long wires.

14 World War One Ammo:
Gordon was told that this was buried alongside the Salisbury Road (A36) below the Australian Badge with a fir plantation to cover it.

15 World War One Picnics:
The building used is still there. It was made into a strong point like a pillbox, with rifle slots and sandbags in World War Two. The youngsters bathed naked in the stream at the back of it.

16 The Ford

17 Eel House:
Eels were collected for food. The trap was an iron griddle in the Eel House.

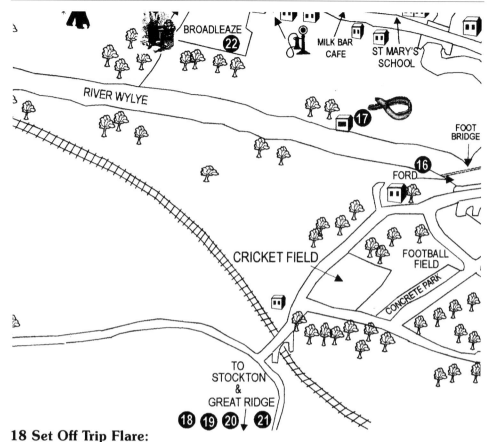

18 Set Off Trip Flare:

'After dismantling the flare in the wood we set it off in a chalk pit. It was probably magnesium and it gave off a lot of smoke.'

19 Dummy Anti-Tank Mines:

Gordon says that they were still *in situ* in recent years.

20 Chased by US Troops:

The boys pinched their shovels and pick axes etc. after the American soldiers had left them unattended when they were making up the road. After being chased the tools were dropped and recovered by the soldiers.

21 Followed Manoeuvres:

Gordon and his pals often shadowed convoys including tanks on to Great Ridge, carrying out their usual scavenging after they had left. Their hauls included blank cartridges, smoke bombs and thunder flashes. The ground would get very wet with deep mud due to constant use, making it impassable for bicycles, which had to be carried.

22 Broadleaze:

'Mr Mizen was what would now be called an entrepreneur. He was the local carrier, bought lots of supplies and also ran a dairy farm. He buried his horse under its favourite apple tree on the present playing field when it died. The apple tree has now gone, the horse is probably still there.'

23 Telephone Exchange:

Was run by Mr Smith who was one of 'The Old Contemptibles' from World War I. I spent many evenings with him as the telephone exchange was situated in his house opposite the Bakery [This is now Wren Cottage, the small house next to the eastern end of the playing field beside the Millennium garden]. His wife died when she was quite young, and his son Albert who had learned to swim in the River Wylye joined the Royal Navy.

In those days telephone numbers were only three digits, all calls were manually connected and logged on small paper pads. To amuse Gordon Mr Smith would build houses of the pads then knock them down and blow smoke from his pipe on to them saying, 'These houses have been shelled!' He would stand the telephone plugs on end to represent the soldiers. Sometimes Mr Smith would listen in to conversations, which made him smile and chuckle as some women were apt to gossip.

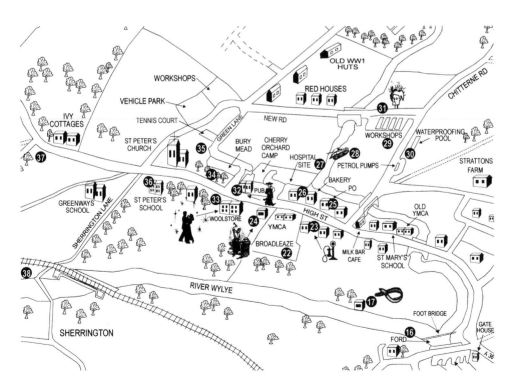

24 The Blacksmith:

25 The Post Office:
This was run by Mr Parker. . . a Communist!

26 Congregational Chapel and Sunday School:

27 Rope Swing:
Was part of the old assault course over the Brook and was left and used long after the troops had gone.

28 The Tank in the Brook:
A Churchill tank, which had been parked in Chitterne Road between Long Hedge and New Road, was supposedly left out of gear and ran away, straight into the Chitterne Brook.

29 Workshops:
'We were able to break into the ammunition stores in a large Nissen hut

Gordon Norris with Bert Smith

where we found blank cartridges, which we emptied out to make fireworks from the cordite. We were able to unlock the door, as security was lax and many locks and keys were left lying around.'

American Doughnuts
'A special vehicle was adapted to serve coffee and doughnuts to the American soldiers. A lady from the American Red Cross would cook the doughnuts in the vehicle while it was parked in one of the large Nissen huts in the evenings.'

30 Waterproofing Pool:
'In Chitterne Road the pool was used to waterproof vehicles prior to the D-Day landings. The jeeps were totally submerged in water apart from the driver's head. The Negro soldiers were furious when their lorries stalled and items would float out of the back.'

The concrete pool was designed to simulate the ramp of a landing craft with a beach contour and an unexpected dip before coming ashore. Small vehicles would enter the water with snorkels. The pool would take most vehicles except tank carriers; they were too long. These would drive into the pool forwards then back out, turn around and reverse in, this ensured the whole vehicle was waterproofed.

31 Scorched Hair:

Gordon and his pals had a mishap while setting fire to thunderflash powder. A Polish soldier lent the boys a match, probably thinking they were intending to use it to light a cigarette! The boys struck the match on the concrete pillars in order to make it light. Its sudden ignition caused them to drop the match into the thunderflash powder, with the effect that it immediately caught alight and went off. Gordon escaped fairly lightly with scorched eyebrows, but his pals George Howard and Tom Jones suffered burnt fingers and scorched hair!

32 *The George*:

'The British Legion Club met at the rear in a room which had old armour, pikes, swords and rifles on the walls. While our parents were playing billiards in the Club we loved to try on the armour and use the various weapons, especially as the rifles could still be fired.'

Three Drunken Priests:

'We had never before seen anyone in black robes with strange hats. Our first experience was seeing three individuals; very much the worse for wear, stumbling out of the *George*. I think they were probably Catholic priests in Codford with the Polish troops at the end of the war.'

33 The Woolstore:

This housed the American Red Cross, and was used as a mess, for billets, dances and film shows.

34 Derelict House:

'The building was west of Green Lane adjacent to the *George*. My sister, cousin and I investigating in candle light discovered a stone coffin, or maybe a horse trough in the cellar, which gave us all a nasty fright.'

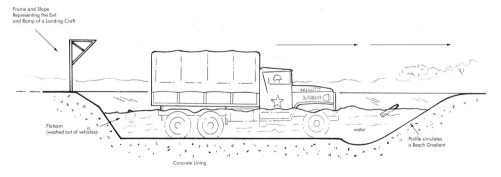

Waterproofing pool, illustrated by Gordon Norris

35 Vehicle Workshop:

This was a huge building in Green Lane on the site of Bury Mead. Gracie Fields gave a concert for the troops there.

36 First School:

'My first school was at St Peter's where I learned to read. All the children walked to school. Some boys wore boots and I remember a girl being sent home because she hadn't worn any shoes. I was not allowed to play with the others as the Head Teacher thought I was too frail. I think I may have made a mess of the Maypole dancing, muddling up the ribbons. The urinal was fenced with galvanised sheets and it was the aim of young boys to 'squirt' over the top.

My favourite game was 'What's the time Mr Wolf!' One person would face the wall while the rest of the class crept forward. One child would shout a time – if 'dinner time' was called everyone would stop, and anyone caught moving was counted out.'

37 Camp opposite Ivy Cottages:

This was used first by the Pioneer Corps and the Conscientious Objectors, then the Italian Prisoners of War, and in 1946 as a demobilisation camp for the Polish Troops.

38 Prostitute story:

'We called the woman who 'comforted' the American soldiers *Withy-bed Winnie* because she lived in a tent amongst young willow trees.'

39 Hillside:
Cookhouse with Underground Kitchen:

Gordon Norris helped his sister Dulcie deliver bread there. The cookhouse was used by the white American soldiers.

Black Americans:

They were camped near Cleeve House at different times. They were not allowed out of camp but were very friendly to the children and loved comics.

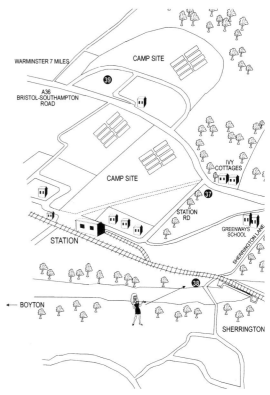

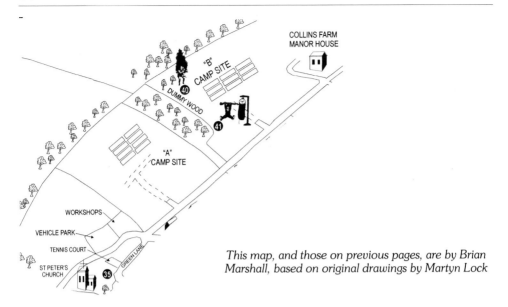

This map, and those on previous pages, are by Brian Marshall, based on original drawings by Martyn Lock

40 Boy Shot At and Hit while pinching a Christmas Tree:

Ken Marden went to the doctor's with pellets in the rear after being shot by an unknown marksman while on Collins Farm.

41 Mizen's Farm and Dairy: Japanese Dummies:

'We were frightened by the dummies hanging in the trees for the American soldiers to use as bayonet practice. At first we thought some Japs had been hung!'

The Way Things Were

Early in the war a thatched wooden barn on Stratton's Farm caught fire and was burned down. Sparks flew from the barn on to the thatch of East Farm House and set that alight. One soldier climbed on the roof and was beating the flames out with his bare hands. As the fire continued to spread across the thatch soldiers helped remove furniture from the building. It was such a great fire that the whole village turned out to watch the spectacle!

Rural pursuits of the wartime children were in some ways exactly the same as for any

Warminster fire engine returning after Stratton's fire

other generation of Codford youngsters. They camped out with the scouts in the surrounding area, including at Sherrington, where they had fun bathing at the mill, and in a cow trough above the strip lynchets. Another favourite picnic and bathing spot was on the Chitterne Brook by the old fish counting station. Gordon remembers one local man, Ginger Chapman, who swallowed some sewage while swimming in this spot and had to go to the doctor. There was a girls' Training Corps run by Doreen Bosworth to familiarise girls for a possible role in the armed forces. They would march along in their navy blue uniforms, consisting of a skirt, a battle blouse and a forage cap. Some of the members were Audrey Goodsall, Phyllis Lock, Beryl Axtell and Gordon's sisters Barbara and Dulcie Norris.

Sometimes Gordon's adventures were frightening! One night while camping with Cyril Bailey on the bank of the River Wylye he heard a vixen scream. He was scared because he had never heard the sound before. Another time the children entered a World War One secure shed and discovered it was full of sacks of animal bones, possibly for glue making. Gordon still recalls the awful smell.

The unique experiences of a wartime childhood surrounded by soldiers and the military paraphernalia of armies everywhere left lasting impressions. The Cherry Orchard Camp at one time had American tank transporters parked near the Brook. The camp was used by the British, Americans and Poles in turn, and German Prisoners of War who worked on this camp to clear the concrete slab paths were guarded by armed Americans. As well as the Officers Mess there was a surgery and an assault course, which made a wonderful play area when not in use by the military. During some work here a skeleton was unearthed but the authorities deemed it to be too old for investigation.

The American Officers Mess in Cherry Orchard had lifesize nudes painted around the walls. The figures were copied by a GI from clothed pin-ups in the *Yank* magazine. Gordon remembers that they made a tremendous impression on the boys, as the models were carrying handbags and wearing hats and shoes, and nothing else.

The memorable characters also imprinted themselves on the youngsters. One, a likeable rogue, was a local man who twice didn't turn up for his own wedding. The second time he was rumoured to have been at a cinema in Salisbury with another girl. At another time he climbed up a ladder through a window into the empty Boyton Manor and camped there with a girlfriend.

The tale of the Rector of Boyton Church who refused to allow the gravedigger to marry his own cousin made a lasting impression. It was said that when the Rector died the gravedigger dug the grave extra deep to make sure his old antagonist stayed underground! Unfortunately I have been unable to discover the identity of either man.

Codford St Mary High Street Before and During World War Two
Gordon Norris

The First YMCA
This was between the Chitterne Brook and St Mary's School, on the site of the two Brook Cottages today. In the background there was a large stable with chalk walls and some straw in the corner. One day we found a pile of sticky bombs underneath. These were probably for Home Guard use, to attack German vehicles in case of Invasion!

Chocolate was rationed. However, whenever I delivered bread rolls from my father's shop to the YMCA on my bicycle, the manager, Mr Dunbar, would give me a Kit-Kat.

The Milk Bar
The manager was 'Carol', an Austrian who had been released from the British Army. At one time he worked in my father's bakery and would make fancy rolls in his spare time. Most days we would deliver loaves and rolls to the Milk Bar. One day when Bill Fry was delivering to the Milk Bar he came off the 'bread bike' and it was run over and scrapped. Carol sold me his army pocket knife for a halfpenny. His son was in Austria during World War Two but came to England later to see his father.

The Hairdresser
He was Mr Mines, who built a large red brick house on the back road just before the turning into Sherrington. When I was young he would singe my hair. He had a daughter named Elizabeth, and an American Army Air Force pilot would drop her messages from a light aircraft to arrange 'dates.' Later the shop was run by Mr Blatch.

The Cycle Shop
This was run by Mr Simper, he would also charge accumulators and sell carbide for cycle lamps. His daughter was called 'Pim,' and I believe that she married Mr Davis, the timber merchant in Green Lane.

The Piano Teacher
She was Miss Ford who lived in a timber house in the High Street, now called Westwood House.

The Blacksmiths

This was opposite Cherry Orchard. Mr Trim the blacksmith would throw iron filings into his forge to make a show of sparks for me. He also loved to play with a large bench drill and I tried boring holes into a piece of steel. I would also watch him making horseshoes and nailing them into horse's hooves. Mr Trim was also head of the Auxiliary Fire Service. When the A.F.S. turned out to practise their fire pump using the water from the Chitterne Brook the whole village would turn out to watch.

The Bakery

By this time sweets, chocolate and ice cream were no longer available, so sales were restricted to bread, cakes and flour, and sometimes food and homegrown vegetables. Some rice and spices were available but not often purchased. The bakery also sold cigarettes, tobacco and matches. Various shop attendants were: Mrs D. Norris, Barbara and Dulcie Norris, Betty Goodenough, Hilda Marden and Millie Rhodes.

The Butcher's Shop

This was opposite the bakers and was run by Mr Pike. Meat was scarce and could only be obtained using coupons. Pigs were killed by the butcher's assistant Mr Macklin at the back of the shop. They must have known they were about to be killed as they had to be caught and gave off horrifying screams.

The Woolstore

This was being used as a cinema, and occasionally films were shown for British soldiers. They were old black and white films or even brown, and they were always breaking down, followed by shouts and jeers. The air was full of tobacco smoke and there were long waits while the film or projector was repaired. When the American army arrived several modern films in colour were shown and the programme changed twice weekly. The favourites were cartoons, especially 'Tom and Jerry', and great cheers accompanied their announcement. There was 'no smoking'; however some chewed cigars and tobacco, most chewed gum.

The Troops
Gordon Norris

The Belgians

Belgian troops were in Codford for a short time and not many spoke English. I can remember that they purchased lots and lots of cocoa from my father's shop, some to send home.

The Italians

The small camp at the corner of Warminster Road and Station Road first held Conscientious Objectors, some destined for the Pioneer Corps or other non-fighting roles. At the time these men were not thought of very highly.

Later the camp, fenced with barbed wire, was used for Italian prisoners. They wore large yellow circular patches on their uniforms, or had British uniforms dyed brown with yellow patches. They were used to clear rivers and water meadows and would cook their lunch, often including nettles and dandelion leaves, on riverbanks. The Italians worked casually but well and were very friendly; they would make rings for us children from three-penny bits. When Italy capitulated they removed their yellow patches and walked freely around the village. One year in the camp they put on a pantomime for the villagers and children, alas all in Italian. One Italian who was a

Ring made out of a threepeny piece by an Italian prisoner of war

blonde Adonis came back to Codford several years running after the war. He was very friendly and would walk in and out of people's homes as if he was part of the family. Some of his countrymen settled in this country.

The Germans

German prisoners were well guarded. They worked hard, also clearing rivers and water meadows between Codford and Sherrington, but were not very friendly and were not camped in Codford. They would walk into a copse and surreptitiously swap rings and badges for razors, knives and aluminium pots. Mr Clarke, a farmer from Tytherington, had several German prisoners of war working on his farm. They slept and ate in a barn with a British Corporal as their guard. They worked well on the farm without supervision and gave no trouble.

I saw a camp for German POWs on Salisbury Plain; it was a compound of barbed wire with no facilities at all! The guards were stationed at a distance with machine guns. Perhaps they were some of the SS who had been naughty and were being allowed to cool off. It quite upset my mother!

The Poles

Several thousand troops had been stationed in Codford throughout World War Two and of course some met girls and later married. I think most married Poles and there are now many families in this area with Polish names. The probable reason they stayed was that they liked England and the British people. They had a hard time fighting through Italy, and some had been prisoners of the Germans, and were always short of food. At the end of the war several others moved on to Canada, where there was plenty of space and immigrants were welcomed to boost the working population.

*   *   *   *

Twice in the twentieth century the villages of Codford St Mary and Codford St Peter were transformed by global conflict on an unprecedented scale. From all over Britain and around the world men arrived to train for combat or to recover from wounds. They came from Australia and New Zealand, from Canada and America, from Poland and other countries in occupied Europe.

We can never truly know the way it was for the young men who were engulfed in two World Wars, those who came to Codford and those who left to fight on far-flung battlefields. They did leave behind something of themselves, offering tantalising glimpses of past times, echoes that can be felt even today. There are the tangible reminders, such as the chalk badge on the hillside, the quiet war grave cemetery, messages on faded postcards, overgrown railway lines, traces of hut foundations in the fields, the blue cobbles, painted shutters, a deserted pillbox and the plaques in the churches.

I can do no better than to paraphrase William Shakespeare :-

Let me speak proudly:- tell the generations they were but warriors for the working-day; their gayness and their gilt were all besmirch'd with rainy marching in the painful field.

Romy Wyeth
Codford
1st May 2002

Index of Persons and Places